The Intergenerational Commission

The Intergenerational Commission was convened by the Resolution Foundation to explore questions of intergenerational fairness that have risen up the national agenda.

This report contains the Commission's conclusions, drawing on a deep and wide-ranging examination of the experiences and prospects of different generations in Britain.

It provides a comprehensive analysis of the intergenerational challenges the country faces and sets out a policy programme to tackle them.

The Commission brought together leaders from business, academia and policy-making to devise a means of repairing the social contract between generations. The Commissioners, who directed the analytical priorities and policy recommendations presented in this report, have been:

- **David Willetts**, Executive Chair of the Resolution Foundation (Commission Chair)
- **Vidhya Alakeson**, Chief Executive of Power to Change
- **Kate Barker**, Chairman of Trustees, British Coal Staff Superannuation Scheme
- **Torsten Bell**, Director of the Resolution Foundation
- **Carolyn Fairbairn**, Director General of the CBI
- **Geoffrey Filkin**, Chairman of the Centre for Ageing Better
- **John Hills**, Professor of Social Policy at the London School of Economics
- **Paul Johnson**, Director of the Institute for Fiscal Studies
- **Sarah O'Connor**, Investigations Correspondent and columnist at the Financial Times
- **Frances O'Grady**, General Secretary of the TUC
- **Ben Page**, Chief Executive of Ipsos MORI
- **Nigel Wilson**, Group Chief Executive of Legal & General

The Commission has been run by the Resolution Foundation, an independent think tank that works to improve the living standards of those in Britain on low-to-middle incomes. Its analysis has been supported by a Technical Panel:

- **Matthew Whittaker**, Deputy Director of the Resolution Foundation (Technical Panel Chair)
- **Kate Bell**, Head of the Economic and Social Affairs Department at the TUC
- **Chris Curry**, Director of the Pensions Policy Institute
- **Anna Dixon**, Chief Executive of the Centre for Ageing Better
- **Bobby Duffy**, Managing Director of the Ipsos MORI Social Research Institute
- **Frank Eich**, Senior Advisor at the Bank of England
- **Laura Gardiner**, Principal Researcher at the Resolution Foundation (Commission Secretary)
- **Paul Gregg**, Professor of Economic and Social Policy at Bath University
- **Andrew Hood**, Senior Research Economist at the Institute for Fiscal Studies
- **David Kingman**, Senior Researcher at the Intergenerational Foundation
- **Abigail McKnight**, Associate Professorial Research Fellow, London School of Economics
- **Rain Newton-Smith**, Director of Economics at the CBI
- **James Plunkett**, Director of Policy & Advocacy at Citizens Advice
- **Jonathan Portes**, Professor of Economics and Public Policy, King's College London
- **James Sefton**, Professor of Economics at Imperial College London
- **Anna Vignoles**, Professor of Education at Cambridge University
- **Kate Webb**, Head of Policy at Shelter
- **Duncan Weldon**, Head of Research at Resolution Group

Publications of the Intergenerational Commission

All publications are available at the Commission's website: *intergencommission.org*

1. *Stagnation generation: The case for renewing the intergenerational contract*
   L Gardiner (July 2016), Resolution Foundation

2. *Votey McVoteface: Understanding the growing turnout gap between the generations*
   L Gardiner (September 2016), Resolution Foundation

3. *Live long and prosper: Demographic trends and their implications for living standards*
   D Finch (January 2017), Resolution Foundation

4. *As time goes by: Shifting incomes and inequality between and within generations*
   A Corlett (February 2017), Resolution Foundation

5. *Study, Work, Progress, Repeat? How and why pay and progression outcomes have differed across cohorts*
   L Gardiner & P Gregg (February 2017), Resolution Foundation

6. *The pay deficit: Measuring the effect of pension deficit payments on workers' wages*
   B Bell & M Whittaker (May 2017), Resolution Foundation

7. *The generation of wealth: Asset accumulation across and within cohorts*
   C D'Arcy & L Gardiner (June 2017), Resolution Foundation

8. *The millennial bug: Public attitudes on the living standards of different generations*
   H Shrimpton, G Skinner & S Hall (September 2017), Resolution Foundation & Ipsos MORI Social Research Institute

9. *Home Affront: Housing across the generations*
   A Corlett & L Judge (September 2017), Resolution Foundation

10. *Consuming forces: Generational living standards measured through household consumption*
    D Hirsch, L Valadez-Martinez & L Gardiner (September 2017), Resolution Foundation

11. *A Budget for intergenerational fairness? Tax and benefit options at the Autumn Budget from the perspective of different generations*
L Gardiner (November 2017), Resolution Foundation

12. *As good as it gets? The adequacy of retirement income for current and future generations of pensioners*
D Finch & L Gardiner (November 2017), Resolution Foundation

13. *The million dollar be-question: Inheritances, gifts, and their implications for generational living standards*
L Gardiner (December 2017), Resolution Foundation

14. *A welfare generation: Lifetime welfare transfers between generations*
G Bangham, D Finch & T Phillips (February 2018), Resolution Foundation

15. *Cross countries: International comparisons of intergenerational trends*
F Rahman & D Tomlinson (February 2018), Resolution Foundation

16. *A silver lining for the UK economy? The intergenerational case for supporting longer working lives*
P Thomson (February 2018), Centre for Ageing Better

17. *The kids aren't alright: A new approach to tackle the challenges faced by young people in the UK labour market*
S Clarke & C D'Arcy (February 2018), Resolution Foundation

18. *Home affairs: Options for reforming property taxation*
A Corlett & L Gardiner (March 2018), Resolution Foundation

19. *Home improvements: Action to address the housing challenges faced by young people*
L Judge & D Tomlinson (April 2018), Resolution Foundation

20. *Technical fault: Options for promoting human capital growth*
K Henehan & A Vignoles (April 2018), Resolution Foundation

21. *Passing on: Options for reforming inheritance taxation*
A Corlett (May 2018), Resolution Foundation

22. *The new wealth of our nation: The case for a citizen's inheritance*
G Bangham (May 2018), Resolution Foundation

Acknowledgements

This report has been prepared by members of the research team at the Resolution Foundation, led by Laura Gardiner (Secretary to the Intergenerational Commission) and Fahmida Rahman.

We are indebted to a wide range of organisations and individuals who have contributed to this work, including the many people who have collaborated on research papers, contributed to events and roundtables and submitted evidence or policy proposals. We are particularly indebted to the Commissioners who have directed this work, and members of the Technical Panel who contributed their time and expertise generously.

Contents

FOREWORD

Society is held together by mutual dependence between the generations. Ten years ago I published *The Pinch*, arguing that we were in danger of breaking these ties because younger generations were having a hard time when it came to their pay, housing and pensions. That was not an attempt to incite generational warfare – one of the strengths of our society is that different generations do still care about each other. Rather, it was an attempt to promote generational thinking.

It is very good news that fairness between the generations has now entered the mainstream political debate. Too often we were drifting into decisions and policies which weakened our generational contract without being aware of what we were doing. Back then it was surprisingly hard to find detailed evidence of what was happening. But the high calibre membership of the Intergenerational Commission emphasises how much attention the issue now commands. By drawing on the fantastic research capacities of our team at the Resolution Foundation and outside experts we have assembled more detailed evidence than ever before on the experience of different generations in modern Britain. We have shown that generational progress has indeed stalled. Moreover, we face significant challenges in providing the health and care that older generations expect. This report brings our findings together and the evidence is compelling. No longer can anyone deny the challenge facing us as a country in maintaining a fair deal between the generations.

If the evidence is so powerful then that means there is an obligation to act. That is the challenge to which the Commission has risen with its carefully developed but ambitious proposals. The Commissioners represent a wide range of organisations and opinions. None of them is bound by every specific proposal in this report. But overall there is a surprising degree of consensus. We can deliver the health and care older generations deserve without simply asking younger workers to bear all the costs. We can do more to promote education and skills, especially for those who are not on the university route. We can and should provide more security for young people, from the jobs they do to the homes they increasingly rent. And we can promote asset ownership for younger generations so that owning a home and access to a decent pension are realities not a distant prospect in 21st century Britain.

The ideas we set out are not easy or comfortable. We are not expecting political parties to embrace them straightaway. Indeed, we look forward to lively debates in the months and years ahead. But we have to tackle substantial long-term problems – they will not fix themselves. We hope that as the important issues we identify are increasingly recognised, our proposals can be a useful guide to action.

David Willetts

Lord David Willetts

Executive summary

Just like our families, society rests on an intergenerational contract

Every day, 14 million parents in the UK bring up their children and 6.5 million of us care for an elderly, ill or disabled relative. Wisdom gets passed on and fresh eyes provide new perspectives, with family resources responding to the shifting needs of their members. This is the intergenerational contract – the principle that different generations provide support to each other across the different stages of their lives. Just as this contract underpins what we do as families, it is fundamental to society as a whole and to the role of government. From education for the young, to extra financial help for those bringing up children, to healthcare and a pension for the old, the intergenerational contract has long defined what the welfare state does.

The intergenerational contract works because everyone puts in and everyone takes out. We are happy to support older generations – indeed we feel obligated to do so – because we believe and expect that we will be treated the same when we are old. And we support children as they develop just as we were supported and nourished when we were young. Indeed, we expect that economic growth and continually expanding social opportunities will mean that our children have more than we did – and we welcome that progress.

We celebrate the good times and deal with the nation's challenges together, across the generations. This feels natural, but that does not mean that we can take the intergenerational contract for granted. Increasingly, there is a sense that it is under threat.

That contract is under threat, with widespread concern that young adults may not achieve the progress their predecessors enjoyed

Commitment to Britain's intergenerational contract remains strong. Large majorities of all age groups in Britain believe both that the success of a society is measured by how we provide for older generations and that each successive generation should have a better life than the one before.

And there are many areas in which we can celebrate significant progress against these goals. **Adults in Britain are positive about young people's access to information and entertainment, travel opportunities and the quality of their education**. While there is still much to do, opportunities for women, ethnic minorities and lesbian, gay and transgender people are much better than for their predecessors.

But while there are strong grounds for optimism in some areas, pessimism dominates overall. **Pessimists about young adults' chances of improving on their parents' lives outnumber optimists by two-to-one**. That marks a dramatic, and very rapid, turnaround in outlook. As recently as 2003, optimists outnumbered pessimists by nearly four-to-one. The gloom that has settled across our society since then is common across advanced economies, though Britain is more pessimistic than most.

This **pessimism is most marked in relation to the key economic aspects of living standards – housing, work and pensions** – where pessimists outnumber optimists by at least five-to-one. It is these areas that have been at the core of the Intergenerational Commission's work.

Our work has first centred on investigating whether the public's pessimism is justified, by examining the experience of different generations. As far as possible we have compared these groups at the same age, allowing us to distinguish specific generational differences in outcomes from the usual differences that arise between age groups at different points in the life course. Intergenerational anxiety has come to the fore only in the period since the financial crisis, so we have also investigated the drivers of any shift in outcomes to see if they were caused by the crisis or have deeper routes.

Overall, we have developed a picture of Britain in the early 21st century as experienced by the generations born in the second half of the previous century. As well as some shared experiences, we find significant differences.

Post-crisis employment has been strong, but young adults have experienced incredibly poor pay outcomes

There has been good news for young people on employment. The unemployment rate for 16-29-year-olds rose less following the financial crisis than it did during the recessions of the early 1980s and early 1990s, and it has been quicker to recover. As a result, **in their late 20s millennials (the generation born 1981-2000) have so far experienced unemployment rates that are around 25 per cent lower than those experienced by baby boomers (born 1946-65) at the same age.**

There is good news on employment for women in particular. Employment rates for baby boomer women have been 5-7 percentage points higher at each age than for the pre-war silent generation (born 1926-45), and women in generation X (born 1966-80) and the millennial generation have experienced big gains on top of those, in the child-rearing years in particular.

While today's young adults have been much more likely to work, however, they have been rewarded very poorly for doing so – with weak pay growth the dominant feature of their working lives so far. While in the past every successive cohort had higher real earnings at each age, **the millennial cohorts born 1986-90 (at age 26) and**

1981-85 (in their early 30s) had similar earnings to the cohorts born 15 years before them when they were that age.

The decade of poor pay growth since the financial crisis has played a big part in this outcome, and has held back cohort-on-cohort pay progress – albeit to a lesser extent – for older adults too. However, **even before the financial crisis the oldest millennials recorded real pay at age 25 no higher than those born five years before them. The suggestion is that generational pay stagnation for today's young adults has deeper roots.**

One such root is the recent slowdown in the rate of human capital improvement. Millennials are the best-educated generation in history, but the very big cohort-on-cohort gains experienced by generation X have not been replicated for them. **The 37 per cent increase in degree attainment recorded between the 1969-71 and 1972-74 cohorts fell to just a 7 per cent improvement between those born in the early and late 1980s.** Crucially, non-degree routes have not picked up the slack.

Another trend that preceded the crisis and has endured even as employment has reached record highs is a shift towards lower-paying and less secure jobs among young people. **Increases in self-employment since the early 2000s have been driven by younger workers without degrees; millennials have been more likely to work part time than generation X at the same age; and the fastest-growing occupations for those in their late 20s have been the lowest-paying ones – elementary, caring and leisure roles.**

Partly as a result of this increase in their exposure to risk, young adults today are taking fewer chances. A decline in job-to-job moves by young people that began in the early 2000s means **millennials have so far been 20-25 per cent less likely to move jobs voluntarily than members of generation X at the same age.** Moving jobs is the surest route to a big pay rise, particularly when young, so this drop off in job moves is likely to be one factor behind millennials' low earnings growth.

Millennials have lower home ownership rates and higher housing costs than their predecessors

Declining home ownership is the most prominent worry about younger generations, and the changes are indeed large. So far **millennial families are only half as likely to own their home by age 30 as baby boomers were by the same age.** An even bigger reduction in access to social housing means that four-in-ten millennial families at age 30 live in the private rented sector, **four times the rate for baby boomers when they were the same age.**

This rise in private renting means that young adults face greater housing insecurity than previous generations did. They are compromising on quality and convenience too. **Adults aged under 45 have slightly less space than they did two decades ago, whereas over 45s have more**. And young adults are commuting longer distances: **millennials are on track to spend 64 more hours commuting in the year they turn 40 than the baby boomers did at that age.**

While home ownership falls take most of the headlines, an even greater problem threatening day-to-day living standards is the pressure that housing costs put on family finances. **Millennials are spending an average of almost a quarter of their income on housing, up from an average of just 8 per cent among the silent generation at the same age.**

These generational shifts are likely to persist. Even **a repeat of the best economic conditions of recent decades would result in millennials only catching up with the home ownership rates of generation X by the age of 45**, and still falling far short of baby boomer rates. **Fast-growing inheritances that are set to double in the coming two decades will help some beyond this age. But they are much less likely to benefit the almost half of 20-35-year-old non-home owners whose parents do not own either.**

Reforms underway are boosting pension saving, but working-age adults bear risks that their predecessors were protected from

Pensioner incomes have performed strongly in this century: median pensioner incomes are now higher than median working-age incomes after housing costs. There are headwinds to maintaining this performance for future retirees, however. That is because **private sector membership of generous 'defined benefit' pensions, for those around age 35, halved for employees born in the early 1980s compared to those born around 1970**. 'Automatic enrolment' of employees into less generous 'defined contribution' pensions does, however, mean that younger cohorts have higher overall pension scheme membership rates than predecessors did at each age.

If more favourable economic conditions returned (and under a simplified assumption of constant investment returns), auto-enrolment plus the move to a flat-rate State Pension mean **future pensioners could achieve broadly similar outcomes to recent retirees on average. However, there are very big risks around these outcomes for younger generations that those currently retiring have not been exposed to.**

Risks include the rate and timing of investment returns. **A 1 percentage point decline in investment returns in each remaining year of working life would reduce retirement incomes for millennial men born 1984-86 by 8 per cent, well below the outcomes enjoyed by recent retirees**. In the defined benefit system it was firms that bore this investment risk rather than individuals. The shift to defined contribution pensions plus new 'pension freedoms' mean people are increasingly having to individually plan for the wide variation in how long they might live. And unlike defined benefit pensions, defined contribution ones rarely provide protection from inflation during retirement, meaning future pensioners will be increasingly exposed to price shocks.

In contrast to older generations, young adults are making no income progress and accumulating much less wealth

Bringing together these trends, **disposable incomes – the best measure of current living standards – are no higher for millennials who have reached age 30 than they were for generation X at that age**. In contrast, older baby boomers have maintained significant income improvements on the silent generation, continuing the pattern of generational progress that was the norm across the age range in the second half of the 20th century.

Our pattern of large historical generation-on-generation gains followed by stagnation or actual income falls – and also declining home ownership rates – marks the UK out in comparison to other advanced economies. We have avoided the truly awful post-crisis outcomes for young adults in parts of Southern Europe, but the scale of our reversal relative to past experience of growth is more marked. Only Spain has experienced a comparable generational 'boom and bust' in both incomes and housing in living memory.

Popular narratives sometimes imply that measuring incomes misses some of what is really going on, with millennials losing out, in truth, because of their excessive spending. But the evidence on spending reinforces the wider findings: **in 2001, 25-34-year-olds were consuming the same as 55-64-year-olds; they are now spending 15 per cent less**.

While incomes faltered following the financial crisis, total **household wealth has grown rapidly throughout the 21st century. Despite this, wealth is only higher for those born before the 1960s compared to predecessors at the same age**. This is because unexpected house price and pension windfalls largely benefit older cohorts with existing wealth. These windfalls are unlikely to be repeated in future.

A look at income and wealth also highlights just how large differences within generations are. **Intra-generational income inequalities have been higher for generation X and the millennials than for the preceding generations at each age, and absolute wealth gaps within cohorts are growing**. Inheritances will get bigger in the coming decades, but with already-wealthy millennials set to inherit more than four times as much as those with no property wealth, they risk amplifying existing wealth gaps. Today's intergenerational differences could create deeper intra-generational gaps in future.

It is not just young adults who are being affected by the challenges to a better Britain

The overwhelming conclusion from our analysis is that today's young adults are having a tough time on key measures of living standards. But while millennials are clearly at the sharp end, there are areas of concern for older generations too. Rising housing costs have held back living standards improvements for all generations alive today – albeit in return for larger houses and the ability to accumulate property wealth in the case of the baby boomers. Older female pensioners have had poorer average pension outcomes than younger women, benefitting from auto-enrolment and a flat-rate State Pension, can look forward to. And insecurities in the labour market can affect older workers too – in some cases precipitating early exit from employment altogether.

The biggest risk for older people is the huge challenge in the coming decades of realising the welfare state's promise to them as they age. The ageing of the large baby boomer generation means we will have more older people, even before factoring in increased life expectancy. Combined with other pressures on health costs, this ageing population means **public spending on health, care and social security is set to rise by £24 billion by 2030 and by £63 billion by 2040**.

The prospects for meeting this challenge weigh heavily on the public's mind. **Healthcare is the most pressing area of worry for British adults: 42 per cent place it in their top three concerns for the country, whereas internationally it ranks in fifth place**. These concerns may be partly anchored in the increasingly parlous state of adult social care services, with the number of older people in England who do not get the care they need having doubled since 2010 to 1.2 million. The baby boomers feel they are at risk of not getting the health and care they need.

The difficulty is that meeting this spending challenge via borrowing or turning to the usual taxes on income and consumption would put disproportionate costs onto younger generations who have borne the brunt of recent living standards pressures. These approaches are both unsustainable in the long run – neither the national debt nor income tax rates can rise forever – and clearly unfair between the generations. We need to avoid breaching the intergenerational contract by either cutting essential support for older generations or putting unsustainable costs onto younger ones most affected by the financial crisis. That means we need new answers.

Families are responding to these challenges, but so far the state has failed to adapt

Families are already finding answers of their own – responding to the twin challenges of supporting older generations as their needs rise, while also looking out for younger ones as the pressure on their living standards and security has intensified. The 'bank of mum and dad' has grown significantly, helping up to half of first-time buyers to purchase a house in recent years. More young adults are living with their parents than a decade earlier. And the number of adults caring for elderly, ill or disabled relatives increased by 11 per cent in the decade to 2011.

Society as a whole faces similar challenges, but we have neither fully recognised nor responded to them. Perhaps this is not surprising because it is not an easy thing to do – requiring new thinking and tough choices. But our view is that it is possible, and indeed essential, if Britain's intergenerational contract is to remain strong in the 21st century.

We can deliver the health and care older generations deserve, need and expect, and do so in a generationally fair way. We can prove to younger generations that Britain can work for them as it did for their predecessors. We can start by addressing the lasting effects of the crisis and overturning long-term policy failures that are holding them back – from housing to technical education. We can, and should, provide more security for young people, from the jobs they do to the homes they increasingly rent. And we can promote asset ownership for younger generations, so that owning their own home and access to a decent pension are a reality, not a distant prospect. The proposals we set out are both practical and deliverable. But our focus is long term, looking beyond what is achievable right now or aligned with the agenda of any particular political party.

Providing the health and care services that older generations deserve, need and expect in a generationally fair way

Giving older generations the health and care they need in the coming decades will not come cheap – but it is the right thing to do. However, asking younger working adults to pay that bill in its entirety risks undermining rather than strengthening the intergenerational contract. A better starting point is to recognise that Britain's booming stock of wealth is increasingly concentrated in older generations and that it is also increasingly lightly taxed.

The most pressing challenge in making good on our welfare promise to older generations is to address the scandal of unmet social care need that is bearing down on families. This means sharing more risk collectively with additional public spending, at the same time as asking individuals able to do so to make a limited contribution towards their own care costs, but with proper protections.

We recommend a public funding increase of more than £2 billion for social care from a replacement to council tax, alongside an increase in property-based private contributions towards care costs. However, these charges should be limited by a strict asset floor and cost cap that mean no-one can be asked to contribute more than a quarter of their wealth for their own care. Such an approach would greatly increase the volume and quality of care provided while leaving over half of older people protected from care charges on the basis of their assets.

To maintain the NHS that the baby boomers were born into as they start to rely more heavily on it, **we recommend a £2.3 billion 'NHS levy' via National Insurance on the earnings of those above State Pension age and limited National Insurance on occupational pension income**. As well as raising funds for health services across the UK from better-off members of the group most likely to use them – four-fifths of revenues are drawn from the richest fifth of pensioners – this approach addresses inequities in the current tax treatment of pensions.

Changes to taxes are never easy and should never be made lightly, but properly funding the NHS and our social care system in the coming decades is essential if we want to deliver our welfare promise to older generations and reshape the intergenerational contract for the challenges of the 21st century.

Reducing labour market risks and restarting progression for young adults

The financial crisis has played a large part in millennial pay stagnation, but the problem started before and has endured since, even as employment has hit record highs. We should therefore be wary of assuming that the problem will quickly unwind as the crisis fades. Just as we responded to the new experience of high unemployment following the recessions of the 1980s and 1990s, the task now is to update our labour market policy for today's challenges.

This means recognising that the current period of high employment is the right time to reduce the levels of insecurity people are bearing in today's labour market. **We recommend boosting employment security via the right to a regular contract for those doing regular hours on a zero-hours contract; extended statutory rights for the self-employed; and minimum notice periods for shifts**. Alongside innovations to support collective bargaining among young workers, this is how we provide them with a stronger base for taking the kind of beneficial risks that drive career improvements.

Getting young people's careers moving cannot be left to chance, especially when lower job moves and a slowdown in human capital improvements represent structural headwinds. **We recommend a new £1 billion 'Better Jobs Deal' that offers practical support and funding for younger workers most affected by the financial crisis to take up opportunities to move jobs or train to progress; and £1.5 billion to tackle persistent under-funding of technical education routes. Both should be funded by cancelling 1p of the forthcoming corporation tax cut**. These steps are designed to ensure businesses get the skilled and confident candidates they need.

Providing immediate housing security while turning around our housing crisis

The housing crisis that Britain faces – which is bearing down most heavily on younger cohorts but affects all of us – is so acute that no single solution will be enough. Action on three fronts is required.

In the short term, with the private rented sector now a tenure in which millions of children are raised and in which more people will spend retirements in future, it is essential to address its poor record for security. **We recommend that indeterminate tenancies should be the sole form of private rental contract, with light-touch rent stabilisation limiting rent increases to inflation for three-year periods and disputes settled by a new housing tribunal.**

In the medium term, we need to rebalance demand so young first-time buyers are in a better position compared to those buying second or subsequent homes. **We recommend replacing council tax with a progressive property tax with surcharges on second and empty properties; halving stamp duty rates to encourage moving; and a time-limited capital gains tax cut to incentivise owners of additional properties to sell to first-time buyers.**

In the long term we need to build more homes, year in, year out, in areas of strong housing demand, while increasing the number of affordable homes, to reduce housing costs. **We recommend piloting community land auctions so local authorities can ensure more land is brought forward for house building, underpinned by stronger compulsory purchase powers; and a £1.7 billion building precept allowing local authorities to raise funds for house building in their area.**

Reducing risks around younger generations' pensions

Recent reforms to the pensions landscape have addressed the persistent decline in saving precipitated by the demise of defined benefit provision, and guaranteed a higher basic rate for the State Pension. But the crucial difference, compared to current retirees, is the sheer scale of risk that future pensioners are being asked to shoulder.

We need to build on these reforms by spreading the benefits to groups that are at risk of remaining outside private pensions saving – including the very lowest earners and the self-employed – and by increasing how much is saved without large numbers of people dropping out of the new system. **We recommend requiring firms contracting self-employed labour to make pension contributions; lowering the earnings threshold above which employees get auto-enrolled; and providing greater incentives to save among low- and middle-earners by flattening rates of pensions tax relief and exempting employee contributions from National Insurance.**

It is also essential that we reduce the risks that individuals are being asked to bear around investment returns, longevity and inflation – risks that those retiring in the past have been comparatively protected from. **We recommend developing a legislative framework for 'collective defined contribution' pensions that better share investment risk; and reforming pension freedoms to include the default option of a guaranteed income product purchased at the age of 80**.

Harnessing the power of assets to boost security and opportunity today and respond to tomorrow's challenges

As well as addressing the issues young adults are facing in the jobs market, the housing market and in saving for retirement, a renewed intergenerational contract means recognising the significance of Britain's growing stock of wealth and the inability of many young people to share in it. Assets are important because they provide individuals with security and a basis for taking chances in their careers.

Inheritances are set to play a bigger role in determining who holds assets, and therefore in what living standards look like for different members of younger generations. But many millennials will not inherit – and even those who will are likely to receive this support shortly before retirement rather than in the expensive family-raising years.

Nonetheless, the coming rise in intergenerational wealth transfers provides an opportunity to show that Britain has something to offer young people, no matter who their parents are. **We recommend abolishing inheritance tax and replacing it with a lifetime receipts tax that is levied on recipients with fewer exemptions, a lower tax-free allowance and lower tax rates. The extra revenues should support a £10,000 'citizen's inheritance' – a restricted-use asset endowment to all young adults to support skills, entrepreneurship, housing and pension saving**. In the medium term, citizen's inheritances of £10,000 should be available from the age of 25 at a cost of £7 billion per year. During an initial transition phase, gradually rising inheritances should be offered at older ages, starting with those turning 35 in 2020.

The effects would be profound. A £10,000 boost today would at least double the wealth of more than six-in-ten adults in their late 20s. It would be enough for half the typical first-time buyer deposit in half the regions and nations of the UK; enough to fund a master's degree or significant retraining; and would add an estimated £45,000 to retirement savings pots if immediately invested in a pension. And by bridging between rental deposits when people move for work, or adding to businesses start-up resources for those in recognised entrepreneurship schemes, it would support the kind of positive labour market risk-taking that is all too lacking for the young at present. Such an approach would represent a bold demonstration that the state's role in delivering the intergenerational contract can evolve for the 21st century.

Renewing the intergenerational contract will not be easy, but it can be done

Families have adjusted to the 21st century's intergenerational challenges, and now as a society we need to do so too. We do not underestimate the task at hand, especially for democratically elected politicians in an era of unstable politics. But people are increasingly concerned about the prospects of other generations within their families and communities, and electoral turnout gaps by age are narrowing. We have presented a policy agenda that addresses the concerns of both old and young, and in so doing rebuilds the intergenerational contract.

We have taken bold steps to strengthen the contract between the generations before. We responded to the needs of those increasingly living beyond working age by introducing the State Pension at the beginning of the 20th century. We built the homes for the children of the baby boom to be brought up in after World War II. And we maintained pay progress and kept our young workers globally competitive via huge increases in access to university education in the 1990s.

If we once again step up to the challenge of keeping the intergenerational contract strong, we will not only have a better Britain but a more united one.

Ten key intergenerational facts

1 Earnings progress has stalled for young adults today. Millennials are earning the same as those born 15 years before them were at the same age.

2 Millennials have so far been 20-25 per cent less likely to move jobs than members of generation X at the same age, and are missing out on big pay rises as a result.

3 Millennial families are only half as likely to own their home by age 30 as baby boomers were by the same age, and are four times more likely to rent privately.

4 All post-war generations are spending more on housing than their predecessors, but millennials are spending more for less. A quarter of their income is spent on housing and they are on track to spend 64 more hours commuting in the year they turn 40 than baby boomers did.

5 Private sector membership of generous 'defined benefit' pensions for those around age 35 halved for employees born in the early 1980s compared to those born around 1970, although auto-enrolment is now boosting overall pension membership.

6 Future pensioners are exposed to retirement income risks that current retirees are largely protected from around investment returns, longevity and price shocks. A 1 percentage point decline in investment returns would reduce retirement incomes for millennial men born in the mid-1980s by 8 per cent.

7 Disposable incomes – the best measure of current living standards – are no higher for millennials who have reached age 30 than they were for generation X at that age.

8 Young adults spent the same as those approaching retirement in 2001, but they are now spending 15 per cent less.

9 Household wealth has grown rapidly throughout the 21st century, but despite this no cohorts born since 1960 are accumulating more wealth than their predecessors.

10 The UK's ageing population means public spending on health, care and social security is set to rise by £24 billion by 2030 and by £63 billion by 2040.

Ten key policy recommendations

1 Increase public funding for social care by more than £2 billion from reformed taxation of property. There should also be an increase in property-based contributions towards care costs, but with strict limits so that no-one pays more than a quarter of their wealth towards their own care.

2 Introduce a £2.3 billion 'NHS levy' via National Insurance on the earnings of those above State Pension age and limited National Insurance on occupational pension income.

3 Boost employment security via the right to a regular contract for those doing regular hours on a zero-hours contract; extended statutory rights for the self-employed; and minimum notice periods for shifts.

4 Introduce a £1 billion 'Better Jobs Deal' that offers practical support and funding for younger workers most affected by the financial crisis to take up opportunities to move jobs or train to progress; and £1.5 billion to tackle persistent underfunding of technical education routes. Both should be funded by cancelling 1p of the forthcoming corporation tax cut.

5 Make indeterminate tenancies the sole form of private rental contract, with light-touch rent stabilisation limiting rent increases to inflation for three-year periods and disputes settled by a new housing tribunal.

6 Replace council tax with a progressive property tax with surcharges on second and empty properties; halve stamp duty rates to encourage moving; and offer a time-limited capital gains tax cut to incentivise owners of additional properties to sell to first-time buyers.

7 Pilot community land auctions so local authorities can bring more land forward for house building, underpinned by stronger compulsory purchase powers; and introduce a £1.7 billion building precept allowing local authorities to raise funds for house building in their area.

8 Require firms contracting for self-employed labour to make pension contributions; lower the earnings threshold above which employees get auto-enrolled; and provide greater incentives to save among low- and middle-earners by flattening the rate of pensions tax relief and exempting employee pension contributions from National Insurance.

9 Develop a legislative framework for new 'collective defined contribution' pensions that better share risk; and reform pension freedoms to include the default option of a guaranteed income product purchased at the age of 80.

10 Abolish inheritance tax and replace it with a lifetime receipts tax that is levied on recipients with fewer exemptions, a lower tax-free allowance and lower tax rates. Use the extra revenues to introduce a £10,000 'citizen's inheritance' – a restricted-use asset endowment to all young adults to support skills, entrepreneurship, housing and pension saving.

SECTION 1

INTRODUCTION

CHAPTER 1

Generational progress – a promise under threat

Chapter summary

Intergenerational fairness has become a major challenge of our times. Its recent prominence in public debates reflects a widespread belief that each generation should have a better life than the previous one, alongside a fear that this may not be the case for today's young adults.

This pessimism does not relate to all aspects of young people's lives – there is recognition of significant progress in technology, personal freedoms and global connectedness delivering real improvements for younger generations.

The downbeat outlook overall is driven by anxieties about the core economic issue of living standards, with jobs, housing and retirement of greatest concern.

The Intergenerational Commission's task has been to understand whether the public is right in its pessimism; whether any slowing of living standards progress is solely down to the financial crisis; and, where problems have developed, what policy response is required to renew the intergenerational contract that underpins society.

The public believes that society is founded on an intergenerational contract of progress and mutual support

Modern states rest on the principle that different generations will provide support to each other at different stages of their lives, a principle that has been recognised at least since Edmund Burke articulated it over 200 years ago:

> *"Society is indeed a contract...It is a partnership in all science; a partnership in all art; a partnership in every virtue, and in all perfection. As the ends of such a partnership cannot be obtained in many generations, it becomes a partnership not only between those who are living, but between those who are living, those who are dead, and those who are to be born."*[1]
>
> Edmund Burke

Public attitudes clearly reflect this principle. A large majority of British adults believe that it is society's duty to provide for older generations, as shown by the left-hand panel in Figure 1.1. While this belief is strongest among older age groups, it is common among young adults too. The British public also believes that each successive generation should have a higher standard of living than the one that came before it: people are more likely to agree than disagree with this statement by a ratio of six-to-one, and this does not shift as we move through the age range. The prospects of both older and younger generations are clearly important issues.

Figure 1.1: Most people support principles of intergenerational support and progress

Agreement with the principles of old-age support and generational progress, by age group: GB, 2017

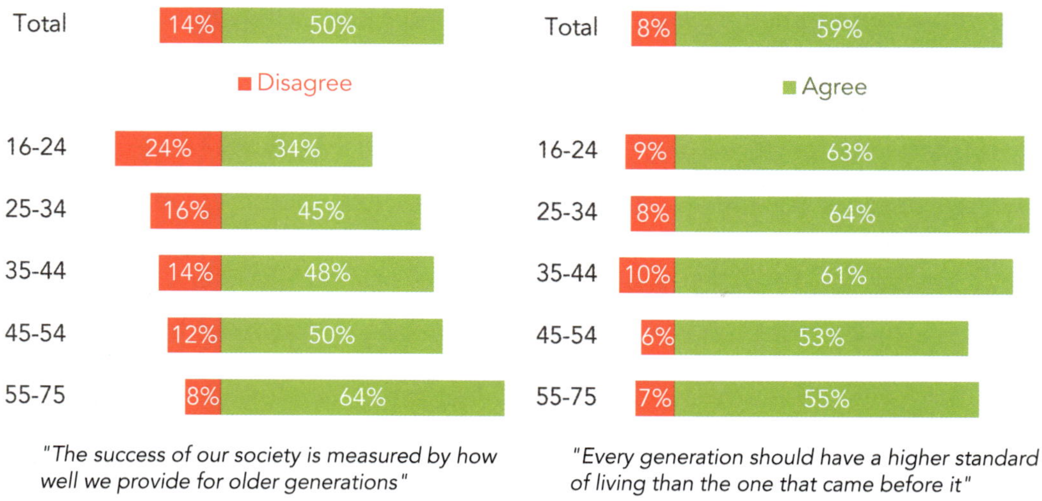

Notes: Adults aged 16-75. For further details, see: *The millennial bug* (Intergenerational Commission report 8)
Source: Ipsos MORI

1 E Burke, *Reflections on the Revolution in France*, Hackett Publishing, 1987

The belief that society should provide for older generations is not surprising – it reflects what families do and the state's core function of providing social insurance over lifetimes. Nor is the belief in improvements for successive generations surprising. A growing economy should mean that each successive generation has a better standard of living at each age, while social reforms and technological advancements continually expand opportunities and choices. Indeed, it is these ongoing improvements that underpin the capacity of younger generations to provide for older ones. But it is difficult for succeeding generations to continue funding generous commitments to previous generations if their own improvements are faltering. This is why any disruption to generation-on-generation improvements should be seen as a shared challenge.

People are concerned that today's young adults may not achieve generational progress

There is widespread concern among the general public that this principle of generational progress is not being honoured for today's younger generations. Those who are pessimistic about young people's prospects of improving on their parents' lives outnumber optimists by two-to-one, as Figure 1.2 shows.

Figure 1.2: British adults are pessimistic about young people's prospects

Opinions about whether young people will have a better life than their parents: GB, 2017

Notes: Adults aged 16-75. For further details, see: *The millennial bug* (Intergenerational Commission report 8)
Source: Ipsos MORI

This pessimism is shared across a broad range of demographic characteristics. There is not a single group in which the balance of opinion about young people's prospects is optimistic across age, sex, region, education level, income, political affiliations, and vote in the EU referendum.

This does not mean there are no differences across groups, but they are often small. For example, the gap between the 53 per cent of 16-24-year-olds who think young people will have a worse life than their parents and the 44 per cent of 55-75-year-olds who are of this opinion is just 9 percentage points. Generally, pessimism about the prospects of today's younger adults is correlated with markers of economic advantage: those who are more educated and have higher incomes are more likely to be pessimistic about generational progress.[2]

Such pessimism is new in Britain. As recently as 2003, 43 per cent of adults thought that their children would have better lives than they did, with just 12 per cent disagreeing. The balance of opinion shifted in the late 2000s and has remained weighted towards pessimism since. A similar switch in opinion was observed in the US over the same period.[3]

It is not just the US that shares Britain's downbeat mood about young people's prospects of late. Similar opinions are observed across advanced economies, although Britain is among the most pessimistic, as Figure 1.3 shows.

Figure 1.3: Pessimism about young people's prospects is common across advanced economies

Attitudes on whether today's youth will have a better life than their parents, by country: 2016

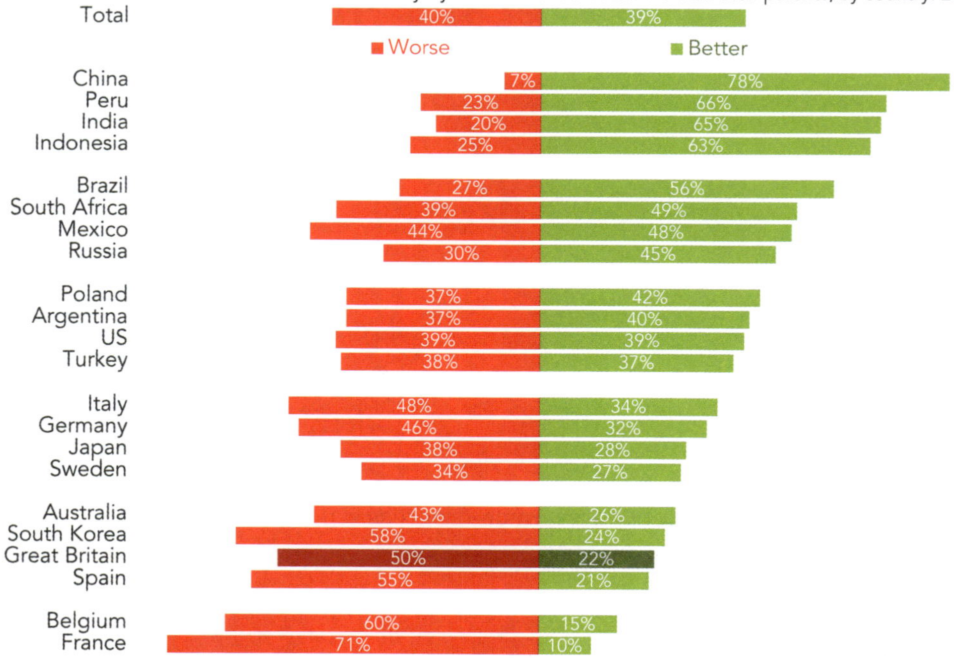

Notes: Adults aged 16+. Results for Great Britain are slightly different to those shown in Figure 1.2 because this analysis is based on a different (slightly earlier) survey. For further details including question wording, see: *The millennial bug* (Intergenerational Commission report 8)

Source: Ipsos MORI, *Global Trends Survey 2017*

2 *The millennial bug* (Intergenerational Commission report 8)

3 These trends over time are based on repeated polling (by Ipsos MORI in the UK and Gallup in the US), albeit using slightly different questions to those discussed elsewhere in this chapter. See: *The millennial bug* (Intergenerational Commission report 8)

Fast-developing countries unsurprisingly have a rosier outlook for their young people, but the degree of pessimism elsewhere is striking. Across more advanced economies the financial crisis, and its effects on those in their formative years when it hit, has been a crucial factor in the rise of intergenerational issues in public debate. In the UK, *The Pinch*,[4] published in 2010, was the first of several books to stimulate debates about intergenerational fairness just as these concerns surfaced among the public on a scale not seen before. But while the financial crisis may be the trigger for much of the current generational pessimism, it is important to ask if there are longer-term drivers.

Pessimism does not extend to all aspects of young people's lives – we should celebrate all the things that are better

There are important areas in which the public does believe that today's young people will experience an improvement on their parents' lives. Access to information, travel opportunities, quality of education and the ability to be true to themselves are all areas in which the optimists clearly outnumber the pessimists, as shown in Figure 1.4.

Figure 1.4: British adults are optimistic about certain aspects of young people's lives

Attitudes on how young people's lives will compare to their parents' lives – areas of optimism: GB, 2017

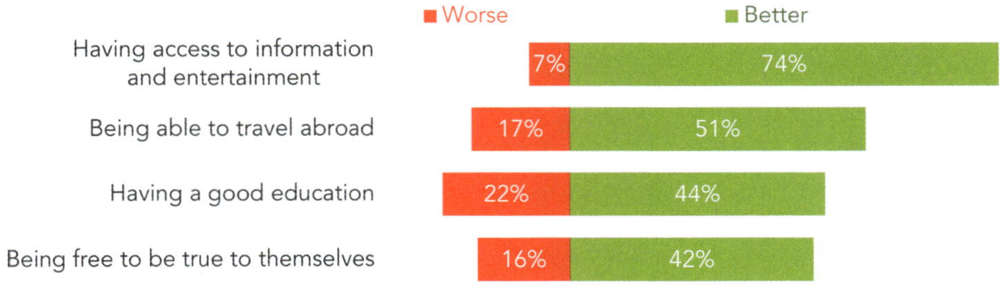

Notes: Adults aged 16-75. For further details including question wording, see: *The millennial bug* (Intergenerational Commission report 8)
Source: Ipsos MORI

Qualitative research conducted alongside this polling shows that adults across age groups view the quality of lives for women, ethnic minorities, lesbian, gay and transgender people and other minority groups as clear areas of improvement through the generations. While there is of course much progress still to be made, many young people in these groups now have opportunities and freedoms that would have been considered a distant dream by their predecessors. Other frequently cited areas in which young people have clear advantages are access to low-cost technology – and the ability to use it effectively – and global connectedness.

These are significant aspects of people's lives which any exercise focusing on headwinds to improvements for young people must not lose sight of. But progress

4 D Willetts, *The Pinch: How the Baby Boomers Took Their Children's Future – And Why They Should Give It Back*, Atlantic Books, September 2010

in these fields is far from new. Many of these advancements in personal liberties, technology and communications in recent decades have come on top of really significant advancements in previous ones. For example female suffrage, colour televisions and washing machines (in very different ways) transformed lives in mid-20th century Britain.

Concern about generational progress is centred on the core aspects of living standards

Despite these areas of optimism, pessimism pervades overall. Areas in which the public believes young people's lives will be worse than their parents' lives are set out in Figure 1.5. These clearly outnumber the areas of optimism shown in Figure 1.4.

Figure 1.5: Pessimism about young people's prospects extends to most areas of their lives

Attitudes on how young people's lives will compare to their parents' lives – areas of pessimism: GB, 2017

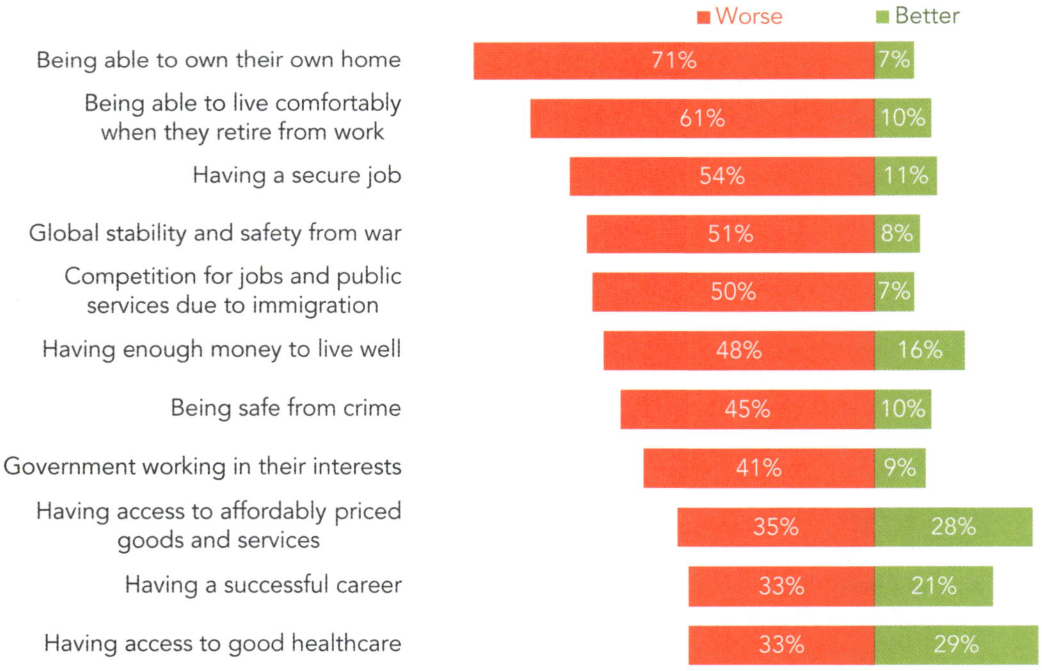

Notes: Adults aged 16-75. For further details, see: *The millennial bug* (Intergenerational Commission report 8)
Source: Ipsos MORI

Despite the breadth of issues across which pessimism holds, the top three areas of concern clearly relate to key aspects of living standards. Across housing, incomes in retirement, and work the pessimists outnumber optimists by around five-to-one or more.

The scope of the Intergenerational Commission

The first task of the Intergenerational Commission's two-year study has been to investigate whether the public is right in its pessimism about the prospects of young people in 21st century Britain. We have sought to offer the most comprehensive assessment to date of differences in the economic experience of generations in the UK, not just at a given point in time but over their life courses.

Taking cues from the issues about which the public is most pessimistic, we have focused our analysis on living standards. This captures incomes (the result of a combination of employment, pay, pensions and taxes and benefits); wealth; and the relative prices and consumption patterns that determine the goods and services that people enjoy. We have not explored in detail all issues of intergenerational relevance, including crucial ones such as climate change or the state of public services. And, while we have included some detailed comparative analysis of the experiences of other advanced economies, this report focuses on the intergenerational challenges facing Britain.

In some areas, such as housing and potentially pensions, there are real questions about whether today's young people will do as well as their parents. In other areas, however – typically those more closely related to economic growth, such as earnings and incomes – such an outcome is almost inconceivable. For that reason, while the public doubts the potential for young adults to do better than their parents, we focus more specifically on gaps between commonly defined 'generations' and between narrower 'cohorts' within them. Our generation and cohort definitions are set out in Box 1.1 overleaf.

Our focus is on the new challenge of inequalities *between* generations, but significant variation exists *within* specific cohorts and generations too. To reflect that we also explore intra-generational differences – particularly by gender and income. This is important when we seek to understand where intergenerational inequalities might exacerbate or reduce intra-generational inequality.

While public pessimism and a more prominent focus on intergenerational issues in political debate emerged alongside the financial crisis, a priority for the Commission has been to establish whether this event is the only driver of these outcomes. We have sought to understand its interplay with more structural factors – including demographic shifts, institutional change and long-term policy choices.

Drawing on a detailed analysis of living standards for different generations and their drivers, the Intergenerational Commission has also considered what changes to policy might be necessary. We've set out to provide both high-level directions and specific policy options that would help renew the intergenerational contract. While both practical and implementable, our focus is long term, looking beyond what might be achieved in the current parliament. Our argument is also about the state of the nation, both now and in the future. And, far from being aligned with the agenda of any particular political party, it should be of relevance to any politician attempting to answer the big questions facing Britain. We also reflect on the challenges of achieving policy change where there are generational differences in political and social engagement. In particular, Brexit has underscored the importance of a credible consideration of generational challenges in politics given stark variation in preferences in the EU referendum by age.[5]

Box 1.1 What are generations?

The dictionary definition of a generation is all the people born and living around the same time, regarded collectively. Generations should be distinguished from age groups (or life stages). A generation may currently be young, for example, but this will of course change over time: its defining feature is its years of birth.

When delineating particular generations comprising those born in between two specific points in time, two other concepts have been advanced:

- That generations have some degree of collective identity, in terms of shared economic experience, shared values or cultural norms;[1]
- That the relative size of generations when they are born and as they age can play an important role in determining these shared experiences.[2]

In referring to generations, we adopt commonly used definitions that have been established in academic and public debates on the basis of population fluctuations and cultural identities.[3] Our definitions are as follows, with the birth patterns they encapsulate summarised in Figure 1.6:

- The lost generation, born 1881-95
- The forgotten generation, born 1896-1910
- The greatest generation, born 1911-25
- The silent generation, born 1926-45
- The baby boomers, born 1946-65
- Generation X, born 1966-80
- The millennials, born 1981-2000
- The latest generation, born 2001 onwards.

1 W Strauss & N Howe, *Generations: The history of America's future, 1584 to 2069*, Perennial, 1991

2 In particular, big generations are often followed by small ones and vice versa. See: T Malthus, *An Essay on the Principle of Population*, Oxford University Press, 1798

3 Precise birth year cut-offs and terminology differ across analyses, we have sought to adopt the most common definitions and terms that fit with the UK's demographic patterns. For a selection of approaches, see: W Strauss & N Howe, *Generations: The history of America's future, 1584 to 2069*, Perennial, 1991; R Fry, 'Millennials surpass Gen Xers as the largest generation in U.S. labor force', *Pew Research Center FactTank*, 11 May 2015; P Bump, 'Here Is When Each Generation Begins and Ends, According to Facts', *The Atlantic*, 25 March 2014; D Willetts, *The Pinch: How the Baby Boomers Took Their Children's Future – And Why They Should Give It Back*, Atlantic Books, September 2010

5 For details on this variation in voting preferences, see: *Stagnation generation* (Intergenerational Commission report 1)

Figure 1.6: Birth patterns have fluctuated over time in the UK

Births per year and generational averages: UK

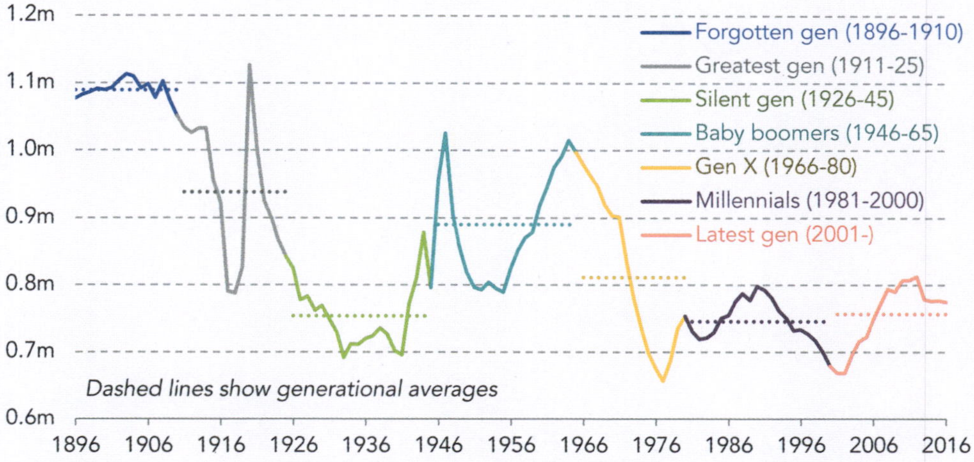

Source: ONS, *Birth Characteristics* (England and Wales); NRS, *Births Time Series Data* (Scotland); NISRA, *Live births, 1887 to 2015* (Northern Ireland)

Within these 15- or 20-year generational groupings we also refer to narrower three-, five- or ten-year birth cohorts to elicit a more detailed understanding. Crucially, these cohorts and generations are – as far as possible – compared at the same age, in order to distinguish the usual differences between age groups at different points in the life course from cohort or generational differences in outcomes.

The structure of this report

- **Section 2** evaluates the **evidence** on the living standards of different generations, with a focus on outcomes so far and a view – where possible – to future prospects. *Chapters 2-5* cover the four key components that determine living standards – the labour market, housing, pensions and interactions with the state.

- **Section 3** reflects on this evidence and what it means for our **overall view of generational living standards** progress and for policy. *Chapter 6* brings the evidence together with an overall view on incomes, consumption and wealth. *Chapter 7* sets out our conclusions from this analysis and the broad shape that any policy response should take.

- **Section 4** provides our **policy recommendations**, including the analytical considerations that underpin the conclusions we have come to. It is set out over four chapters (*Chapters 8-11*), again covering the labour market, the housing market, the pensions system and the state.

- **Section 5** provides concluding remarks.

SECTION 2

OUTCOMES AND PROSPECTS FOR LIVING STANDARDS ACROSS GENERATIONS

CHAPTER 2

Jobs and pay – work in progress

Chapter summary

Unemployment is at a 40-year low, with millennials in their late 20s around 25 per cent less likely to be unemployed than baby boomers were at the same age. Today's record levels of employment are in part driven by historical improvements for women.

But cohort-on-cohort pay progress has stalled, with the oldest cohort of millennials recording earnings at age 30 only slightly higher than the cohort born 15 years before them.

The financial crisis played a large part in this. Average real pay is still £15 per week below pre-crisis levels.

However, cohort-on-cohort pay progress was declining for younger cohorts even before the crisis. Key to this longer-term trend has been a shift towards lower-paying and less secure jobs among young people, alongside a slowing in the rate of human capital improvement.

Increases in low-paid self-employment and 'atypical' work mean young adults today are shouldering more risk than their predecessors. This increase in risk is one reason younger workers themselves are taking fewer risks by way of job-to-job moves, which depresses their pay.

The labour market is the primary engine of generational living standards progress

The labour market represents the major source of household incomes (and therefore consumption) over people's working lives, and is the vehicle through which much saving for retirement or a house deposit takes place. What happens in it is therefore vitally important to trends in living standards across generations. Particularly key are changes in both the quantity of work – the number of people in a household in employment and the hours they work – and the pay received for it. But these two elements have moved in very different directions over recent years, with important generational consequences.

Today's young adults have avoided the high unemployment previous generations faced

Unemployment increased after the recession of 2008-09, but by less than most people expected. As Figure 2.1 shows, despite the unusual depth and duration of the post-crisis downturn, the unemployment increase was no higher than was recorded following the recessions of the early 1980s and early 1990s. A similar pattern held for youth unemployment too, rising by 10.5 percentage points in the early 1980s (against the backdrop of a 5.3 percentage point fall in output) but just 5.4 percentage points in the late 2000s (when output fell by 6.1 percentage points).

Figure 2.1: Despite a deep recession, the post-financial crisis increase in youth unemployment was relatively muted

Change in output (%) and unemployment rate (percentage points) from pre-recession peak: UK, 1979-2017

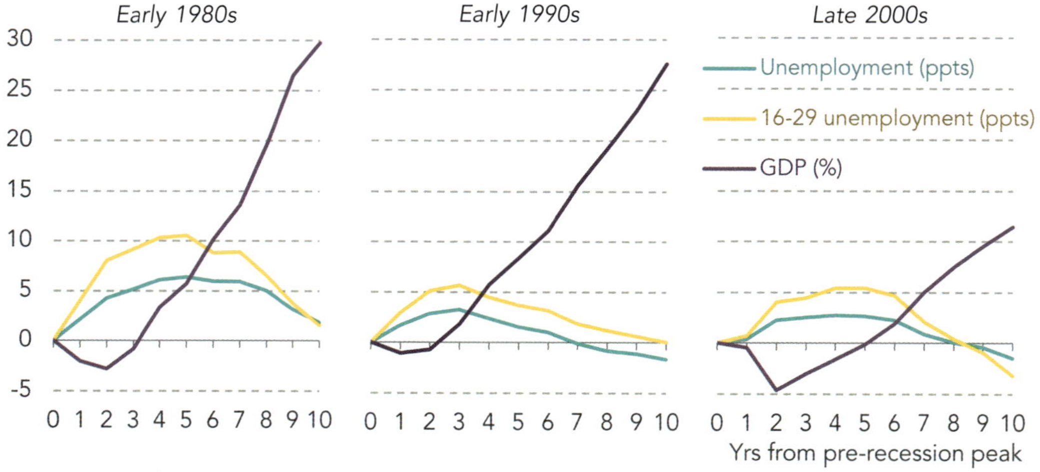

Notes: Periods over which change is measured are 1979-89, 1989-99 and 2007-17. Figures for 16-29-year-olds are derived from a weighted average of estimates by single year of age, with published unemployment rates used as control totals in order to create a consistent series over time.

Source: RF analysis of ONS, *Labour Force Survey*; ONS, *Labour Market Statistics*; ONS, *GDP estimates*

The speed of the employment recovery after the financial crisis also stands in contrast to the earlier experiences. Youth unemployment did not recover to pre-recession levels at any point in the decade after the 1980-81 downturn, and it took a full ten years to recover after the spike that followed the 1990-91 recession. In the most recent recession, youth unemployment took just eight years to return to its previous level.

One way in which younger adults fared less well in the most recent recession relates to their relative position in the jobs market. Increases in unemployment were disproportionately higher among 16-29-year-olds following each of the last three recessions, but they were most skewed towards younger people in the late 2000s. In that instance the increase for 16-29-year-olds was twice as high (104 per cent) as the overall rise, whereas it was only 65 per cent higher in the early 1980s and 79 per cent higher in the early 1990s.

Notwithstanding this finding, the recent story on unemployment remains a more positive one than we might have anticipated a decade ago. And the UK experience has been very different to that of some other advanced economies. Youth unemployment rose in high-income countries across the globe following the recession in 2008, with some especially large increases in Southern Europe. The 15-30-year-old unemployment rate peaked above 40 per cent in Spain and Greece, compared to a high of 16 per cent in the UK. And, while youth unemployment has since recovered across advanced economies, the UK is one of the few countries in which it had fallen back to a similar level to its pre-crisis low by 2016.[1]

Unemployment is of course deeply troubling for each individual and family affected, but it now sits at a 40-year low and a higher proportion of people aged 16-64 is participating in the labour market than ever before. As a result, in their late 20s millennials have so far experienced unemployment rates that are around 25 per cent lower than those experienced by baby boomers at the same age, and are similar to those of generation X.[2]

Big improvements in female employment have been maintained

Complementing this generational decline in unemployment rates have been record levels of employment. Three-quarters (75 per cent) of the UK's working-age population are now in employment, higher than at any other point since comparable records began in the early 1970s. Underpinning this are historic improvements in female employment.

While employment rates have been broadly unchanged for men in each of the last three generations to reach adulthood, Figure 2.2 shows a big increase for women in generation X relative to the baby boomers (with a further slight improvement to date among millennial women). And baby boomers themselves recorded consistently

1 *Cross countries* (Intergenerational Commission report 15)

2 *Stagnation generation* (Intergenerational Commission report 1)

Figure 2.2: **Women have made great generational gains in employment since the silent generation**

Employment rates, by age, sex and generation: UK, 1975-2017

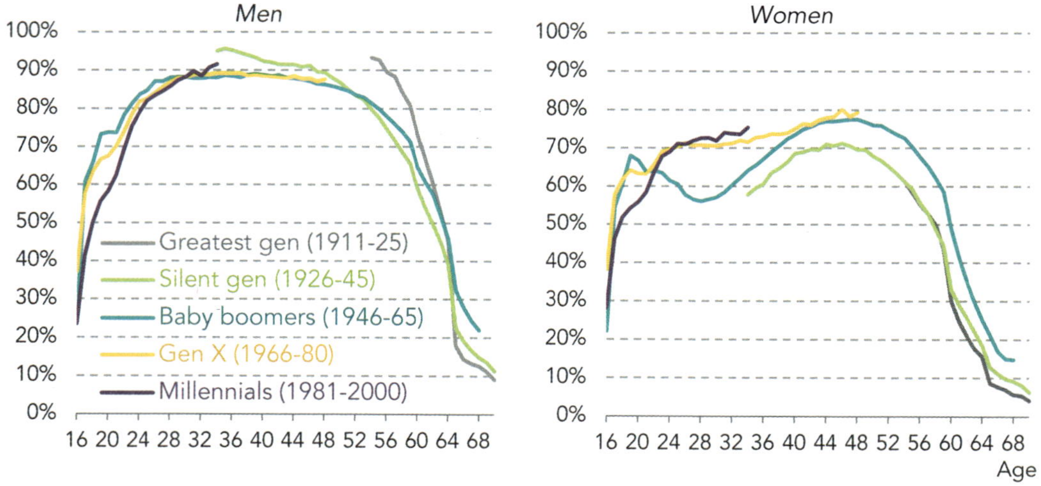

Notes: See notes to Figure 11 in: *Stagnation generation* (Intergenerational Commission report 1)
Source: RF analysis of ONS, *Labour Force Survey*; ONS, *Labour Market Statistics*

higher employment rates at all ages (of about 5 to 7 percentage points) than the silent generation coming before them. These strong employment outcomes for women should not be taken for granted. While societies have generally become more equal across the globe in recent decades, many other advanced economies – notably the US – have experienced much smaller labour market gains for women in the face of similar demographic and industrial pressures.[3] The UK experience has been driven by a concerted policy effort, including equal pay legislation, enhanced employment rights around childbirth and improved childcare support. Box 2.2 later in this chapter takes up the subject of the experiences of different sexes in the labour market in more detail.

There have also been large strides over recent years in employment among people from ethnic minority backgrounds, particularly women. Although the employment rates of Bangladeshi and Pakistani women remain around half those of white women, there has been a steady catch-up over the past 14 years. There have also been big improvements in employment for Black African and Black Caribbean women. For Black men, employment rates fell substantially post-crisis and were slow to recover, but have since rebounded to record highs. However, unemployment rates for Black, Bangladeshi and Pakistani men (at 8 per cent to 12 per cent) remain higher today than was the case for white men even during the recession.[4] These differential experiences by ethnicity will be reflected in the experiences of those from ethnic minority backgrounds within younger generations.

3 *Cross countries* (Intergenerational Commission report 15)

4 A Corlett, *Diverse outcomes: Living standards by ethnicity*, Resolution Foundation, August 2017

But young adults' pay has performed unprecedentedly poorly

In contrast to overall positive trends in employment, the recent story on pay has been much more disappointing. Pay growth failed to keep pace with inflation for the six years between 2009 and 2014. Following two years of modest recovery, this 'pay squeeze' returned in 2017 – prompted by a spike in inflation associated with the Brexit referendum. As a result, average pay was still £15 a week below pre-crisis levels in real terms in early 2018, a decade on from the financial crisis.[5] Unlike the speedy recovery that has characterised the post-crisis story on unemployment, pay is currently projected to take nearly two decades to return to its pre-recession peak.[6]

Across advanced economies the magnitude of the UK's post-crisis pay squeeze was second only to Greece – a country which experienced a much deeper and longer period of economic stagnation than the UK. But the UK experienced the greatest divergence of pay experiences by age in this period, with young adults faring much worse than older workers.[7]

The generational consequences of these trends are shown in Figure 2.3. Prior to the post-crisis pay squeeze, all generations, other than the millennials, had experienced large gains when compared to their predecessors. These gains have subsequently narrowed, but some progress remains. In contrast, the pay trajectory of millennials is

Figure 2.3: Today's young adults are earning less than the generation before them did at the same age

Median real weekly employee pay (CPIH-adjusted to 2017 prices), by age and generation: UK, 1975-2017

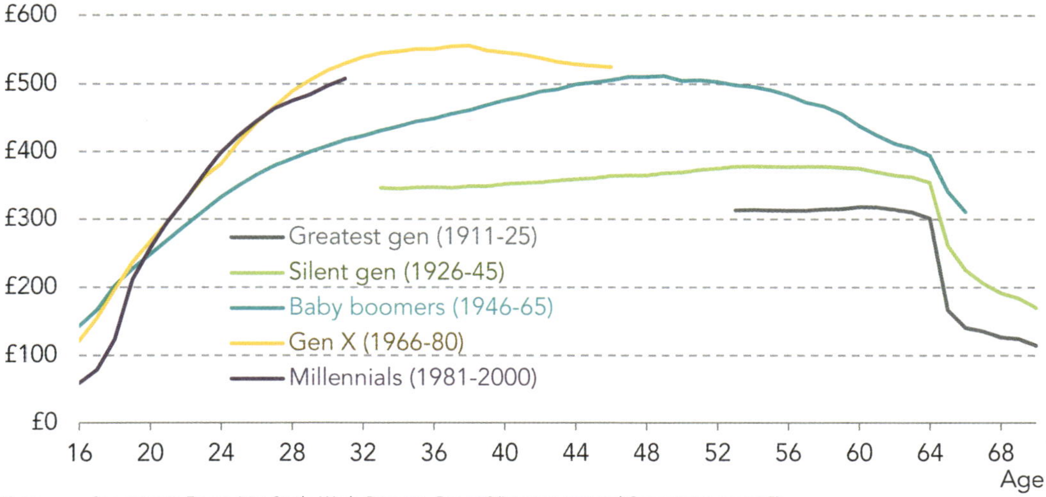

Notes: See notes to Figure 1 in: *Study, Work, Progress, Repeat?* (Intergenerational Commission report 5)

Source: RF analysis of ONS, *Labour Force Survey*; ONS, *Annual Survey of Hours and Earnings*; ONS, *New Earnings Survey Panel Dataset*

5 Here and throughout this report, unless otherwise specified, we deflate using CPIH. Source: ONS, *Labour Market Statistics*

6 Resolution Foundation, *Sugar rush: Spring Statement response*, March 2018

7 *Cross countries* (Intergenerational Commission report 15)

largely tracking that of generation X. Those millennials who have so far reached their 30s are earning less than their generation X counterparts at the same age.The broad patterns set out in Figure 2.3 are helpful for getting a summary picture of trends over a long time-frame. But not all members of each generation have reached the ages displayed (we only include generations at a given age when at least five birth years are present in the data), so the picture may change in future as younger members of the generation come through.

By way of digging into that thought, Figure 2.4 looks in more detail at the pay trends for five-year cohorts. It highlights the extent to which the earnings of younger cohorts have fallen back the most in recent years. For example, following years of cohort-on-cohort progress, median real earnings among the various baby boomer cohorts have dipped below earnings for those born five years before them when measured at the same age. But within generation X, earnings are no higher than for those born *ten* years earlier. Shifting to the two millennial cohorts, we can see that both those born 1986-90 (at age 26) and 1981-85 (in their early 30s) had similar earnings to the cohorts *15* years before them at the same age.

Figure 2.4: All cohorts have been affected by weak earnings growth, but younger cohorts have been hit the hardest

Median real weekly employee pay (CPIH-adjusted to 2017 prices), by age and cohort: UK, 1975-2017

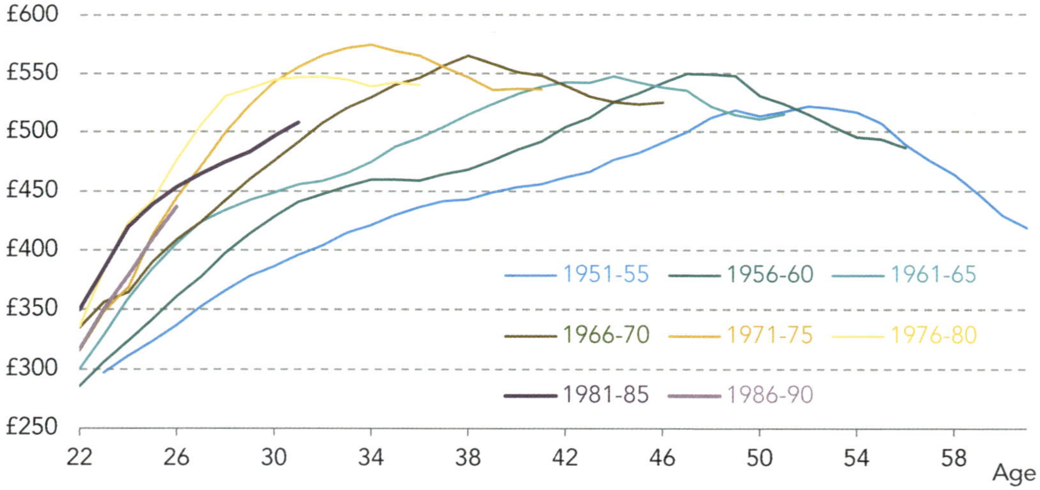

Notes: See notes to Figure 2 in: *Study, Work, Progress, Repeat?* (Intergenerational Commission report 5)
Source: RF analysis of ONS, *Labour Force Survey*; ONS, *Annual Survey of Hours and Earnings*; ONS, *New Earnings Survey Panel Dataset*

These outcomes are reflected in the experience of both lower and higher earners within generations. For example, the degree of generational earnings stagnation is similar for millennials at different skill levels compared to their counterparts in generation X.[8]

8 *Study, Work, Progress, Repeat?* (Intergenerational Commission report 5)

This disappointing pay performance has deeper roots than just the financial crisis and its aftermath

The fact that cohort-on-cohort pay progress has stalled in recent years owes much to the financial crisis, but it had been slowing – and even stagnating – before this. Figure 2.5 shows this by setting out the cohort-on-cohort earnings gains recorded at age 25 across six successive cohorts, spanning the period from 1981 to 2009. It shows that each of the three generation X cohorts achieved lower gains than those enjoyed by the youngest baby boomer cohort, with the oldest millennial cohort then experiencing almost no gain relative to those born five years earlier.

Figure 2.5: Pay progress had started to slow even before the crisis

Change in median real weekly employee pay (CPIH-adjusted) compared to the preceding cohort at age 25, by cohort: UK, 1981-2009

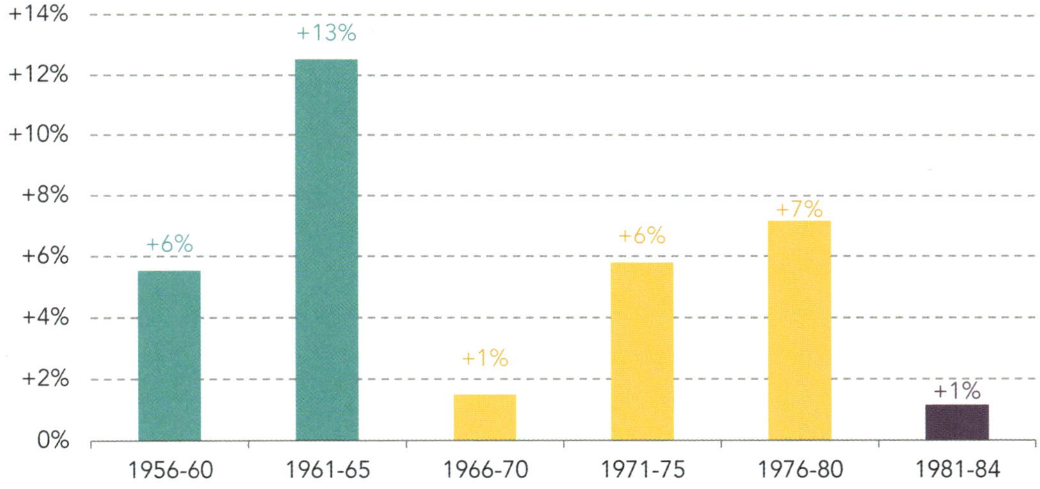

Notes: See notes to Figure 2 in: *Study, Work, Progress, Repeat?* (Intergenerational Commission report 5)
Source: RF analysis of ONS, *Annual Survey of Hours and Earnings*; ONS, *New Earnings Survey Panel Dataset*

Poor pay outcomes therefore started before the crisis and have endured beyond it, even as unemployment has dipped to its lowest level in decades. The implication is that the drivers of the poor generational pay performance are related to the financial crisis but are also partly structural, reflecting far deeper shifts in our labour market.

A major non-recession-related contributor to these longer-term trends has been stalling cohort-on-cohort growth in qualifications for millennials. The millennials form the best-educated generation to date, but what matters for cohort-on-cohort pay improvements is not only *levels* of educational attainment, but also the pace of *change*. The upskilling of successive cohorts is central to productivity and pay growth.

Figure 2.6 shows that each cohort has been more educated than the previous one over the past 50 years. On average, around 35 per cent of older millennial cohorts had a degree by their late 20s, compared with 23 per cent of generation X at the same age. But the large cohort-on-cohort gains in degree attainment experienced by generation X have not been replicated for the millennials: the 37 per cent increase recorded between the 1969-71 and 1972-74 cohorts dwindled to just a 7 per cent improvement between the 1981-83 and 1984-89 cohorts.

Figure 2.6: Improvements in human capital accumulation have slowed in recent years

Highest qualification held at age 25-28, by cohort: UK, 1992-2017

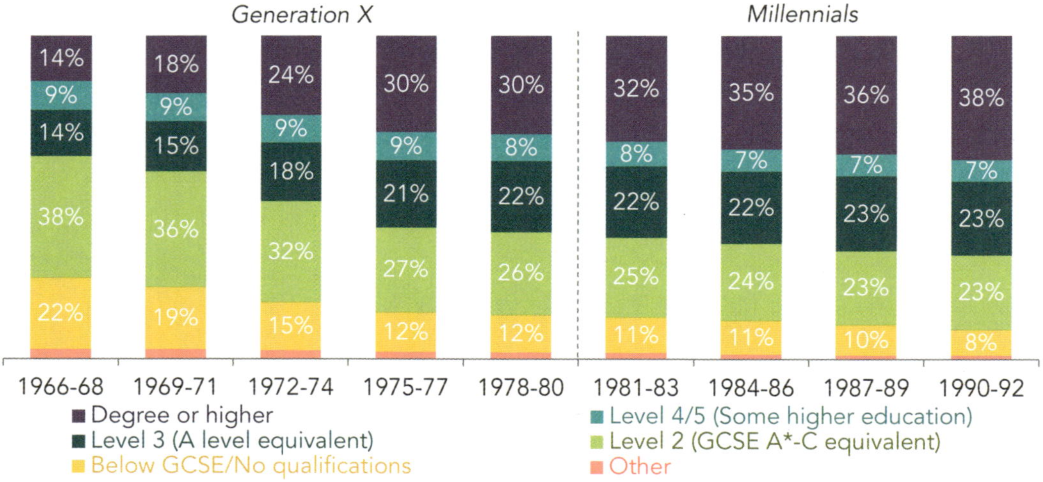

Source: RF analysis of ONS, *Labour Force Survey*

While the growth in the share of each cohort going into higher education has slowed, other routes for cohort-on-cohort human capital progress have not picked up the slack. Between the 1966-68 and 1978-80 cohorts, the proportion of adults with qualifications at Level 2 or below (equivalent to GCSE grades A*-C) fell from 63 per cent to 38 per cent. But since the 1978-80 cohort this proportion has fallen at a much slower rate, only declining to 32 per cent in the 1990-92 cohort. The trend towards greater participation in higher education is common across advanced economies, as is the slowdown of human capital growth. However, this slowdown has been especially marked in the UK (along with France and Spain).[9]

The emergence of defined benefit pension deficits and the necessary plugging of these gaps by many established firms has also been identified as a potential structural factor holding back pay growth, but does not appear to have made more than a small difference across the economy. These effects are summarised in Box 2.1.

9 *Cross countries* (Intergenerational Commission report 15)

Box 2.1 The impact of defined benefit pension deficits on wages

Across the UK economy, the share of overall employee compensation accounted for by non-wage elements such as employer pension contributions has increased substantially since 2000. This increase was driven in no small part by increased payments by employers to plug defined benefit deficits, necessary because of increases in longevity and lower-than-expected interest rates. Increased deficit-funding contributions accounted for around £19 billion of the overall £37 billion elevation in non-wage employer contributions in 2016 relative to the 2000 position. The coincidence of these contribution increases with the pre-crisis pay slowdown and subsequent pay squeeze led to speculation as to whether the two phenomena are linked. This question has generational implications: with 85 per cent of defined benefit schemes closed to new members and 35 per cent also closed to future accrual, the population with most to gain from closing scheme deficits is likely to have limited overlap with the population affected by any associated reduction in pay, or for that matter investment.

A report for the Intergenerational Commission – *The pay deficit* – empirically tested the firm-specific impact of deficit contribution payments on wages using a large dataset of linked firm-employee records.[1] It identified a strongly significant negative correlation between deficit payments and employee pay levels, such that these payments are estimated to directly lower employee pay by between £1.4 billion and £2.2 billion a year. Roughly half of private sector employees work in firms with defined benefit schemes, and the average annual pay effect within this group is in the range £145-£225. These effects are stronger for current members of the pension scheme, but are present even among non-members when looking at the bottom end of the pay distribution where workers tend to be younger.

At the macro level, these firm-specific effects are not large enough to explain more than a small part of the generalised slowdown in pay growth that has occurred since the early 2000s. Nevertheless, the micro firm-level effects are sizeable and have generational implications. In addition, subsequent research has identified potential effects on dividends and investment.[2]

1 *The pay deficit* (Intergenerational Commission report 6)

2 P Bunn, P Mizen & P Smietanka, *Growing pension deficits and the expenditure decisions of UK companies*, Bank of England, February 2018

Wider shifts are also increasing the labour market risks young people now bear

Weak pay performance for younger cohorts is also partly a reflection of some deeper trends that have profoundly affected young adults in particular by increasing the risk they bear in the labour market. These are broadly characterised by a rise in 'atypical' forms of working, which transfer risk from the employer onto the worker. The result is weakened employment rights and reduced certainty of income relative to traditional full-time employees with permanent contracts.

The first of these trends is a rise in self-employment. This has been one of the big stories of the post-crisis period, but the share of self-employed people has actually been rising since the early 2000s. Snapshots of self-employment across the age distribution in 2001-03 and 2015-17 are shown in Figure 2.7. Additionally, it contrasts rates among those with and without a degree. The lines slope upwards, indicating that the propensity to be self-employed increases with age. More significant, however, are shifts in the educational profile of the self-employed. In both periods, younger people were more likely to be self-employed if they did not hold a degree, whereas older workers were more likely to be self-employed if they were degree-educated. Relative to the 2001-03 baseline, the proportion of degree-holding older workers who were self-employed had fallen in 2015-17. In contrast, the proportion of younger non-degree-holders working in this way increased sharply. This latter group is more likely

Figure 2.7: Self-employment has grown for younger non-graduates in the 21st century

Self-employment as a share of all employment, by age and educational attainment: UK

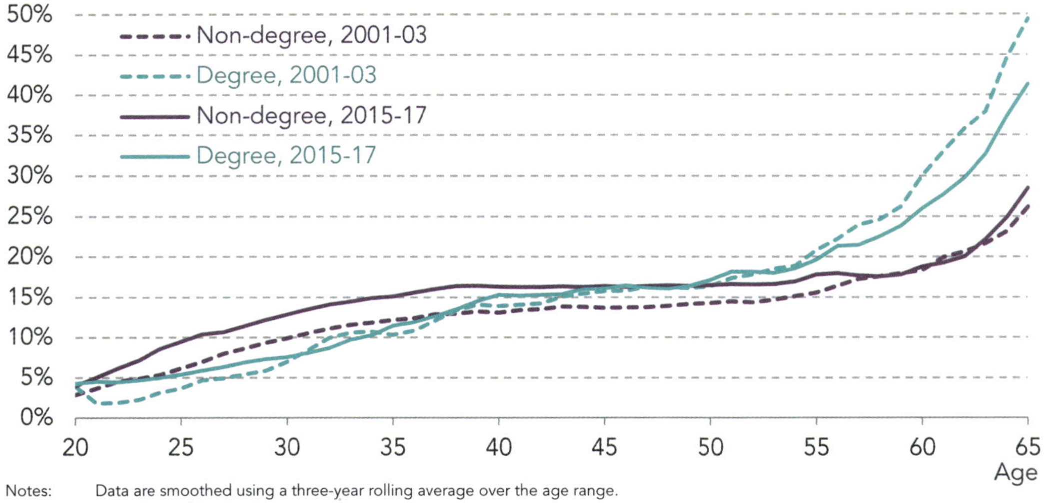

Notes: Data are smoothed using a three-year rolling average over the age range.
Source: RF analysis of ONS, *Labour Force Survey*

to be in low-skilled and insecure self-employment, in contrast to those seeking to work more flexibly or boost earnings on the run-in to retirement for example.[10]

These shifts are not directly reflected in the headline earnings data, which only covers employees. But more limited data suggests the millennial earnings position would look no better, and in some cases worse, if the self-employed were included. For those born during 1981-85, the fall in real earnings at age 30, compared with those born a decade earlier, increases from 7.1 per cent to 9.3 per cent with the inclusion of the self-employed.[11]

Young adults also appear to have disproportionately shouldered the risk associated with the rise in recent years of zero-hours contracts (ZHCs) and agency working. ZHCs comprise only a small proportion (2.8 per cent) of the workforce,[12] but, despite a marginal decline in the latest data, this proportion has risen rapidly in recent years (albeit largely due to greater recognition of the term among survey respondents as it hit the headlines in 2013). These increases are strongly concentrated at the bottom of the age range, and particularly among cohorts newly entering the labour market. One-in-twelve workers aged under 25 is on a ZHC, compared to around one-in-fifty of those aged 25-64. And while 6 per cent of the 1991-95 cohort reported being on a ZHC at age 21, just 1 per cent of the 1986-90 cohort did so.[13]

At 2.6 per cent of employment, agency workers also represent only a small proportion of the workforce: but there has been a rise of over 30 per cent since 2011. And this has again been concentrated among workers under 30, who are around twice as likely to be agency workers as those in their 50s and 60s.[14]

These growing forms of atypical employment sit alongside a wider increase in part-time working, which has roots far beyond the crisis. Figure 2.8 shows significant generation-on-generation increases in part-time working among millennials of both sexes in their early- to mid-20s, followed by declines for women in their 30s, but continued increases for men relative to their predecessors. While potentially reflecting some element of active choices within families, the generationally-skewed growth in men working part time is concerning, because these increases have been strongly concentrated in low-wage work. This is an issue explored in further detail below and in Box 2.2.[15]

---

10 D Tomlinson & A Corlett, *A tough gig? The nature of self-employment in 21st Century Britain and policy implications*, Resolution Foundation, February 2017

11 These estimates are necessarily based on mean earnings, rather than the median referred to elsewhere in this chapter. Source: RF analysis of ONS, *Labour Force Survey*; DWP, *Family Resources Survey*

12 *The kids aren't alright* (Intergenerational Commission report 17)

13 *Study, Work, Progress, Repeat?* (Intergenerational Commission report 5)

14 *The kids aren't alright* (Intergenerational Commission report 17)

15 D Tomlinson, 'No country for young men?', *Resolution Foundation blog*, 9 February 2017

Figure 2.8: Part-time working has risen for young men in particular

Proportion of those in employment working part time, by age, sex and generation: UK, 1992-2017

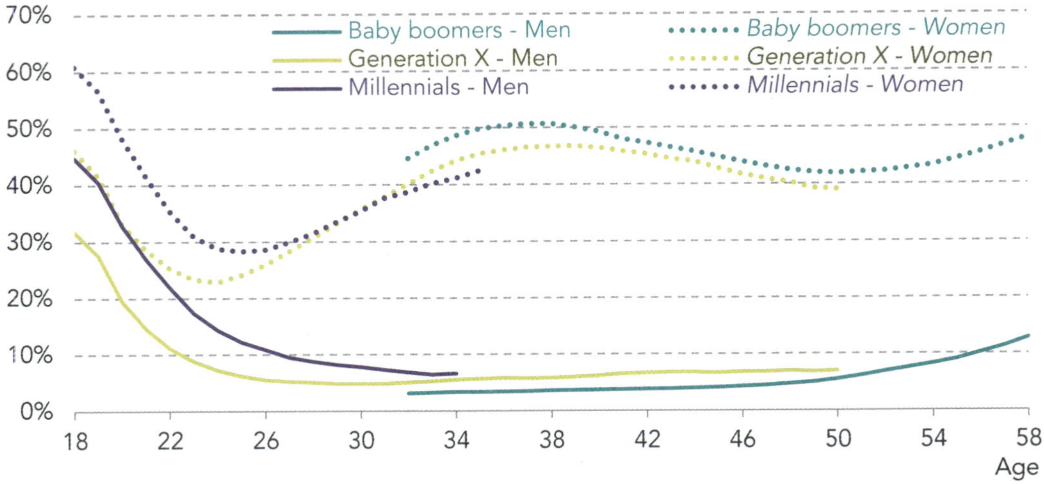

Notes: Data are smoothed using a three-year rolling average over the age range.
Source: RF analysis of ONS, *Labour Force Survey*

Atypical working arrangements suit many workers, particularly those seeking to supplement other household income sources or those who enjoy the flexibility of these types of contracts. In particular, older workers stand out as a group who may benefit from the lower hours and employment flexibility these contracts entail. At best they can be a good way of maintaining employment in later life. But many older workers value security too, meaning these contracts can also precipitate early exit from the labour market.[16]

Indeed, there is a sizeable minority of workers on such terms who desire a more regular relationship with their employer: 12 per cent of part-time workers would prefer to work full time; 20 per cent of the self-employed would like to be employees; 27 per cent of those on temporary contracts would like a permanent role; and only a slim majority of those on a ZHC are happy with their lack of guaranteed hours. And it would appear that younger workers are in some instances more likely to be unhappy with atypical work: 17 per cent of those aged 16-34 working part time would like a full-time role, compared with 12 per cent of those aged 35-54 and 8 per cent of those over 55.[17]

Lower and less secure pay has been underpinned by a downward shift in the occupations and sectors young adults work in

A trend that is less visible for our labour market as a whole, but has affected young adults, is a shift towards employment in lower-paying occupations. Figure 2.9 shows how the share of younger workers working in the nine main occupational groups changed in two consecutive five-year birth cohorts compared to those born a decade earlier.

16 *A silver lining for the UK economy* (Intergenerational Commission report 16)

17 ONS, *Labour Market Statistics*; C D'Arcy & L Gardiner, *Just the job – or a working compromise? The changing nature of self-employment in the UK*, Resolution Foundation, May 2014; D Tomlinson, 'Zero-hours contracts: casual contracts are becoming a permanent feature of the UK economy', *Resolution Foundation blog*, 9 March 2016

Figure 2.9: **Young people have experienced a shift towards employment in lower-paying occupations**

Change in employment composition of 26-30-year-olds, by occupation and cohort: UK, 1992-2015

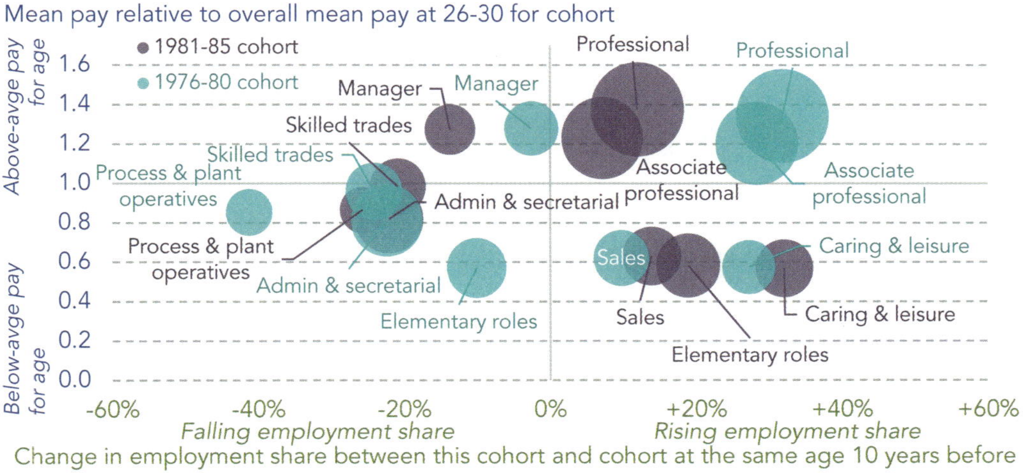

Notes: See notes to Figure 6 in: *The kids aren't alright* (Intergenerational Commission report 17)
Source: RF analysis of ONS, *Labour Force Survey*

Looking first at the cohort born 1976-80, we can see that there was a 32 per cent increase in the share of people working in professional roles compared to the 1966-70 cohort. At the lower-paid end of the labour market there was a 27 per cent rise in the share of people working in caring and leisure roles, a 10 per cent increase in the share of people in sales roles, and a marked decline in people in mid-paying roles such as skilled trades.

The next five-year cohort, born 1981-85, recorded a much slower increase in the share of people in higher-paying roles relative to those working a decade before them. It also recorded a faster increase in the share of people in lower-paying roles. For example, the share of younger workers in professional roles increased by only 12 per cent for this cohort, whereas the share of younger people in caring and leisure roles and elementary roles increased by 32 per cent and 19 per cent respectively. Importantly, this is not an economy-wide trend but a youth-specific one. The experience of older workers has been the opposite over the same period – for those in their late 50s the three fastest-growing occupational groups have been the three highest-paying.[18]

This trend has been especially marked among young men. Employment growth in the two lowest-paid occupational groups, sales and basic service jobs, has been largely driven by increases in the number of young men in these jobs, with an associated increase in young men working part time. In fact the number of men working part time in these jobs has increased four-fold since 1993. In total, the proportion of low-paid work done by young men has increased by 45 per cent between 1993 and 2015-16. In comparison, the number of women (both younger and older) working in

18 *Study, Work, Progress, Repeat?* (Intergenerational Commission report 5)

these sectors has fallen.[19] But this is against a backdrop of young women remaining far more likely to work part time or in lower-paying roles. Increased numbers of men in these roles have therefore served to reduce gender pay differences up to a certain point. This is explored in further detail in Box 2.2.

Box 2.2 The jobs young men and women do and the generational gender pay gap

The gender pay gap has narrowed for every generation of women since the greatest generation, and has done so at every stage of their working lives. For women in their 20s, the gap fell from an average of 16 per cent for baby boomers to 9 per cent for women in generation X. It then nearly halved to just 5 per cent for millennials. Although this pay gap reopens once children enter the scene,[1] there have been welcome improvements in the position of women in the labour market.

This generational progress on gender pay differences reflects a number of positive trends and policy interventions. These include improved equalities legislation, maternity rights and welfare support, as well as rising higher educational participation, which women in particular have benefited from. All this has meant more women breaking into higher-paying occupations and staying in them. But this is only part of the full story.

On the flipside, the higher concentration of young men in lower-paid and part-time jobs, as set out above, has had an overall negative effect on their pay. Millennial men have earned less than men in generation X in each year of their 20s. If you add this up, the pay deficit totals a striking £12,500 per person by the time they reach the age of 30.[2] It is true of course that millennial men still earn more than millennial women, and some of the narrowing of the pay gap for people in their 20s will have been caused by rebalancing of gender roles within the household. But poorer pay performance of many young men compared to their predecessors is clearly not the optimal way to reduce the gender pay gap.

1 L Gardiner, 'Is the gender pay gap on the brink of closure for young women today?', *Resolution Foundation blog*, 4 January 2017

2 D Tomlinson, 'No country for young men?', *Resolution Foundation blog*, 9 February 2017

The combined effect of trends towards lower-paid and more insecure work, along with smaller boosts resulting from human capital gains, has had a compositional effect on pay growth statistics. That is, relative to older generations, shifts in the jobs younger people do have structurally dragged down cohort wage improvements for millennials. This should warn us against ascribing all changes in cohort earnings patterns to the financial crisis and the pay squeeze that followed.[20]

19 D Tomlinson, 'No country for young men?', *Resolution Foundation blog*, 9 February 2017

20 *Study, Work, Progress, Repeat?* (Intergenerational Commission report 5)

Rates of job mobility and progress out of low pay have slowed for young people as risks have increased

Moving jobs is important for individuals, and for young people in particular, because it is usually associated with promotions and often with substantial pay rises. In 2016 the typical pay rise for someone who remained in their job was just 1.7 per cent, whereas job changers received a typical pay rise of 7.8 per cent.[21] High rates of job mobility may also have wider pay effects across economies, for example by reallocating labour to fast-growing, higher-productivity (and higher-paying) firms more quickly, or by prompting pay increases for those who remain in firms after a loss of staff, to prevent further resignations.

Figure 2.10: Job-to-job moves have declined for each generation since the baby boomers

Proportion voluntarily moving from one job to another each year, by age and generation: UK, 1992-2017

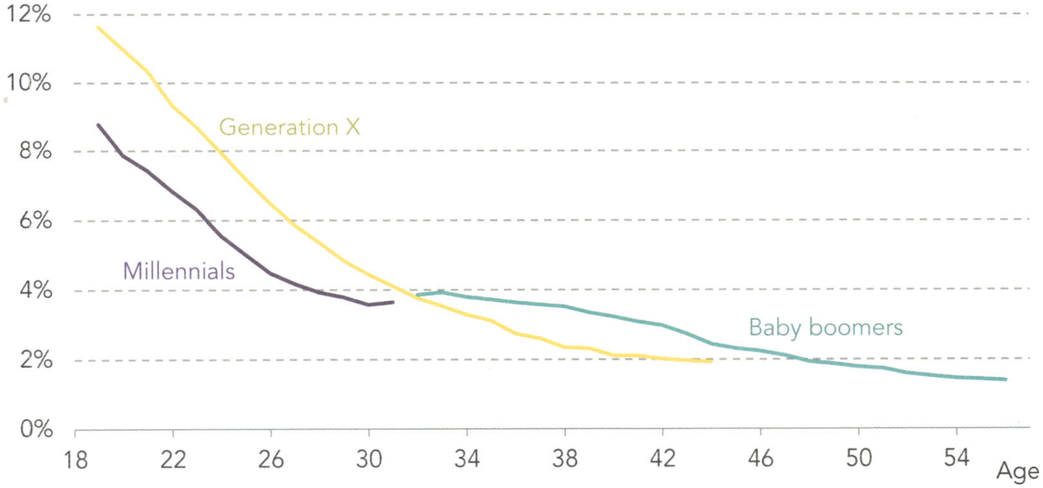

Notes: Data are smoothed using a three-year rolling average over the age range.
Source: RF analysis of ONS, *Labour Force Survey*

However, there has been a significant decline in voluntary job-to-job moves (those precipitated by resignations rather than redundancies or contracts ending) since the early 2000s. Figure 2.10 shows the rate of these moves for successive generations. Millennials are so far 20-25 per cent less likely to move jobs voluntarily than members of generation X at the same age. Because job moves are pro-cyclical, the financial crisis is a big factor in this outcome. But the higher risk shouldered by young adults today may also be a culprit, given youth job mobility has not recovered to the levels of the early 2000s even as employment has hit record highs.

21 Source: RF analysis of ONS, *Annual Survey of Hours and Earnings*

The pattern of job-to-job moves has followed a similar path in the US, albeit the decline started earlier and (from a higher starting point) has been steeper there. However, the UK has fared particularly poorly in recent years. Following a large post-crisis drop, job mobility for young adults remains substantially lower in the UK today than it was in the 2000s, but has recovered in the US.[22]

The effects of decreased job mobility on young people's pay progress have been compounded by declines in the proportion of young people moving from region to region for work. While people who change job benefit from pay rises 5.5 times as large as those who remain in the same job, people who move employer *and* region experience typical pay rises 6 times as large. It is therefore relevant to weak pay growth that the rate of regional job-to-job moves for under 35s has declined from 1.7 per cent to 1.4 per cent between 2001 and 2016.[23]

But weak pay growth for the young is not just about their lower levels of mobility. For the increasing share of young people who are remaining with their employers for longer periods, the return to doing so has declined significantly. As such, the gap between the average pay rise received by young people when they move jobs and the pay rise they receive when they remain with the same employer has widened. For instance, at ages 24-26, the cohort born 1975-77 received an annual pay rise of 14.6 per cent when moving jobs and 6.9 per cent when they remained with their employer for 2-5 years. The equivalent figures for the cohort born 1987-89 are 13.8 per cent and 3.9 per cent respectively. Coupled with the decline in both job-to-job moves and regional job-to-job moves, the decline in pay improvements for job stayers has contributed a further drag to young people's pay.[24]

The good news is that younger millennials, who entered the labour market after the worst effects of the recession had worn off, are starting to move jobs more frequently. And, as shown in Figure 2.10, there is evidence of a very recent uptick in job-to-job moves for older millennials too. This suggests that more young people are now likely to be receiving the higher pay rises associated with this. Additionally, the latest data on changes in pay associated with longer job tenures shows a pick-up in recent years. However, a collapse in starting wages means that this group of younger millennials is building from a much lower base.[25] As a result, this newer cohort of young adults faces a much steeper climb if they hope to achieve higher earnings at each age than the cohorts that came before them.

22 *Cross countries* (Intergenerational Commission report 15)

23 S Clarke, *Get A Move On? The decline in regional job-to-job moves and its impact on productivity and pay*, Resolution Foundation, August 2017

24 *Study, Work, Progress, Repeat?* (Intergenerational Commission report 5)

25 *Study, Work, Progress, Repeat?* (Intergenerational Commission report 5)

An uncertain future for today's and tomorrow's young workers

Today's young people have faced a labour market that is far less dynamic than it was in the past. They are making progress in relation to human capital, but at a much slower rate than previous generations did. They are also more likely to be doing low-skilled and atypical work. These fundamental shifts in our labour market mean that young people are not only being paid less but are shouldering more risk than their predecessors did. As a result, they are taking fewer voluntary risks, with implications for their pay and progression. Importantly, this has been a result of more than just the financial crisis. And the concern is that, without effective intervention, this lack of dynamism means that the problem will persist.

The good news has come in the form of improvements in the employment rate, especially among women. However, questions remain about how we can maximise this across the life course – reducing drop outs as a result of parenthood and supporting older-age working are key considerations. That the UK has had historically low unemployment levels in recent years reflects in part the lessons that we learnt from the enduring damage done by long-term unemployment in the 1980s and 1990s. The challenge now is to renew our labour market policy to respond to today's experience, while continuing to fend off yesterday's challenges. How we might do this is outlined in Chapter 9.

The financial crisis has been characterised by poor earnings for everyone. Britain's poor productivity performance since the crisis is central to this, because productivity is the long-term driver of real pay. We return to this in Chapter 6, considering the impact of future productivity growth on young people's pay prospects. However, stagnant productivity alone cannot explain why younger workers' pay has performed more poorly than older adults' pay. The damage of entering the labour market during the crisis is combining with structural labour market challenges, identified in this chapter, in a way that should make us worry about young adults' futures even as the crisis fades. Therefore any policies that aim to tackle poor generational pay performance must address these longer-term issues which have borne down on the young.

Having examined earnings and the security of jobs in today's labour market, we turn next to the biggest-ticket spending item – housing – and the security of people's living conditions. The nature of the housing challenge demolishes the idea that intergenerational difficulties are just about the crisis. Rather, we see that structural problems have been building cohort-on-cohort since World War II. Again, millennials are worst affected, but instead of being because of the crisis, it is by virtue of being the most recent generation to reach adulthood after decades of policy failure. These issues are taken up in the next chapter.

CHAPTER 3

Houses – not so safe

Chapter summary

Millennials are half as likely to own a home at age 30 as baby boomers were. This is due to increased barriers to entry caused by higher house prices, low earnings growth and tighter credit availability post-crisis. In the 1980s it would have taken a typical household in their late 20s around three years to save for an average-sized deposit. It would now take 19 years.

Because millennials also have less access to social housing than earlier generations, almost four-in-ten of them rent privately at age 30; double the rate for generation X and four times that for the baby boomers at the same age.

Millennials are now spending an average of nearly a quarter of their net income on housing, three times more than the pre-war silent generation did in their 20s. But they are getting less for their money: they are commuting longer distances than their predecessors and have less space.

While millennials are at the sharp end, they are not the only generation to face challenges in the housing market. Declining home ownership rates have been a feature for all cohorts born since the 1950s, and every generation alive today has devoted a higher share of their income to housing than their predecessors.

These generational shifts are likely to persist. Even very favourable economic conditions are likely to result only in millennials catching up with the home ownership levels of generation X by the age of 45. Fast-growing inheritances will help some, but nearly half of young non-home owners have parents who do not own either.

Huge home ownership falls for millennials are a core focus of generational concern

Chapter 1 showed that home ownership is the leading cause of generational pessimism. This concern is warranted: since 2003 the share of families owning their home has been in decline,[1] driven by sharp reductions among young people that began well before the turn of the millennium. Figure 3.1 shows that, as a result, millennials who have reached the age of 30 have been only half as likely to own their home as baby boomers at the same age. So on home ownership, the public is right to think that millennials are doing worse not just than the previous generation, but than their parents' generation.

Figure 3.1: Millennials have secured lower rates of home ownership than predecessors

Home ownership rates, by age and generation: UK: 1961-2017

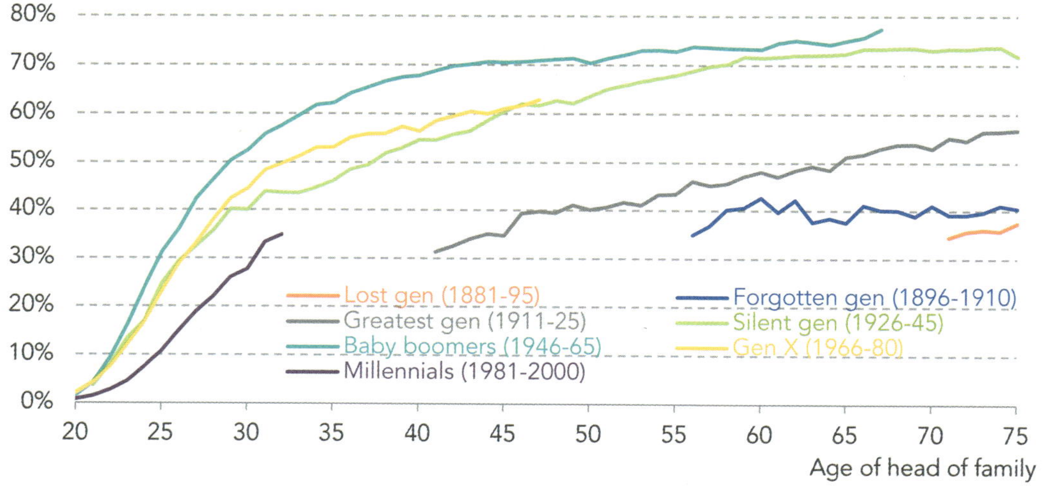

Notes: See notes to Figure 3 in: *Home Affront* (Intergenerational Commission report 9)

Source: RF analysis of ONS, *Family Expenditure Survey*; ONS, *Labour Force Survey*

Home ownership for young families is lowest in London but, as Figure 3.2 sets out, declines have occurred across the country. What *does* appear to be different is that ownership in London has fallen consistently over the past 30 years, whereas rates in some other parts of the country declined more slowly before the early-2000s but very rapidly thereafter.

While declining home ownership is a trend shared by a number of other countries, including Australia, Spain and the US, the UK's 'rollercoaster' experience stands out. The UK recorded a much bigger surge in generation-on-generation progress for older generations, and subsequent declines among younger generations have also been much more marked.[2]

---

1 Our preferred measure of home ownership refers to families rather than households. For further details, see Box 1 in: *Home affront* (Intergenerational Commission report 9)

2 *Cross countries* (Intergenerational Commission report 15)

Figure 3.2: Home ownership for young families has fallen across the country

Home ownership rates for families headed by 25-34-year-olds, by region (selected regions only)

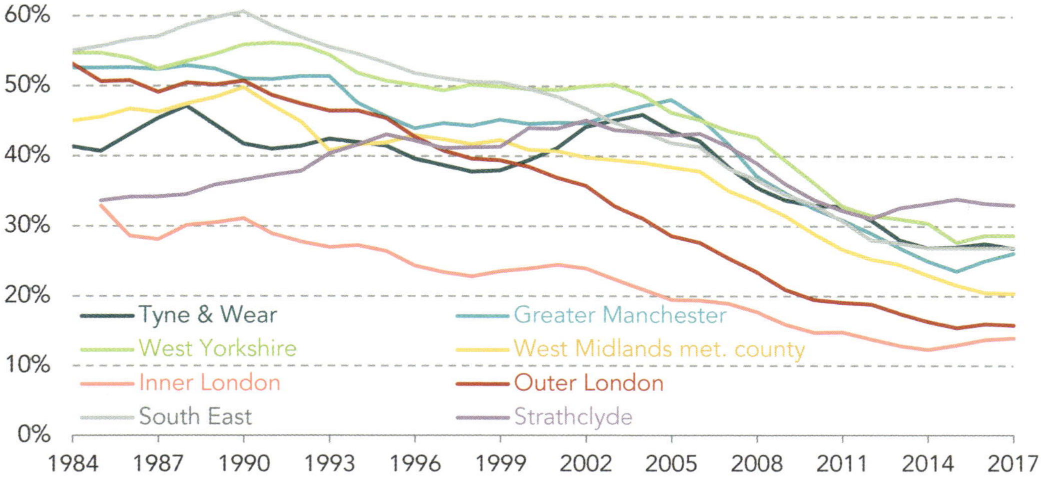

Source: RF analysis of ONS, *Labour Force Survey*

It is likely that societal and demographic shifts have contributed to lower ownership rates for young adults today. Housing choices are closely related to life events, with the transition from renting to home ownership particularly strongly correlated with partnering and having children. Moreover, longer periods in education mean that by the age of 30 many millennials have spent significantly less time earning (and therefore saving for a deposit) than previous generations.

These shifts may result in some young adults renting or living with parents for longer. But this only accounts for part of the decline in home ownership rates, at least for the millennials. For those aged 30-32, identifiable demographic differences only explain one-third of the gap between home ownership rates in 2016 and those observed in 1984-85.[3] Instead of changing lifestyles and personal choices driving most of the decline in home ownership, deeper trends are at work.

The headline trend has been huge increases in the price of homes, significantly outstripping growth of incomes. For young adults buying their first home, this creates a major barrier to entry: the upfront cost of a deposit. As shown in Figure 3.3, it would have taken a typical family headed by a 27-30-year-old around three years to save for an average-sized deposit in the 1980s: today the figure stands at 19 years.

3 Calculated using an estimate of what the home ownership rate would have been in 2016 if young adults had the same levels of labour market exposure, partnering and child bearing as in 1984-85. See: *Home affront* (Intergenerational Commission report 9)

Figure 3.3: The time required to save for a typical first-time buyer deposit has spiralled in recent years

Estimated years required to save for a first-time buyer deposit for households headed by 27-30-year-olds: UK

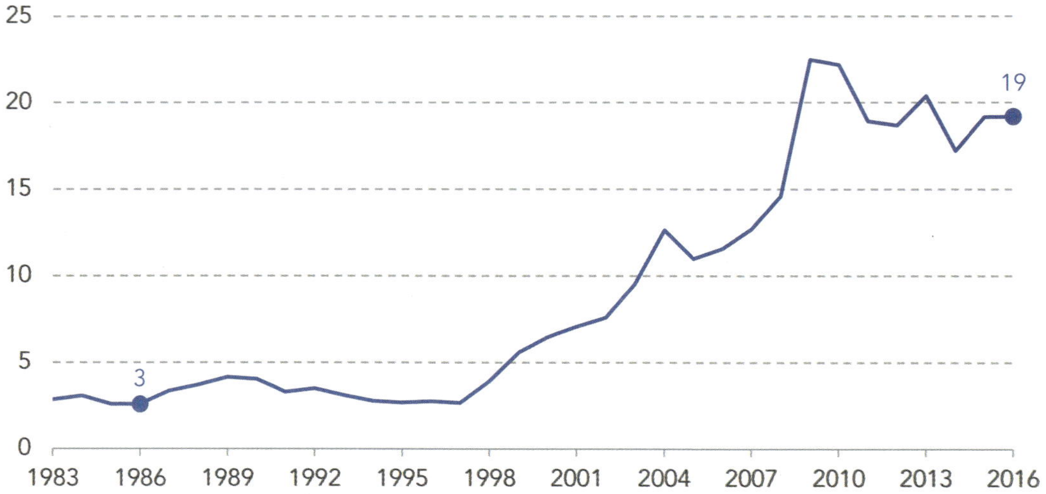

Notes: Calculated by applying the median first-time buyer loan-to-value to the average first-time buyer house price in each year. The level of household savings is based on putting aside 5 per cent of disposable income a year at five-year average interest rates. Appropriate stamp duty charges are added to the cost of the required deposit.

Source: RF analysis of DWP, *Family Resources Survey*; *UK Finance*

House prices alone do not determine the size of the deposit required. Shifts in credit conditions over time also play a key role, with more available credit at times making it easier for a particular generation to get on the housing ladder but with a feedback loop to house prices then having the opposite effect on future generations. Young people keen to buy in the 1960s and 1970s benefited from low house-price-to-income ratios, but faced limited access to credit markets. After credit was liberalised from the 1980s onwards, it was easier to get a mortgage which covered a greater part of the purchase price, or even 100 per cent in some cases. That same easier credit was a key factor in pushing up house prices. But prior to the crisis, high loan-to-value mortgages had minimised the effect of house prices rises on the size of deposits needed.

After 2008, house prices fell briefly and are now growing at a slower rate than in the 2000s. However, high loan-to-value lending has become more restricted, first as a result of the credit crunch and then more formally – since 2014 – following the mortgage market review (MMR) which, among other things, tightened rules for interest-only mortgages. The combination of rapid house price growth pre-crisis (and post-crisis in some parts of the country), stricter lending rules and weak income growth has made it increasingly difficult for today's young adults to raise a deposit by saving from income.[4]

4 *Home affront* (Intergenerational Commission report 9)

More worrying is the huge increase in the burden of housing costs

Home ownership falls take most of the headlines, but an even greater problem threatening day-to-day living standards is the pressure from housing costs on family finances, be that via rent or mortgage interest payments.

As Figure 3.4 shows, housing costs have been taking up a growing share of incomes for each generation throughout the 20th century. Millennials are spending an average of almost a quarter of their income on housing – with many spending much more – up from an average of just 8 per cent among the pre-war silent generation at a similar age. Generation X and the baby boomers also experienced big increases, though in the latter case the increase came in exchange for higher home ownership rates.

Figure 3.4: On average millennials spend almost a quarter of their incomes on housing

Proportion of net income spent on housing costs, by generation: GB, 1961-2016

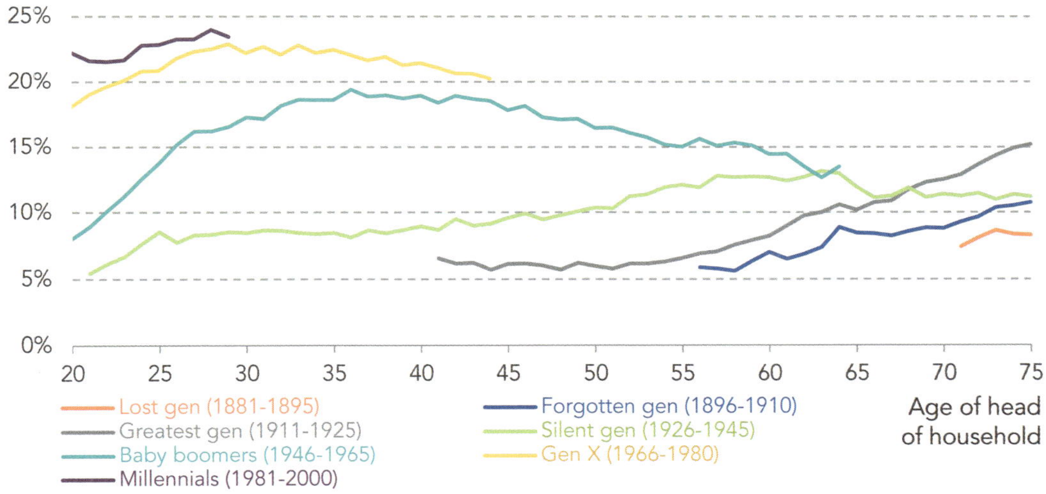

Note: This analysis refers to households, not families as in our analysis of tenure. See notes to Figure 20 in: *Home Affront* (Intergenerational Commission report 9)

Source: RF analysis of IFS, *Households Below Average Income*; DWP, *Family Resources Survey*

It is not just that housing costs in the UK have been taking up a greater share of income since the 1980s; those costs are at a high level by international standards too. In 2015, the UK had one of the highest housing-cost-to-income ratios for working-age people in Europe – surpassed only by Greece (which has had the deepest post-crisis economic slowdown affecting incomes) and Denmark (where a tax freeze implemented in 2002 has contributed to rising house prices).[5] The amount of income spent on housing by working-age people has risen relative to that of older people in most European countries over the decade between 2005 and 2015. But the UK is one of only two countries, the other being France, in which working-age people had

5 Z Smidova, *Betting the house in Denmark*, Organisation for Economic Co-operation and Development, November 2016

already surpassed the share of income spent on housing by older people by 2005.[6]

Different groups within each generation have, of course, fared very differently. The more limited group of millennials that has managed to buy a property with a mortgage is doing comparatively well. For those of them born in the first half of the 1980s, record low interest rates mean housing costs (largely mortgage interest) as a share of income around age 30 are 8 percentage points lower than those of millennials as a whole. And the average cost-to-income ratio of 15 per cent recorded by this group is much lower than the more than 25 per cent ratio faced by the equivalent group of baby boomers born 1961-65 when paying off mortgages in the early 1990s.[7]

This does not mean the baby boomers had a tougher time becoming owners. First, those high housing costs did not last, falling back to around 15 per cent of incomes by their 40s. Secondly, the actual cost of the house, or the mortgage principal, is typically excluded from calculations of housing costs because it represents the purchasing of an asset rather than an ongoing cost of housing. If we include those payments, which do not feel very different from interest repayments in reducing the amount of disposable income people have available, the picture changes significantly. This is because each younger generation has bought houses at higher prices than any prior generation, and lower inflation has pushed up the effective ongoing cost of principal repayments. Up until generation X, each subsequent generation of mortgagors spent higher proportions of their incomes on housing (including mortgage principal) than their predecessors. While housing costs for mortgaged home owners relative to incomes on this broader measure have dropped for millennials in recent years, they still remain higher today than they were for the baby boomers when they were young.[8]

Both ownership and cost trends are long-standing – it is not just the millennials who have been affected

The millennials have certainly fared the worst on housing outcomes but, as the analysis above shows, theirs is not the only generation to be affected by falling ownership and rising costs. Swift generational progress on home ownership peaked with baby boomers, while housing costs have risen relative to incomes for each and every generation alive today.

A number of post-war cohorts, from the younger baby boomers onwards, therefore find themselves spending more to accumulate lower levels of property wealth than previous generations. Figure 3.5 shows that older cohorts accumulated property wealth at a rapid pace, with this largely due to the windfall effect of the house price boom of the mid-1990s to the mid-2000s. Indeed, four-fifths of net property wealth growth since the early 1990s has been the product of the 'passive' effect of rising prices, rather than 'active' steps like moving, improving houses, or paying off mortgage debt.

6 *Cross countries* (Intergenerational Commission report 15)
7 *Home affront* (Intergenerational Commission report 9)
8 *Home affront* (Intergenerational Commission report 9)

Figure 3.5: Cohort-on-cohort property wealth progress has stalled for those born since the 1960s

Mean real family net property wealth per adult (CPIH-adjusted to 2017 prices), by cohort: GB, 1993-2016

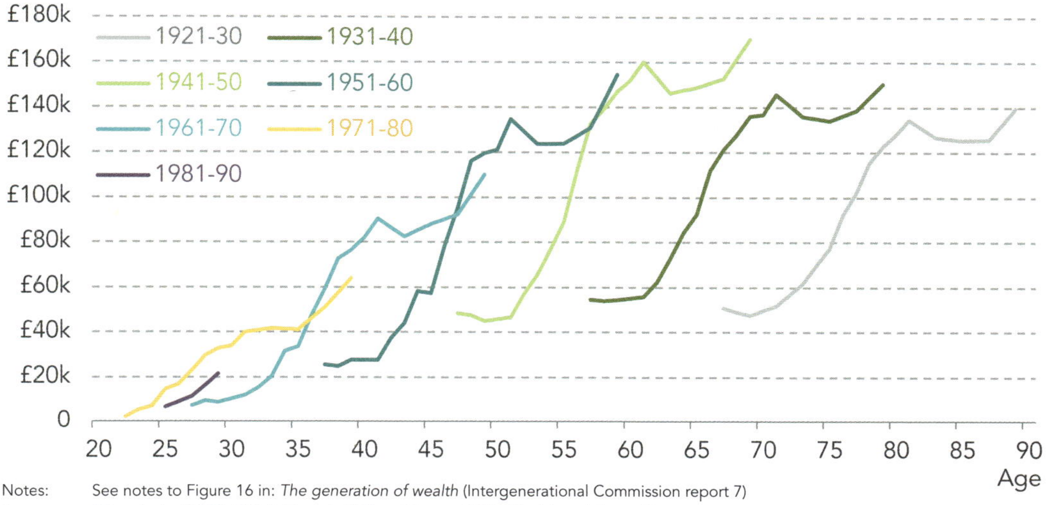

Notes: See notes to Figure 16 in: *The generation of wealth* (Intergenerational Commission report 7)
Source: RF analysis of ISER, *British Household Panel Survey*; ONS, *Wealth and Assets Survey*

These windfall effects were concentrated among those born in the 1950s and before, who owned at the time of these house price booms.[9] The process of big and swift property wealth accumulation, exceeding that enjoyed by previous generations, came to a close for those cohorts born from the 1960s onwards. As a result, at age 29 the 1981-90 cohort had one-third less net property wealth (in real terms) than the 1971-80 cohort did at the same age.

Of course home ownership is not everything. House prices can go down as well as up, and a fall would reduce wealth for those who already own, and present potential financial problems for some – especially those in younger generations who are more likely to be highly leveraged. Ownership can also limit mobility, especially when negative equity occurs, and entails more responsibility and costs associated with upkeep than renting. Nevertheless, these downsides are offset by the ability to build up wealth and to hedge against future housing cost changes, along with security of location. These very real benefits are increasingly out of reach for younger generations.

But millennials do face specific housing problems in the insecurity they experience

Steep declines in home ownership among young people have come alongside a much less remarked upon trend – big falls in their access to social housing. In fact the proportion of families aged 25-34 in social housing has declined even faster than the proportion of home owners, as stocks have been run down relative to population size by Right to Buy and an end to significant state building programmes in the 1980s (we return to these issues in Chapter 9).

9 *The generation of wealth* (Intergenerational Commission report 7)

Taken together, falling home ownership and access to social housing have produced a huge increase in the number of millennials in the private rented sector – a shift that has been only slightly offset by a rise in single adults living in their parents' home (see Box 3.1). Figure 3.7 shows that only one-in-ten baby boomer families was renting privately at the age of 30. This doubled to two-in-ten for generation X, before doubling again to four-in-ten among millennials at the same age.

Box 3.1 Changing family lives

In recent years, popular narratives about intergenerational issues have emphasised a rise in young people living with their parents as a result of high housing costs and poorly paid or insecure work.[1] Yet, as Figure 3.6 shows, the proportion of young adults in this position has increased by only 6 percentage points since 2001. This is roughly one-third of the increase in the rate of young people renting privately over the same period.

Figure 3.6: Private renting has increased rapidly for young families

Proportion of families headed by 25-34-year-olds in each tenure: UK

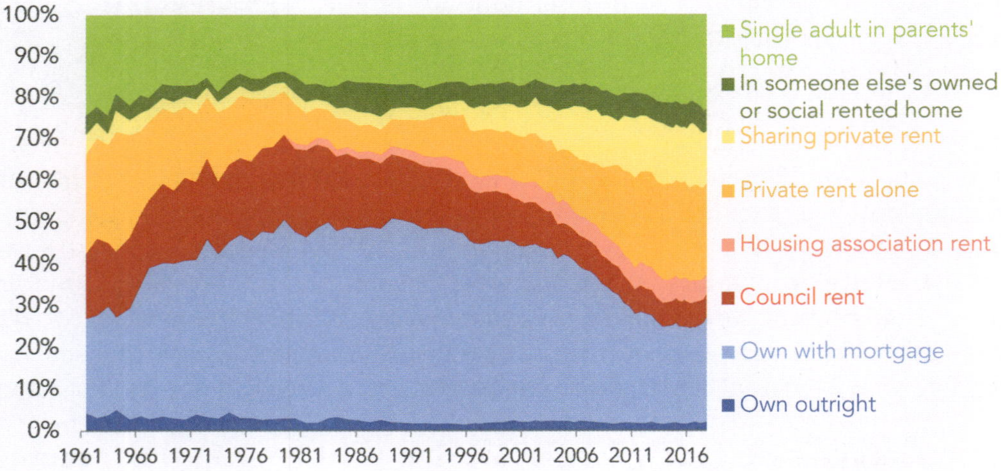

Notes: See notes to Figure 1 in: *Home Affront* (Intergenerational Commission report 9)
Source: RF analysis of ONS, *Family Expenditure Survey*; ONS, *Labour Force Survey*

1 Office for National Statistics, *Why are more young people living with their parents?*, February 2016

While the proportion of young adults living in their parents' home has fluctuated over time, it has always been a fairly significant tenure. Historically, said fluctuations have been a response to social and economic conditions. For example, there was a rise at the start of the 1980s due to an increase in unemployment levels, and again after the financial crisis. Increased participation in higher education has also contributed to a small part of the increase in this tenure type, as has the increased share of the population accounted for by non-UK-born adults in younger cohorts. This has however had a greater effect on the proportion of young adults renting privately.

There are now fewer parents coming back to live with their children in old age. This is partly due to welcome improvements in longevity and better health as they age. But changing social norms, including improvements in female employment, may also provide part of the explanation.[2]

2 *Home affront* (Intergenerational Commission report 9)

Figure 3.7: Millennials are four times as likely to be private renters as baby boomers were

Rates of private renting, by age and generation: UK, 1961-2017

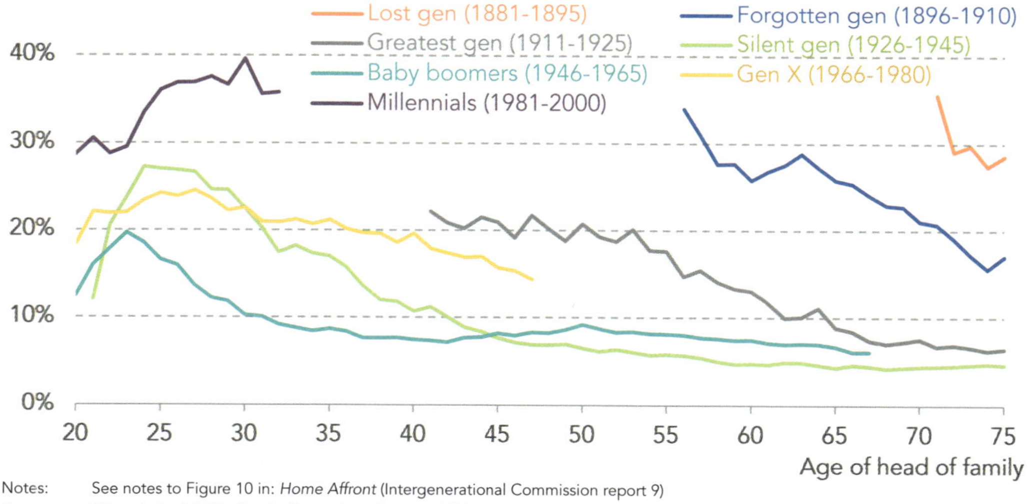

Notes: See notes to Figure 10 in: *Home Affront* (Intergenerational Commission report 9)

Source: RF analysis of ONS, *Family Expenditure Survey*; ONS, *Labour Force Survey*

As a result, young adults now face greater insecurity than previous generations. The rights of private tenants in the UK have been eroded relative to other countries. From the 1960s through to the 1980s, the majority of private tenancies were either regulated or controlled and landlords would struggle to evict tenants unless there was a breach of contract. Indeed, tenancies could even be passed on after death to partners living in the property. The introduction of the assured shorthold tenancy in 1988 marked a sea change for renters, however: tenants with such contracts could be given just two months' notice to vacate.

Many millennials are now renting well into their 30s, when the proportion of people settling down and having children rises. Alongside old age, the family-raising years are when stability of location is most important, but increasing numbers of households with children now face the insecurity associated with private renting.

Millennials are compromising on quality and convenience too

Private renting also has the worst record of all tenures for housing quality. While mass slums, outside toilets and inadequate running water are thankfully almost entirely things of the past, many people live in homes that fail to meet today's 'decent homes standard'. This includes over 30 per cent of privately rented homes – compared to 20 per cent and 15 per cent for owner occupied and social rented homes respectively.[10] While older people are far more likely than younger people to live in non-decent homes, particularly in the private rented sector, the sheer number of young adults in this sector raises concerns about the quality of the housing that they occupy.

Something else important has been compromised for younger generations: space. Figure 3.8 shows the change in floor space available to various household types between 1996 and 2013-15. Although the mean amount of space overall has not changed significantly over time, the distribution between tenures and age groups has altered significantly. Each person living in the private rented sector now has on average $8m^2$ less space today than they did in 1996. In contrast, those who live in an owned property enjoy an extra $4m^2$ each. Since younger households today are more likely to be private renters

Figure 3.8: Under 45s now have less space per person than they did in the 1990s

Average floor space per household member, by tenure and age group: England

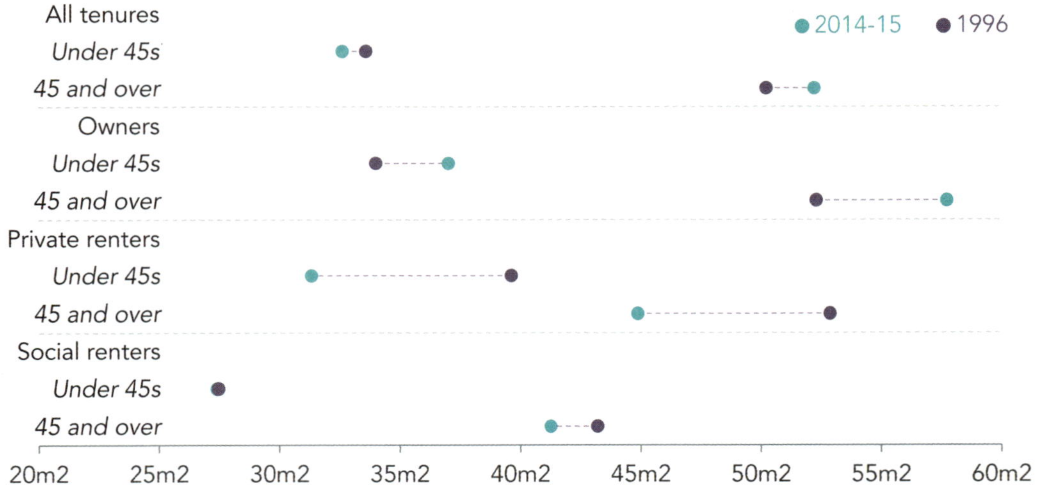

Source: RF analysis of MHCLG, *Survey of English Housing*; MHCLG, English *Housing Survey*

10 *Home affront* (Intergenerational Commission report 9)

than owners, they now have slightly less space on average per household member. In contrast, older households have more space than they did in the 1990s.

Younger households are also more likely than previous generations to live in homes that are deemed to be overcrowded.[11] While generation X, baby boomers and the silent generation have all fared similarly when it comes to overcrowding, the rate for millennials is higher during their 20s than it was for generation X. Just under one-in-ten households headed by millennials in their late 20s now live in overcrowded conditions.

Figure 3.9 shows that commuting patterns have also shifted, with younger generations facing longer commutes than older generations did at the same ages. If these differences between the average commuting times of each generation endure, millennials will spend 64 more hours (or almost three full days) commuting in the year they turn 40 than the baby boomers did at the same age.[12]

Figure 3.9: Millennials spend more time commuting than predecessors at the same age

Mean travel-to-work time in minutes, by age and generation: UK, 1992-2016

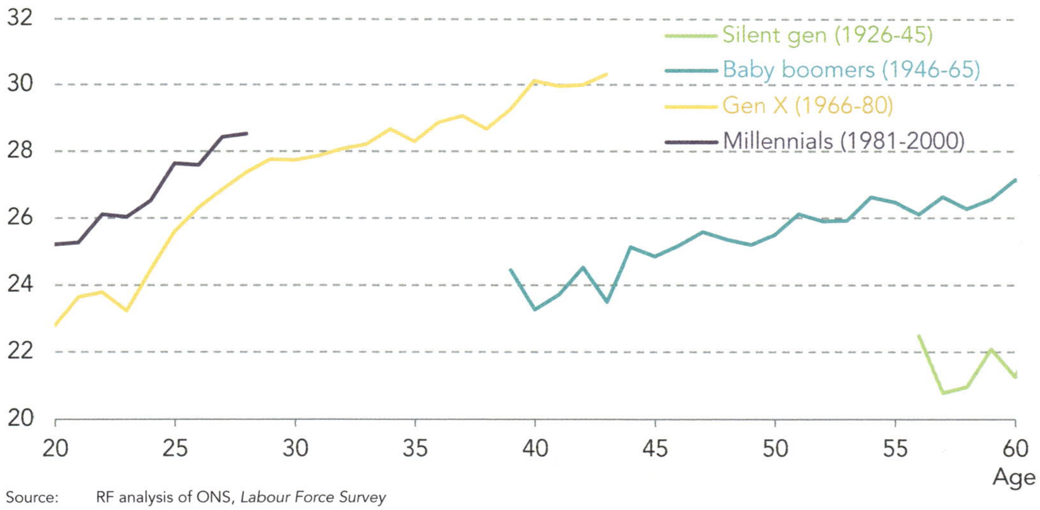

Source: RF analysis of ONS, *Labour Force Survey*

These longer commutes raise the question of location. Box 3.2 shows both that a greater concentration of young people is now living in cities (despite facing longer commutes) and that older and younger people are increasingly living apart. This has potential implications for social cohesion and the strength of the intergenerational contract.

11 Overcrowded homes are defined as those that do not meet the bedroom standard. For further details, see Box 2 in: *Home affront* (Intergenerational Commission report 9)

12 *Home affront* (Intergenerational Commission report 9)

Box 3.1 Generations apart? Generational mixing by place

In the mid 1980s both cities and non-cities housed similar proportions of old and young people, mixing the generations. However, migrations of younger people into our major cities and older people out of them has changed this. Figure 3.10 shows the proportion of families living in select city regions across the age range. By 2017 a clear age-related pattern had emerged: 41 per cent of families headed by someone aged 30 lived in these selected city regions, compared to 25 per cent of families headed by 70-year-olds.

Figure 3.10: Young and old people are increasingly divided between urban and rural areas

Proportion of families living in selected city regions, by age: UK

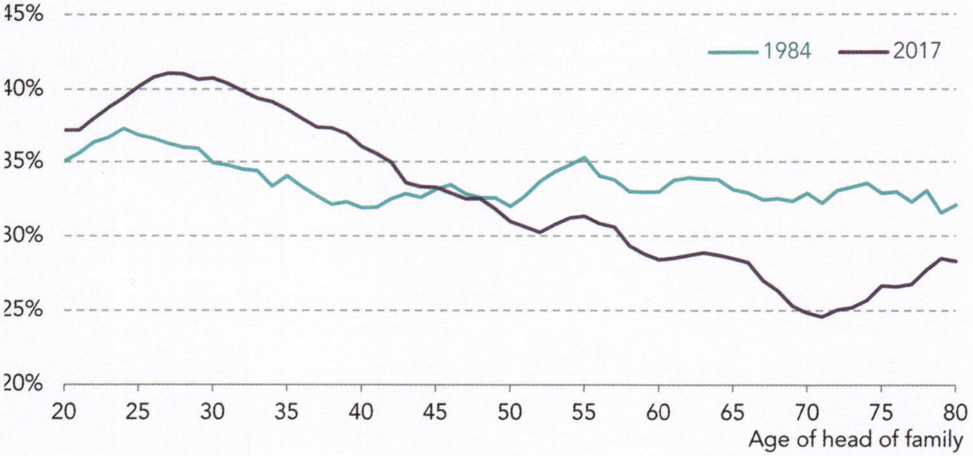

Notes: City regions included are Tyne & Wear, Greater Manchester, Merseyside, West Yorkshire, South Yorkshire, West Midlands metropolitan county and London. Data are smoothed using a five-year rolling average over the age range.

Source: RF analysis of ONS, *Labour Force Survey*

There is also evidence that workplaces are quite segregated. In 2004 a survey of businesses found that, "9 per cent of employees in workplaces were aged between 16 and 21 but 15 per cent of workplaces had at least one-quarter of their workforce in this age group", with similar workplace concentration noted for older workers.[1]

Age segregation can present problems for overall social cohesion. With generations increasingly living apart, the danger is that generational sympathies reduce with possible policy and political implications.

1 D Willetts, *The Pinch: How the Baby Boomers Took Their Children's Future – And Why They Should Give It Back*, Atlantic Books, September 2010

Different age profiles across cities and regions place challenges on local councils: places with a greater share of older residents face greater demands on health and social care, while additional housing may be more in demand in younger areas. Responding to these different challenges poses a problem, given the lack of flexibility local areas often have over how they spend money. Much of the money received from central government is allocated for specific issues such as potholes and schools, meaning councils are limited in the extent to which they can prioritise according to differing age profiles.[2]

2 A Carter & P Swinney, 'Where are the UK's youngest and oldest city populations?', *BBC*, 19 March 2018

The challenges of rising insecurity and high costs will not fix themselves

Tenure is often (although not always) a critical determinant of housing outcomes. While there are risks associated with home ownership, as discussed above, it remains by far the preferred tenure.[13] Although there is no 'right' level of home ownership, we have examined the future home ownership prospects of the current young generation for this reason.

While we expect home ownership to pick up in the next few years as we move further away from the financial crisis, there is significant uncertainty about the scale of any recovery. Considering historical market conditions and the interaction of house prices, incomes, credit availability and supply, we model an 'optimistic' scenario that assumes the underlying conditions that prevailed in the decade with the strongest home ownership growth (1981-91) are replicated in the coming years.[14] In this scenario – shown in the left-hand panel of Figure 3.11 – the share of the oldest millennials owning homes would reach similar levels to members of generation X by the age of 45.[15] Even in this optimistic scenario, the proportion of owners would remain around 6 percentage points lower among the oldest millennials than it was for the baby boomer generation.

Conversely, if the experience of the poorest-performing home ownership decade (2002-12) were to be repeated, less than half of the oldest millennials would own a home by the age of 45, compared to over 70 per cent of baby boomers who had done so by that age (our 'pessimistic' picture, shown in the right-hand panel in Figure 3.11). Such a scenario could have wide-ranging consequences politically (with renting eventually becoming the majority tenure) and financially (with big implications for wealth accumulation and inequality).

13 E Attar Taylor, *Public attitudes to housing in England*, NatCen, July 2011

14 For details, see Annex 3 in: *Home affront* (Intergenerational Commission report 9)

15 We stop at 45 because although ownership did continue increasing beyond this age in older cohorts, in today's context taking out mortgages beyond the mid 40s becomes much less common or practically possible. See: *Home affront* (Intergenerational Commission report 9)

Figure 3.11: Even in an optimistic scenario, millennials would not catch up with baby boomers' home ownership rates by 45

Actual and projected home ownership rates, by age, birth year and scenario: UK: 1961-2027

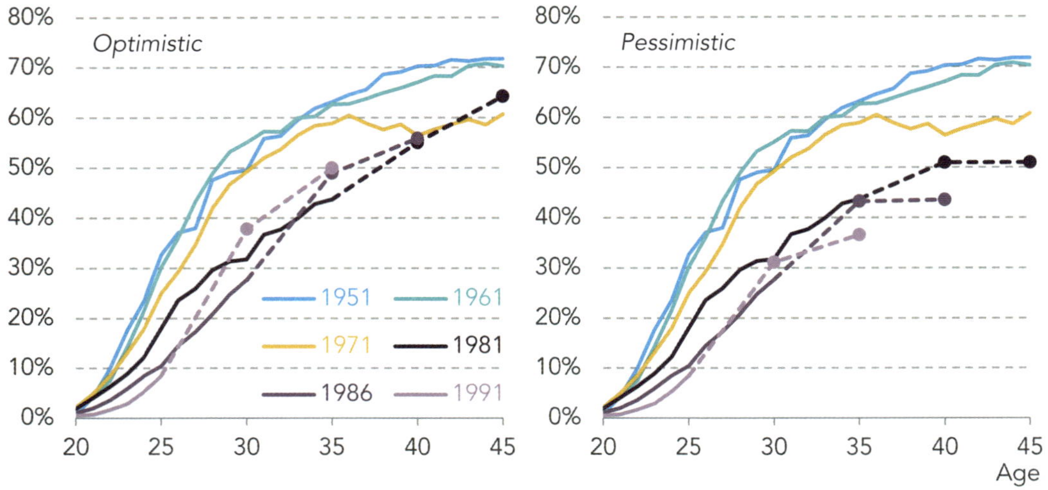

Notes: Solid lines show out-turn; dashed lines show projections. For details of the modelling approach, see Annex 3 in: *Home Affront* (Intergenerational Commission report 9)

Source: RF analysis based on ONS, *Family Expenditure Survey*; ONS, *Labour Force Survey*

These projections are necessarily limited; for example, they ignore the potential role for older family members to come to the aid of younger ones. Many in older generations recognise the challenge their children face. That ownership among millennials is not lower still owes much to the help received from the family to get a deposit for a house together. Estimates from the Council of Mortgage Lenders suggest that the proportion of first-time buyers getting help from parents or grandparents has risen from around 30 per cent in 2005 to more than 50 per cent in 2014.[16]

This significant expansion of the role played by the bank of mum and dad – and, in future years, of inheritances – is an important feature of future home ownership potential. But it highlights the interaction of intra- and inter-generational trends that arises in many of the areas we have looked at. In this instance, the intergenerational reduction in home ownership opportunities facing millennials increases the importance of having access to additional family resources – thereby helping to accentuate existing intra-generational inequality. For example, nearly half (46 per cent) of 20-35-year-olds who do not own a home do not have parents with any property wealth.[17] So while intergenerational wealth transfers might help many non-owners get into property ownership in future (and in particular beyond the age of 45 when our scenarios above cease), there is a sizable group of millennials for whom such an outcome appears much less likely.

16 B Clarke, 'New CML data shows nearly half of first-time buyers didn't use the 'bank of mum and dad'', *Council of Mortgage Lenders news*, 5 March 2015

17 *The million dollar be-question* (Intergenerational Commission report 13)

The potential persistence of reduced rates of home ownership into future decades has a social cost too. Private renting in old age is most associated with non-decent housing and its transience may be particularly unsuitable for those towards the end of their lives. So a greater share of older people renting privately in future is an issue of deep concern at the individual level. But it is also a collective concern, because a majority of those renting above pension age depend on the state to cover their housing costs – the pensioner housing benefit bill stood at £6.3 billion in 2016.

We have considered how these costs might change in future by combining our optimistic and pessimistic scenarios for ownership up to the age of 45 with our projections for the pattern of property inheritances (and their size and timing) across millennial owners and non-owners.[18] Our modelling suggests that the share of pensioners owning homes in 2060 (when the group will largely be composed of millennials) will be lower than today's figure of 77 per cent – falling to 73 per cent under our optimistic set of assumptions and 66 per cent with a more pessimistic outlook. Combined with sensible assumptions about the social/private renter split amongst pensioners and housing benefit eligibility, we estimate that this degree of tenure change alone would push up state spending on housing benefit for pensioners by between 15 and 50 per cent, or between £1 billion and £3.2 billion.[19]

Add in growth in the pensioner population, and the pensioner housing benefit bill doubles at least; rising by £6 billion in our optimistic scenario and £9.8 billion in our pessimistic one. These estimates are only illustrative and the range is very broad, but it is clear that the future housing outcomes of today's young adults are of national, not just individual, interest.

Given the deep-seated desire for home ownership, the benefits it can bring, and the implications for state spending if lower ownership rates persist, the focus of politicians on how higher levels of ownership can be supported is understandable. But with many of today's young adults now spending much of their lives renting in the private sector, we also need to consider how the benefits of ownership – cost control, security and quality – can be delivered in other ways. Alongside setting out how demand can be rebalanced such that more young adults' desire for home ownership can be satisfied, this is one of the challenges confronted in Chapter 9.

It is not just ownership itself, but also *costs* relative to incomes which are a key problem for younger generations. Even optimistic projections for a catch-up in ownership would not deliver a reduction in housing costs. The fundamentals of the supply and demand of housing are the long-term driver of these. Chapter 9 also considers these.

Having considered what later life looks like in different housing scenarios above, we turn in the next chapter to the most direct way in which individual assets and state support combine to deliver living standards in retirement – pensions.

18 For details of this modelling, see: S Clarke, 'The future fiscal cost of 'Generation Rent'', *Resolution Foundation blog*, 17 April 2018

19 These figures are expressed in 2016 GDP terms, for comparability with current spend on housing benefit for pensioners.

CHAPTER 4

Pensions – an uncertain future

Chapter summary

Wholesale reform of the UK's pension system has been delivered in the past decade. 'Auto-enrolling' workers has made 'defined contribution' pension saving the norm, and a new flat-rate structure for the State Pension has been introduced.

If we return to more favourable economic conditions in the coming years, and assuming constant investment returns, future pensioners have the potential to achieve broadly similar pension outcomes to recent retirees. But crucially there are very big risks around these outcomes for younger generations, from the rate and timing of investment returns to longevity and inflation risks. These are risks that those currently retiring have been largely protected from.

Men in generation X and women who have already retired stand out as doing less well than other groups, and no generation – including the already-retired – looks set to achieve what is commonly accepted as an adequate retirement income compared to their working-age earnings.

Concern about pensions around the turn of the century led to transformation of the state and private systems

At the turn of the 21st century, a political consensus had formed that the UK's system of pension provision – both state and private – was in need of attention. The case for action was a mixture of rising longevity, a State Pension that had been falling in relation to earnings for two decades, and the decline of 'defined benefit' (DB) pension schemes that provide a guaranteed income in retirement.

Against this backdrop the government established the Pensions Commission in 2002, chaired by Adair Turner. The Commission's final report in 2006 presented a range of recommendations which were broadly accepted by the government of the day, setting in motion reforms to the State Pension and private savings schemes. The key pillars of the recommendations were:

- A State Pension age rising in line with longevity;
- Transition to an increasingly flat-rate State Pension that would maintain its value in relation to working-age incomes, as a clear and understandable base to underpin greater private saving; and,
- Automatic enrolment of employees (with a right to opt-out) into pension saving via their workplace, and a modest level of compulsion on employers to match individual contributions.[1]

Even before the Pensions Commission, the State Pension age was being equalised for men and women. In keeping with the Commission recommendations, it is also now set to rise roughly in line with longevity improvements (posing challenges in terms of timing and of accurately capturing longevity changes).

The State Pension has since 2011 been uprated using the 'triple lock', in part reflecting a wish to support pensioner incomes after the financial crisis. This mechanism ensures the State Pension is uprated each year by the highest of inflation, earnings and 2.5 per cent. The triple lock does a good job of boosting the value of the State Pension relative to earnings and has made up some of the ground lost over previous decades, as Figure 4.1 shows. It is however a rather arbitrary and unpredictable mechanism, and its high cost – an extra £4 billion relative to earnings uprating[2] – has helped put pressure on welfare spending for working-age adults, as discussed in the next chapter.

1 Pensions Commission, *A New Pension Settlement for the Twenty-First Century: The Second Report of the Pensions Commission*, November 2005

2 *As good as it gets?* (Intergenerational Commission report 12)

Figure 4.1: **The triple lock has boosted the value of the State Pension relative to earnings**

State Pension as a proportion of median weekly earnings: UK

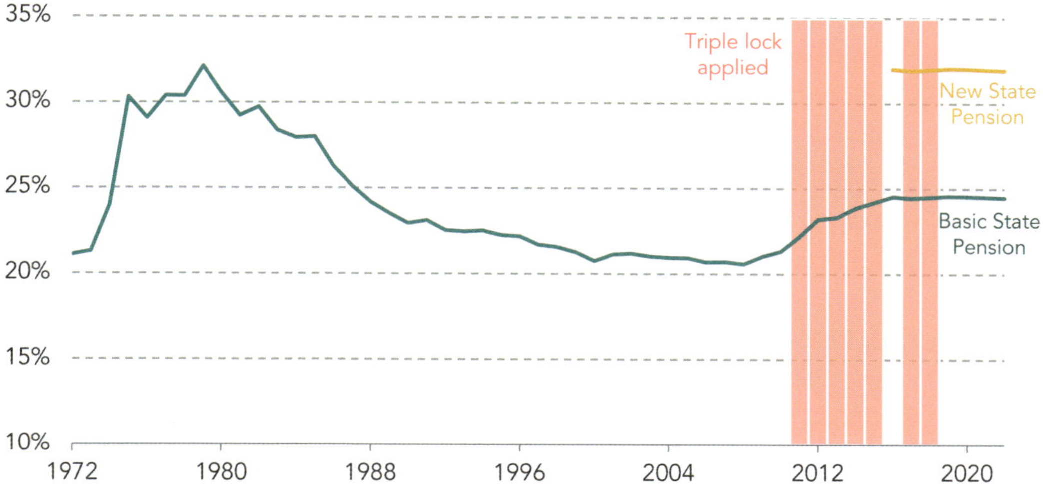

Source: RF analysis of DWP, *Abstract of statistics*; OBR, *Economic and Fiscal Outlook*

New pensioners now also receive the single-tier 'new State Pension', which significantly increases the basic level of entitlements (relative to earnings) to close to the high watermark of the late 1970s, as Figure 4.1 also makes clear. This is an improvement for lifelong low earners in the first cohorts retiring under the scheme and the self-employed, but brings an end to a system of earnings-related State Pension top-ups that benefitted higher earners.[3]

However, those earnings-related accruals have been protected for those currently retiring, taking their overall State Pension entitlement above the 'new State Pension' level in many cases. This protection (and associated spending) will gradually phase out as future cohorts move into retirement having spent less of their working lives under the old system. Because that spending will not be reallocated elsewhere in the pensioner benefit system, this approach is more generous to retirees in the coming years than to younger generations. We return to this issue in Chapter 10.

Auto-enrolment into 'defined contribution' (DC) private pensions (which offer no guaranteed retirement income level) began in 2013 and so far has done well. At the end of 2017, over 9 million employees had been auto-enrolled at a low minimum contribution level.[4] Those minimum contribution requirements are now rising.

As Figure 4.2 shows, these reforms have arrested cohort-on-cohort declines in pension scheme membership driven by the demise of DB schemes outside of the public sector.

3 The previous SERPS (State Earnings Related Pension Scheme) system also provided an individualised mechanism for ensuring successive cohorts secured higher pensions, in line with the practice in most advanced economies. The restoration of an earnings link in relation to the basic State Pension and new State Pension plays the same role on a cohort-wide basis.

4 Department for Work and Pensions, *Automatic Enrolment Review 2017: Analytical Report*, December 2017

Private sector DB membership around age 35 more than halved between employees born around 1970 and those born twelve years later. But a surge in membership of DC schemes means that overall pension coverage at age 35 has increased above preceding cohorts among the oldest male millennials. Cohort-on-cohort improvements for women (who were historically less likely to be in DB schemes outside of the public sector and who are most likely to be newly saving via auto-enrolment) have been even more rapid.[5]

Figure 4.2: **Defined benefit is in decline, but overall pension scheme membership has surged**

Occupational pension scheme membership among private sector employees, by age, sex and cohort: GB, 1997-2016

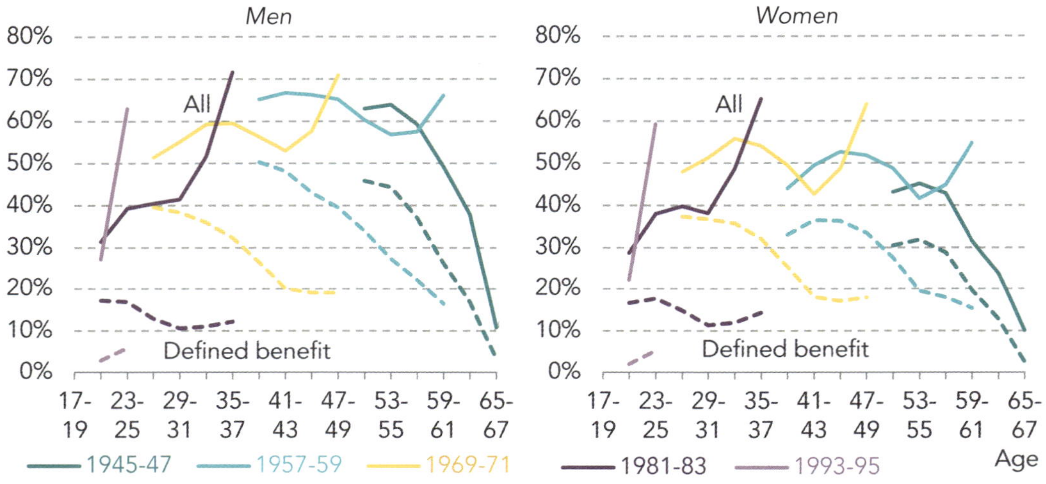

Source: RF analysis of ONS, *Annual Survey of Hours and Earnings*

Today's pensioners are doing relatively well, raising the question of whether this performance will be maintained for future pensioners

Pensioner incomes have performed strongly in this century, driven by the introduction of Pension Credit in the mid 2000s and recent cohorts of pensioners reaching retirement with higher employment rates and private savings than their predecessors.[6]

Historically, poverty in the UK has been disproportionately concentrated among pensioners. But now typical pensioner incomes are actually *higher* than working-age incomes after housing costs, as Figure 4.3 shows. This is a substantial change in the distribution of income between age groups. And, while far from all pensioners are well off, these gains have been made at the top and bottom of the income distribution. As a result, pensioner poverty has fallen by one-third during this century.[7]

5 For further details, see: *As good as it gets?* (Intergenerational Commission report 12)

6 *As time goes by* (Intergenerational Commission report 4)

7 24 per cent of pensioners had incomes after housing costs below 60 per cent of the median in 2002-03, falling to 16 per cent in 2016-17. See: Department for Work and Pensions, *Households Below Average Income: an analysis of the UK income distribution: 1994/95 to 2016/17*, March 2018

Figure 4.3: Typical pensioner incomes are now higher than typical working-age incomes

Real household net annual income after housing costs (CPI-AHC- adjusted to 2017 prices), by life stage: UK

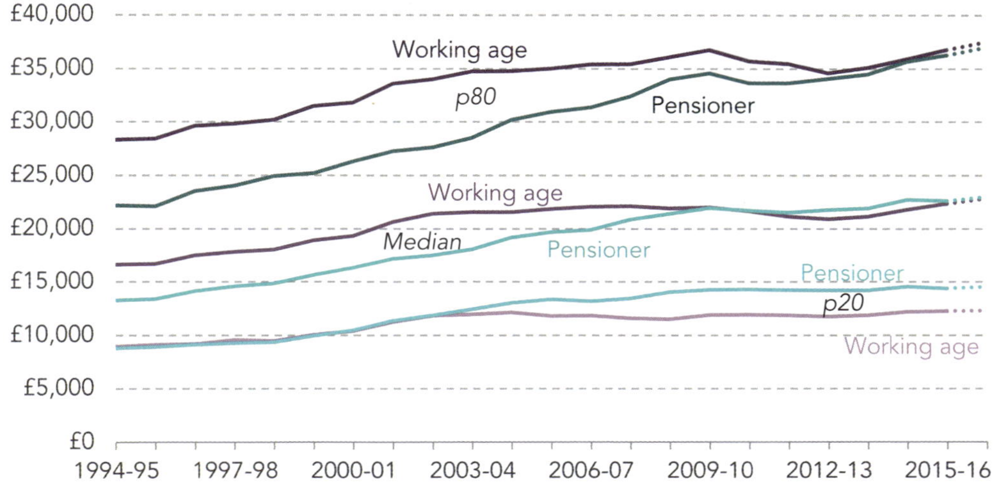

Notes: 'p20' refers to incomes at the 20th percentile within each age group; 'p80' refers to incomes at the 80th percentile within each age group. Dotted lines show 2016-17 nowcast. Incomes are equivalised to account for differences in household size. See notes to Figure 1 in: *As good as it gets?* (Intergenerational Commission report 12)

Source: RF analysis of DWP, *Family Resources Survey*; RF nowcast

If we return to more favourable economic conditions, and under the simplified assumption of steady investment returns, the new system could deliver for millennials

Good news around pensioner incomes and reductions in pensioner poverty are outcomes to be celebrated, but the question is whether this performance can be maintained for future generations of retirees.

To answer that question we can project the level of future retirement incomes. We do so on the significant assumption that our economy returns towards a pre-crisis level of performance, with real earnings growing at 2.3 per cent per year,[8] and real pension pot investment returns of 3.6 per cent a year.[9] We assume these growth rates are constant, an approach that unavoidably hides what in reality would be significant variation over time and across the population.

Actual and projected average incomes just after retirement for different cohorts are summarised in Figure 4.4 for men and women separately. Average incomes have grown relative to earnings for recent cohorts of retirees of both sexes, covering the silent generation and the oldest baby boomers. This has been driven by growing private pension income for men in particular (an increase for men of 106 per cent between the 1927-29 and 1945-47 cohorts), along with rising State Pension income for women (rising 18 per cent through the same cohorts).

8 This is in line with the Office for Budget Responsibility's long-run assumption prior to recent downward revisions. See: Office for Budget Responsibility, *Fiscal sustainability report – January 2017*, January 2017

9 Other key assumptions include: auto-enrolment covers 80 per cent of private sector employees once fully rolled out; defined contribution pensions are fully converted into an income (annuitised) at retirement, which is assumed to happen at State Pension age; the new State Pension is uprated by earnings after the triple lock expires at the end of the current parliament. Our modelling approach is set out in detail in: *As good as it gets?* (Intergenerational Commission report 12)

Figure 4.4: Future pension incomes fall then rise for men but are flatter for women

Average real individual annual income at retirement (earnings-adjusted to 2017 values), by sex, birth cohort and income component: GB, 1995-2060

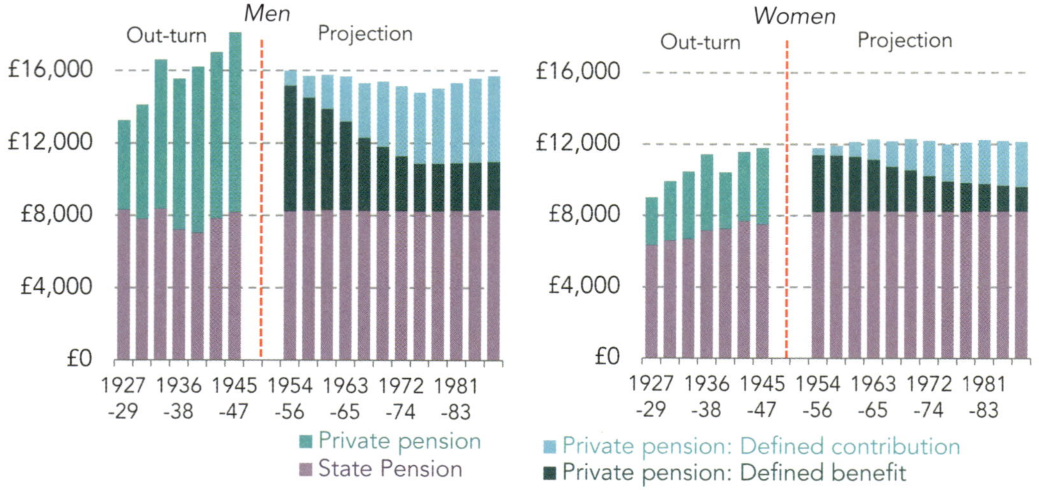

Notes: Out-turn and projection estimates are drawn from different sources and based on different methodologies, thus they are not directly comparable. Incomes are gross of taxes and other deductions. Income levels are expressed in constant-earnings terms; this is common in analyses of retirement income adequacy, allowing an assessment of long-run results in terms of whether retirement outcomes are keeping pace with returns from the labour market. For full details on the projection methodology, see: *As good as it gets?* (Intergenerational Commission report 12)

Source: RF analysis of ISER, *British Household Panel* Survey; ISER, *Understanding Society*; ONS, *Annual Survey of Hours and* Earnings; ONS, New *Earnings Survey Panel Dataset*; RF lifetime model; Pensions Policy Institute dynamic model

The most recent cohorts of male retirees enjoy high average incomes compared to both past and projected future outcomes. This is because the average is pushed up by high-earning men within these cohorts with either generous DB provision or earnings-related State Pension top-ups.[10] High earners in future cohorts will much less frequently have the very highest pension incomes that the luckiest current retirees benefit from.

While State Pension income settles at a flat (earnings-adjusted) rate across the sexes in these projections, the shift from DB to DC private pension income is very visible. This is driven by the assumption that all private sector DB schemes eventually close (only 500,000 private sector workers today are in schemes still open to new members).[11] This shifts the risks around these projected outcomes, as we discuss below.

On the basis of the return to more favourable economic conditions noted above, average retirement incomes for younger baby boomer men (born 1954-65) would be somewhat below those of the male cohorts that have retired most recently. Average retirement incomes then dip for men in generation X – with those in the younger half of this generation recording income levels up to £1,000 a year lower than those who came before them. In this scenario, average retirement incomes then pick up

10 These findings for recent retirees confirm those in: Department for Work and Pensions, *Pensioner income projections*, March 2015

11 Office for National Statistics, *Occupational Pension Schemes Survey: UK, 2016*, September 2017

again, such that outcomes among younger male millennials are similar to those of the youngest baby boomer men. For women, projected retirement income levels relative to earnings are flatter across future cohorts. They appear to maintain but not accelerate the modest increases in average retirement incomes recorded for recently retired cohorts under the assumption of favourable economic conditions and steady investment returns.

Similar patterns are evident when we switch to a focus on earnings 'replacement rates': that is, the extent to which post-retirement income replaces pre-retirement employee earnings. Figure 4.5 compares projected retirement incomes to the pre-retirement earnings distribution of different cohorts for both sexes combined. It shows that gross earnings replacement rates are lower for higher earners in all instances, as has historically been the case for a group that experiences higher pre-retirement taxation and larger consumption drops upon retirement.[12] Beyond this, we can see that replacement rates across the earnings distribution (apart from at the very bottom) are broadly comparable to the recent out-turn for those retiring since the turn of the century. As implied by Figure 4.4, this average out-turn performance across the silent generation and the oldest boomers masks improvements in income levels for the very latest cohorts of retirees.

Figure 4.5: Replacement rates for future retirees looks set to fall short of adequacy benchmarks

Median individual earnings replacement rate, by half-generation and pre-retirement employee earnings quintile: GB, 1995-2060

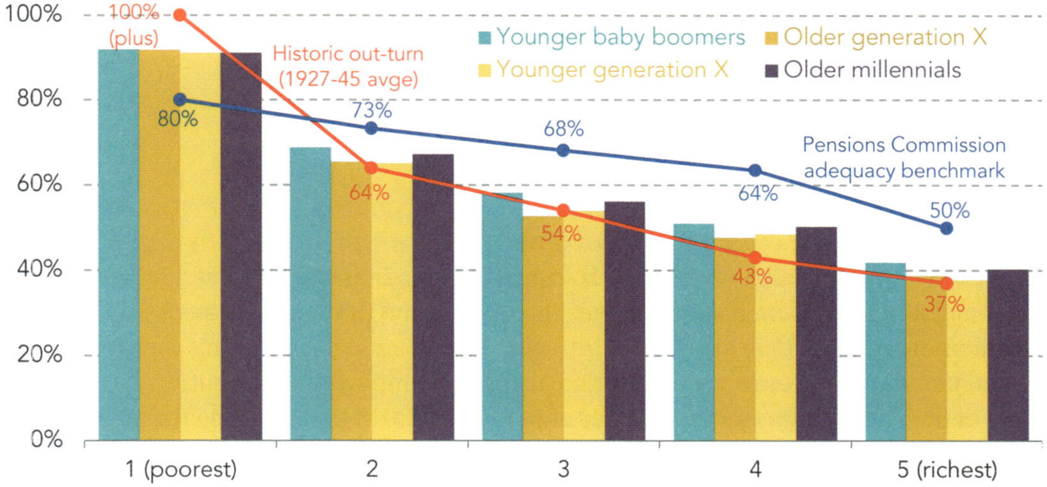

Notes: Earnings replacement rates capture average gross private pension and state benefit income at retirement as a proportion of average gross earnings in the 15 years before retirement. Out-turn and projection estimates are drawn from different sources and based on different methodologies, thus they are not directly comparable. For full details on the projection methodology, see: *As good as it gets?* (Intergenerational Commission report 12)

Source: RF analysis of ISER, *British Household Panel Survey*; ISER, *Understanding Society*; ONS, *Annual Survey of Hours and Earnings*; ONS, New *Earnings Survey Panel Dataset*; RF lifetime model; Pensions Policy Institute dynamic model

12 This analysis excludes those who spend the vast majority of working-age lives not in employee jobs due to self-employment or worklessness. For a fuller discussion of earnings replacement rates across the distribution and the benchmarks set for these by the Pensions Commission, see Box 1 in: *As good as it gets?* (Intergenerational Commission report 12)

Apart from the lowest earners, it is also clear that replacement rates consistently fall short of the benchmarks for adequacy recommended by the Pensions Commission. As that Commission set out, achieving these would require a much greater level of voluntary private saving than is currently happening or planned.

There are risks that could throw these outcomes off course, with future retirees bearing much greater individual risk than their predecessors

Crucially, the assumptions that underpin these projections mask both policy and outcome risks that younger generations bear in a way that current retirees do not. Private pension outcomes are always subject to four key uncertainties: the trajectory for pay growth among savers; investment returns; variation in life expectancies; and the extent to which pension incomes retain their purchasing power over the course of retirement. But the move from a largely DB world to a largely DC one brings with it a switch in *who bears* risks. Today's system is thus far more precarious than its predecessor in terms of what cohorts can be sure it will deliver for them.

Looking first at future pay growth – a risk that individuals bear in both a DB and DC world – it is worth noting that the Office for Budget Responsibility (OBR) has downgraded its medium-term pay projections since publishing its last long-term fiscal outlook (on which we base our pay assumption above). This suggests that a less rosy view of the long-term position might be warranted. Because private pension contributions or entitlements are generally a function of pay levels, lower pay growth would feed through to lower private pension income (but not lower earnings replacement rates) for future cohorts of retirees.[13] These effects would be greatest for those with more of their working lives still ahead of them. This uncertainty around future earnings is a topic that we return to in Chapter 6.

Beyond the long-term performance of pay itself, outcomes for future retirees could be more immediately thrown off course by weak short-term pay growth if it affects the ongoing roll-out of auto-enrolment into private pension saving. The key success of auto-enrolment thus far has been lower rates of opt-out than many expected. However, while many more people are saving into pensions, they are not saving very much: the initial phase of auto-enrolment entailed minimum employee contribution rates of just 1 per cent. The minimum rose to 3 per cent in April 2018 and will rise further to 5 per cent in April 2019. These increases, coming at a time of relatively weak pay growth, look set to wipe out the entirety of the projected pay rise for an affected average earner between 2017 and 2019.[14] Such pressure on short-term living standards – coming on the back of a weak decade for young adults' incomes – raises the risk that opt-out rates within the generally lower-earning auto-enrolled group might increase.

---

13 It should be noted that private pension income would be lower in nominal or price-adjusted terms, but of course not in relation to earnings, which is how results in Figure 4.4 are presented.

14 *As good as it gets?* (Intergenerational Commission report 12)

To illustrate the damage that a big rise in opt-outs would cause, Figure 4.6 re-states earnings replacement rates across the distribution in a higher opt-out scenario. This scenario entails private sector coverage of 65 per cent (around the mid-point between our baseline long-run 80 per cent assumption and pre-auto-enrolment rates). This significantly reduces replacement rates in the bottom three-fifths of the earnings distribution for younger cohorts in particular, with a reduction of 5 percentage points to 8 percentage points among older millennials. The result would be markedly lower earnings replacement rates for low- and middle-earning millennials compared to low- and middle-earning younger baby boomers.

Figure 4.6: Higher auto-enrolment opt-out rates would reduce replacement rates for lower earners

Median individual earnings replacement rate, by half-generation, pre-retirement employee earnings quintile and auto-enrolment opt-out scenario: GB, 1995-2060

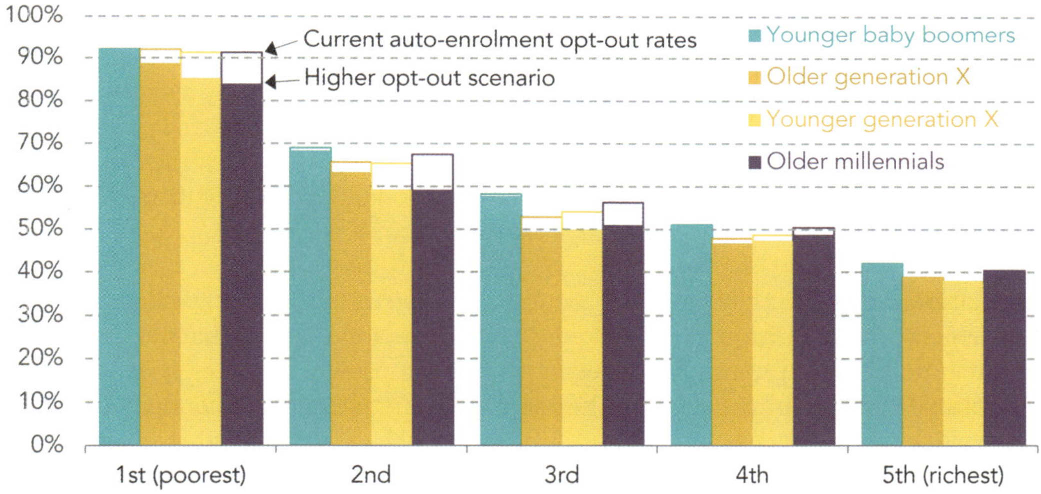

Notes: The baseline scenario entails 80 per cent of private sector employees contributing to a pension; the low auto-enrolment scenario entails 65 per cent, with opt-out relative to the baseline scenario assumed to be concentrated among lower earners. Earnings replacement rates capture average gross private pension and state benefit income at retirement as a proportion of average gross earnings in the 15 years before retirement. For full details on the projection methodology, see: *As good as it gets?* (Intergenerational Commission report 12)

Source: RF analysis of ISER, *British Household Panel* Survey; ISER, *Understanding Society*; ONS, *Annual Survey of Hours and* Earnings; ONS, *New Earnings Survey Panel Dataset*; RF lifetime model; Pensions Policy Institute dynamic model

Auto-enrolment's success to date and design features such as periodic re-enrolment give grounds for optimism.[15] But this scenario demonstrates the potential long-term consequences for younger generations of any destabilisation of the auto-enrolment success story during this current tricky phase.

In addition, while auto-enrolment is spreading private pension saving further through current working-age cohorts than the old system ever did, there are groups who still miss out. These include employees earning too little to qualify (the auto-enrolment trigger point is currently set at earnings of £10,000 per year) and the self-employed. Recent

15 Continuously employed workers who have opted out of contributing to pensions will be re-enrolled every three years. See: The Pensions Regulator, *Detailed guidance for employers: Opting out: How to process 'opt-outs' from workers who want to leave a pension scheme*, April 2017

growth in self-employment has been mainly drawn from younger non-graduates, a group less likely to be building up resources for retirement in other ways than older and more qualified self-employed people. Should they remain self-employed for significant periods, the danger is that a significant minority within younger cohorts miss out on one of the fundamental pillars of the new pensions system.

Turning next to the risks associated with investment performance, we can see that individuals in DC pensions are exposed to risks which under a DB system are almost always borne by firms. If returns come in lower than expected, then individuals saving into a DC scheme with no guaranteed level of retirement income will find themselves holding smaller pension pots than they had anticipated. And such an outcome can arise even over a period in which investments perform well on average. Our baseline assumes a constant rate of return, but a dip in the decade before retirement followed by an uptick in the decade after would leave those unlucky pensioners retiring just before the uptick much worse off.

Figure 4.7 demonstrates the impact that somewhat lower investment returns would have on average retirement income levels for future retirees. We show the effects of assuming a 2.6 per cent real rate of return (still based on the simplified assumption of constant returns), 1 percentage point below the 3.6 per cent used above. Such an outcome would leave millennials of both sexes worse off on average than their younger baby boomer counterparts: for men born 1984-86, overall retirement income would fall 8 per cent compared to the projections above.

In relation to the third key pension outcome risk – variation in life expectancies – the uncertainty is again large. The latest longevity estimates suggest that a man aged 65 might expect to live for another 19 years on average, to 84. However, mortality rates over the post-65 period are such that he has around a 30 per cent chance of dying before 80 and a similar chance of living to 90 or beyond. Such variation has obvious implications for how far a given pension pot will stretch. Under DB the longevity risk sits with the firm, but the shift to DC saving has again transferred risk to the individual.

To insure against this longevity risk, those with DC pensions were in the past required to convert at least some of their pension savings into an annuity – providing a guaranteed income stream for life. But 'pension freedoms' reforms removed this requirement from 2015, leaving individuals to decide how they wished to use their pension savings upon retirement. More freedom and flexibility is often a positive thing, but viewed in the round it's clear that pensioners in this new world can now be exposed to a range of risks that they may not be well-placed to manage.

Consider for instance that there is around a two-in-five chance that two men aged 65 today live to ages at least 10 years different to one another.[16] With either DB pensions or DC savings turned into annuities, at any given level of pension saving these men would have identical incomes in each year of their remaining lives. But individuals

16 Based on 2014-16 life expectancies. Source: ONS, *National Life Tables*

Figure 4.7: Low investment returns would dent millennials' retirement incomes

Average real individual annual income at retirement (earnings-adjusted to 2017 values), by sex, birth cohort, income component and investment returns scenario: GB, 2020-60

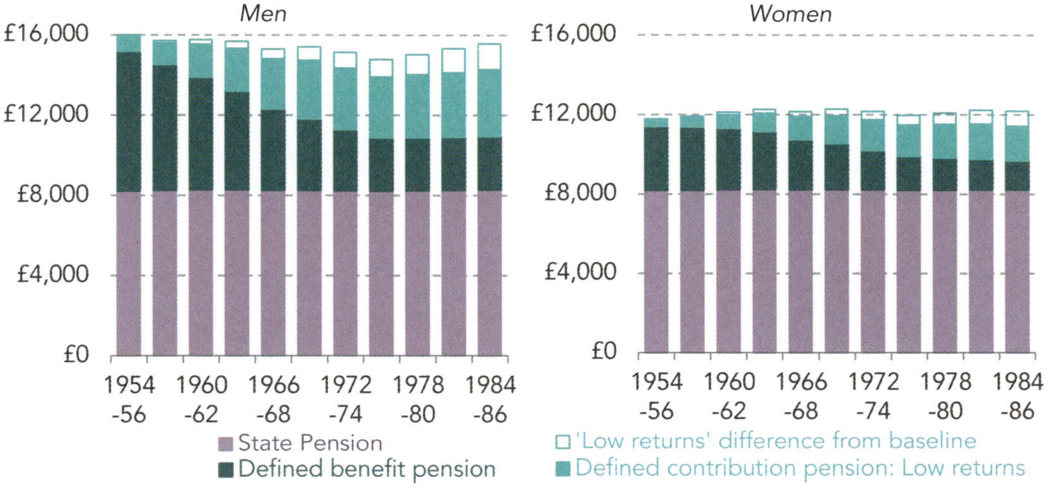

Notes: In the low investment returns scenario we assume that defined contribution pension pots grow at an average long-term real rate of 2.6 per cent per year, compared to 3.6 per cent per year in the baseline scenario. Income is gross of taxes and other deductions. For full details on the projection methodology, see: *As good as it gets?* (Intergenerational Commission report 12)

Source: RF analysis of ISER, *British Household Panel* Survey; ISER, *Understanding Society*; ONS, *Annual Survey of Hours and* Earnings; ONS, *New Earnings Survey Panel Dataset*; RF lifetime model; Pensions Policy Institute dynamic model

are increasingly having to manage this variability in their potential retirement income requirements themselves. The danger is that this will leave them either holding on to too much of their savings as a precaution, or facing big living standards falls if they live longer than expected.

Somewhat counterintuitively, shifts in investment performance and life expectancies are the mechanisms that have driven rapid *increases* in pension wealth for older cohorts in recent years. Box 4.1 summarises why this has happened and how much it has boosted the pension wealth of older generations.

The final area of risk for future cohorts of pensioners is the purchasing power of incomes over retirement. DB awards are inflation-linked, protecting an individual's purchasing power throughout retirement from any price rises. Moreover, three-quarters of DB schemes still uprate income before and during retirement using the RPI measure of inflation (which has fallen out of favour due to flaws in its calculation, but produces consistently higher estimates than CPI-based measures).[17] In contrast, estimates from the Department for Work and Pensions (DWP) suggest that only 6 per cent of annuities are linked to inflation, the remaining 94 per cent being sold as flat-rate cash ('level') products.[18] These pay the same cash amount in each remaining year of life and therefore decline in real terms over the course of retirement, with individuals bearing the risk of any big price rises.

17 Department for Work and Pensions, *Security and Sustainability in Defined Benefit Pension Schemes*, February 2017

18 Department for Work and Pensions, *Framework for the analysis of future pension incomes*, September 2013

Box 4.1 Pension wealth and 'valuation' effects

Private pension 'wealth' is hard to measure, and has only recently been captured consistently in household surveys. The challenge is how to compare those in retirement with an income stream for the rest of their lives from a DB pension or an annuity, with those before retirement who have either accrued rights to a future annual income within a DB scheme or who have a certain amount saved in a DC pot. The *Wealth and Assets Survey* overcomes this challenge by converting *pensions in payment* and future DB rights into the size of DC pot that would be required to purchase that level of income on the market today, at prevailing annuity and discount rates.

Falling annuity rates (due to falling interest rates and rising life expectancies) over the past decade have inflated the implicit value of these pension promises in terms of the DC-equivalent pot that would be required to buy them at a given point in time. This 'passive' effect dominates 'active' changes to pension wealth associated with things like accruing more years in a DB scheme or making contributions to a DC one: it accounted for three-quarters of the growth in pension wealth between 2006-08 and 2012-14.[1] This wealth-boosting effect for those with DB wealth or who have purchased annuities is essentially the inverse of the downside investment and life expectancy risks presented in this chapter for future cohorts with largely DC pensions.

The result is big surges in pension wealth for older generations. For example, median real (CPIH-adjusted) pension wealth in the 1946-50 cohort increased from £78,000 at age 59 to £140,000 at age 67.[2] Such shifts, and the fact that they are unlikely to be repeated, should make us cautious about concluding too much from the fact that millennials and those in generation X have typical levels of pension wealth in 2014-16 that are comparable to what immediately preceding cohorts had at the same age. For example, the 1976-80 cohort had median real private pension wealth of £14,500 at age 37, compared to £13,800 for the 1971-75 cohort at the same age.

1 *The generation of wealth* (Intergenerational Commission report 7)

2 Data captures family wealth per adult. For further details, see: *The generation of wealth* (Intergenerational Commission report 7)

There may be good reasons for preferring a higher real income in early retirement than in old age. But it remains the case that declining DB coverage, an annuities market mainly composed of flat-rate products, and the new freedoms to avoid annuitisation altogether, mean an increasing share of pensioners are exposed to inflation shocks as they age. This may not appear to be a problem in the current environment of relatively low inflation, but a return to the fast-rising prices of previous decades would swiftly erode the value of pensioners' incomes. For example, income from a flat-rate annuity taken in 1970 would have lost 70 per cent of its real value a decade later in 1980.[19]

19 Calculated using historic estimates of CPI inflation.

The system is transforming, but significant risks remain

While there is good cause to build upon rather than disrupt progress that recent pension reforms have created, we are faced with a major issue of intergenerational unfairness in our pensions system: the question of who bears risk. We have chosen to increase very significantly the level of risk that younger generations are being asked to bear, from investment returns to their own longevity and inflation shocks. Reducing that risk, while building on recent increases in pension saving, should be the key objective of public policy.

In addition, while the State Pension will deliver fairly flat outcomes across most future cohorts upon retirement, how much each generation gets relative to the old system deserves more attention. These policy questions are the topic of Chapter 10.

How we fund our living standards in retirement has always been a key intergenerational question, which individuals, firms and the state have to grapple with. From the state's perspective this extends beyond the State Pension to broader welfare provision, particularly health and care. The generational implications of this challenge are the subject of the next chapter.

CHAPTER 5

The state – in it together

Chapter summary

While the short-term deficit burden has eased, the UK's ageing population is set to put pressure on the public finances in the 2020s and beyond. Projected additional costs amount to £24 billion per year in just over a decade, and £63 billion by 2040.

Borrowing to meet these costs would mean debt rising above 230 per cent of GDP by the 2060s, passing the burden on to future generations who are already set to inherit higher debt levels following the financial crisis. This approach would not be sustainable.

The alternative of reducing the generosity of the welfare state would mean older generations not receiving the health and care services they deserve, expect and need.

A third option of raising current taxes on income and consumption to meet these additional costs would weigh particularly on millennials and generation X, pushing taxes up by 7 per cent of GDP by the 2060s.

Each of these three approaches would breach the intergenerational contract: instead we need to rethink the way we fund our welfare state.

In considering the country we pass on to future generations, it is not just debt that should concern us but the wider 'social inheritance' we leave – UK net worth is increasingly dominated by property, and rates of both public and private investment have been falling.

The welfare state has been tilted away from young adults towards those in retirement in the recent past

From the availability of social housing to changes in pension saving, the decisions of policy makers and the actions of successive governments have played a central role in shaping living standards outcomes for different generations. But the most direct way in which people interact with the state throughout their lives is in the taxes they pay and the benefits and services they receive. These interactions are the topic of this chapter.

Scrutiny of tax and benefit policy tends to focus on outcomes for different household types or at different levels of income. Differential impacts between age groups or generations are much less discussed. In the current decade, however, such differences have been very significant indeed. For example, the objective of benefit spending restraint as part of deficit reduction has been achieved entirely via reduced generosity for working-age adults and children, mainly due to freezes to their benefits and cuts to Universal Credit. Real per-person spending within this group is set to be nearly 15 per cent lower in 2022-23 than it was in 2010-11. In contrast, benefit spending per pensioner will have increased by 2022-23, not least due to the triple lock.

Together with modest cuts to income tax that have benefitted households across the age range, the overall impact is to lower annual household incomes at the end of the current parliament by £475 on average for families in their 20s and 30s. In contrast, these tax and benefit changes will lift incomes by £35 on average for families headed by those over 65.[1] The distribution of these impacts across the age range is shown in Figure 5.1.

Figure 5.1: Recent benefit cuts have been concentrated on those aged under 50

Mean change in annual net family income from tax and benefit policy changes implemented during the current parliament, by age: UK, 2022-23

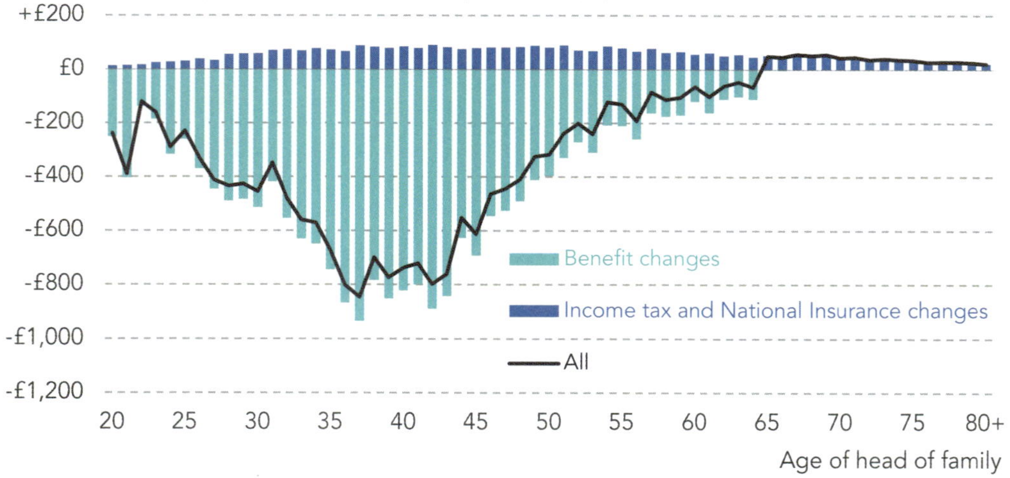

Notes: Income is measured before housing costs, and expressed in cash terms. See notes to Figure 1 in: *A welfare generation* (Intergenerational Commission report 14)

Source: RF analysis using the IPPR tax-benefit model

1 2022-23 prices, cash terms, incomes before housing costs.

These differences reinforce rather than ameliorate the divergence of living standards between different age groups in recent years. We have seen that labour market trends are putting downward pressure on the current living standards of younger working-age adults in particular, making the focus of recent benefit reductions on them look all the more tough. However, this form of analysis is by no means comprehensive. Generations progress up the age distribution over lifetimes, so today's 'losers' might be tomorrow's 'winners' if policy did not change further in the years ahead.

For a fuller generational picture it is necessary to extend our thinking beyond specific policy changes at a given point in time, to consider how different cohorts interact with the welfare state over their lives. Differences within cohorts will always be large, with those with lower lifetime resources tending to be net beneficiaries, and those with higher resources net contributors, due to the state's redistributive function. But far from just being about rich and poor, a key part of this function – and one with strong public support – is that the state redistributes from those in working age to the old and young.

This is not a stable balance however: changes in demographics, the economic backdrop and policy all affect each cohort's average experience of putting in and taking out from the welfare state over lifetimes. In the coming decades, profound demographic shifts as Britain's population ages, and the nature of our policy response to them, will determine how generations are treated by the welfare state over their lifetimes.

The challenge of the 2020s is the fiscal pressure of the large baby boomer generation retiring

With the government's current budget now broadly in balance, some have hailed the end of the fiscal pressure-led austerity of recent years. The deficit does indeed look much better than it has over the past decade.[2] However, managing the public finances will still require big decisions in the years ahead. That is partly because the stock of national debt remains high, at double pre-crisis levels, and is projected to fall only slowly, if at all, in the coming years. At the same time, the ageing of the big generation of baby boomers will push up public spending if current commitments on the NHS and social care are maintained.

A long-term driver of population ageing is continued improvements in life expectancy across successive birth cohorts. Life expectancy at birth increased by 17 years for men and 14 years for women between the silent generation and the millennials.[3] While recent life expectancy estimates indicate a slowdown in the projected rate of increase in cohort survival,[4] the key outcome remains that lives for today's younger generations will be much longer on average than for today's oldest ones.

---

2 Resolution Foundation, *Sugar rush: Spring Statement response*, March 2018

3 For more detail on these trends and wider demographic shifts, see: *Live long and prosper* (Intergenerational Commission report 3)

4 Office for National Statistics, *Past and projected data from the period and cohort life tables, 2016-based, UK: 1981 to 2066*, December 2017

Longer lives are a living standards gain in themselves, and something to be celebrated. Families and the state are adapting to these new realities in a myriad of ways. People are having children later and working until they are older, in part due to increases in the State Pension age.[5] Nonetheless, rising longevity implies more people at those ages where they tend to rely on the resources of others and of the state. This implies relatively greater welfare spending for the state.

Alongside rising longevity, the demographic headwinds that Britain currently faces result from cohorts being different sizes. The baby boomers are so named because more of them were born per year than was the case for generations immediately before or since. The transition of this large generation into the later stages of their lives is a key factor now driving population ageing.

In particular, the transition of baby boomers from working age into retirement means that we have passed a crucial turning point in the dependency ratio (the ratio of older adults and children to 20-64-year-olds) in the last 10 years. Having been falling for decades, it is now rising, as shown in Figure 5.2. Between the mid 1970s and the early 2010s, dependency fell (despite rising longevity) because the large baby boomer generation was of working age, with small generations in front of and behind it. However dependency has been rising since 2010, and is set to increase rapidly over the next two decades as the baby boomers move into and through retirement age.

Figure 5.2: After four decades of demographic tailwind, the dependency ratio is rising

Dependency ratio ((under 20 and 65+ population)/20-64 population) in different scenarios: UK

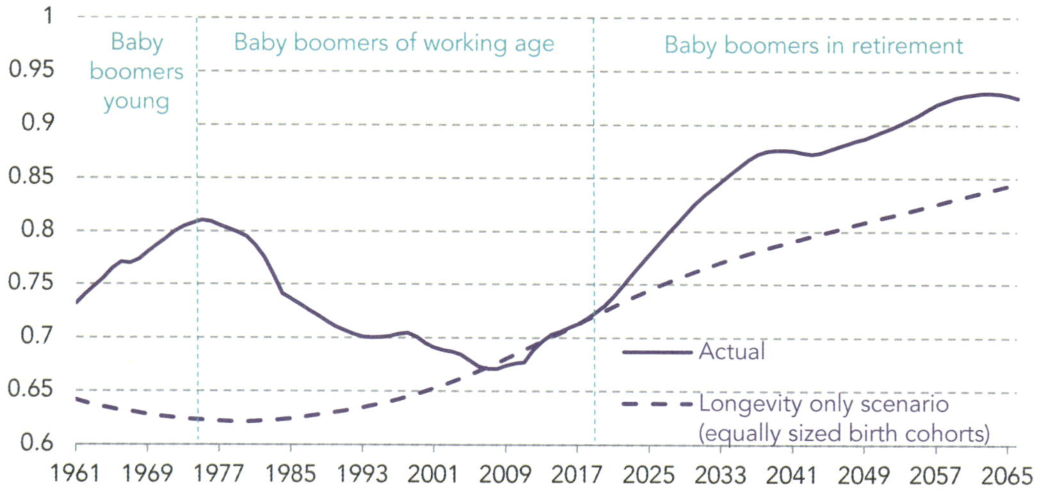

Notes: 'Longevity only' scenario provides a dependency ratio assuming an equal number of births each year, as well as an even gender balance. The life stages of the baby boomer cohort are taken from the mid-point of the generation at age 20 and age 65.

Source: RF analysis of ONS, *2016-based mid-year population estimates*; ONS, *2016-based population projections*

5 *Live long and prosper* (Intergenerational Commission report 3)

'Dependency' is of course a simplistic – even offensive – measure because older people contribute in many ways, both formally and informally.[6] Nevertheless it does capture patterns of public spending in the welfare state because many entitlements are defined by age. The 'longevity only' scenario in Figure 5.2 emphasises the role of cohort size in driving this trend by showing what the dependency ratio would look like if all birth cohorts were of equal size: longevity itself accounts for less than half of the projected increase over the next two decades.

While these trends are striking, many other advanced economies face the prospect of steeper rises in dependency ratios.[7] Both here and abroad, these trends underpin any analysis looking at the long-term role of the welfare state through a generational lens.

An ageing population and rising health costs look set to significantly increase welfare spending in the coming decades

The history and projected future path of spending on the three main elements of the welfare state – education, social security benefits and health – is set out in Figure 5.3.[8] It highlights the rapid expansion of the welfare state in the period following World War II – spending grew 2.5 times faster than the economy in the three decades between

Figure 5.3: Welfare spend is set to rise, driven by health spending

Historic and projected welfare spend as a proportion of GDP: UK

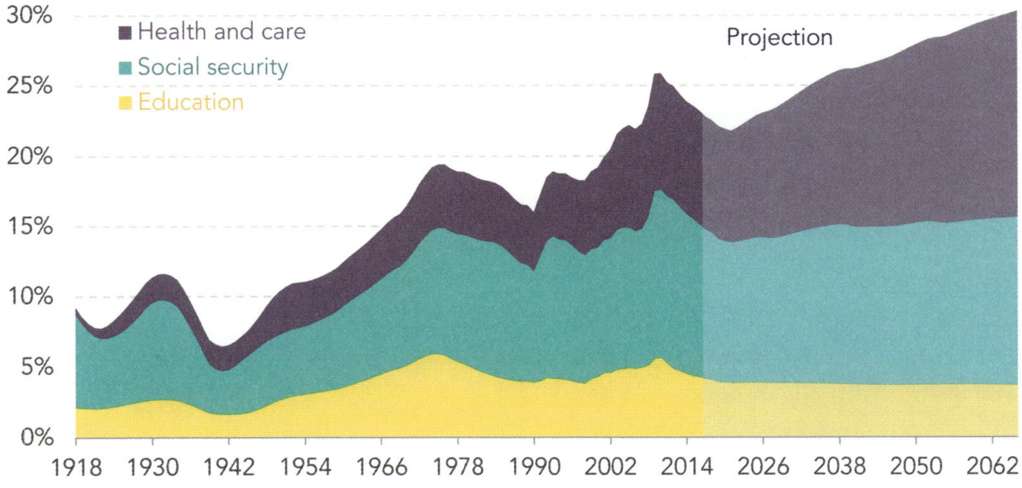

Notes: Data for years prior to 1966 are presented as five-year rolling averages. Total spend is based on the categories used in Hills (2004), so does not map precisely to HM Treasury and OBR totals.

Source: RF analysis of OBR, *Fiscal sustainability report – January 2017*, January 2017; HMT, *Public Expenditure Statistical Analyses*; J Hills, *Inequality and the State*, Oxford University Press, October 2004

6 As people live for longer the working life tends to lengthen and health outcomes at given ages improve, reducing the validity of a purely age-based concept of 'dependency'. However, such measures remain instructive. See: *Live long and prosper* (Intergenerational Commission report 3)

7 *Cross countries* (Intergenerational Commission report 15)

8 Projections are drawn from the OBR's central long-term estimates.

1945 and 1975. Since then spending has fluctuated with political and economic cycles. Looking forward, after a few more years of decline due to factors including the rise in the State Pension age, welfare state spending is set to rise substantially over the following four decades.

It is benefits and services for the baby boomers themselves which are the key drivers of these projected increases in spending. Social security spending is forecast to rise by around 2 per cent of GDP over the same time period. Health costs (and the social care costs that run alongside them) dominate the outlook for the coming decades. Health spending is forecast to reach 12.6 per cent of GDP in 2066, up from 7.3 per cent in 2016-17.

Like the increase in State Pension spending, shifting demographics are a fundamental part of this outcome; but they are not the only driver. The OBR's assessment points to rising health spending at all ages, for example due to the startling increase in certain chronic conditions that Britain is set for. Box 5.1 summarises these pressures and how

Box 5.1 Demographics, health and the challenges of ageing

Longer lives are a mark in themselves of living standards improvements across cohorts, but a lot depends on the state of health in which the increasing years of life are spent. Overall, increases in projected life expectancy and healthy life expectancy have roughly tracked one another.[1] However, simulations suggest that larger numbers of older people are set to produce striking increases in certain conditions in the population aged 65 and over between 2015 and 2035. For example, the prevalence of diabetes is projected to rise by 118 per cent. Importantly, increases such as this will lead to a doubling in multi-morbidity prevalence (the proportion of older adults with four or more diseases or impairments) over the same period.[2]

1 Public Health England, *Health profile for England*, July 2017

2 A Kingston et al., 'Projections of multi-morbidity in the older population in England to 2035: estimates from the Population Ageing and Care Simulation (PACSim) model', *Age and Ageing*, January 2018

How families, and health services, adapt to this environment will shape people's experience of old age in the coming decades.

These shifts also have a bearing on projections for rising health spending. Reflecting the experience of recent decades, the OBR assesses that a significant amount of the increase projected over its forecast period is accounted for by factors other than pure demography alone.[3] These 'non-demographic' costs include the increasing prevalence of chronic conditions at certain ages and the tendency for technological advancements to be cost-escalating. In effect, these trends mean that projections include a ratchet effect on health costs in order to deliver a comparable public service to future cohorts to that which their predecessors received.

3 M Licchetta & M Stelmach, *Fiscal sustainability and public spending on health*, Office for Budget Responsibility, September 2016

they relate to the important question of what longer lives mean for experiences of good health and ageing.

The clear conclusion from these projections is that, for reasons centred on but not limited to population ageing itself, increased demand for services which governments are committed to deliver means that welfare state spending looks set to increase very substantially in the coming decades. Spending projections proceed on a relatively steady path that racks up an additional 7 per cent of GDP between 2016 and 2066. More immediately, expressed in today's terms, the additional spending pressure amounts to £24 billion a year in just over a decade (by 2030) and £63 billion a year a decade after that.[9]

The assumptions underpinning these projections are, however, subject to a lot of uncertainty. For example, technological advances might begin to support health cost efficiencies, or fertility and migration might hold back increases in the dependency ratio. A range of outcomes that might occur under alternative assumptions for demographic change and health costs is highlighted in Figure 5.4. These trajectories generally vary from the central assumption as would be expected. However, the 'lower migration, lower fertility, higher life expectancy' scenario reduces spending in the nearer term because of accelerated State Pension age increases and reduced pressure on the education budget, before spending comes in higher as the effect of an older age structure dominates.[10]

Figure 5.4: There is a large degree of uncertainty around projected spending requirements

Projected welfare spend as a proportion of GDP under different scenarios: UK

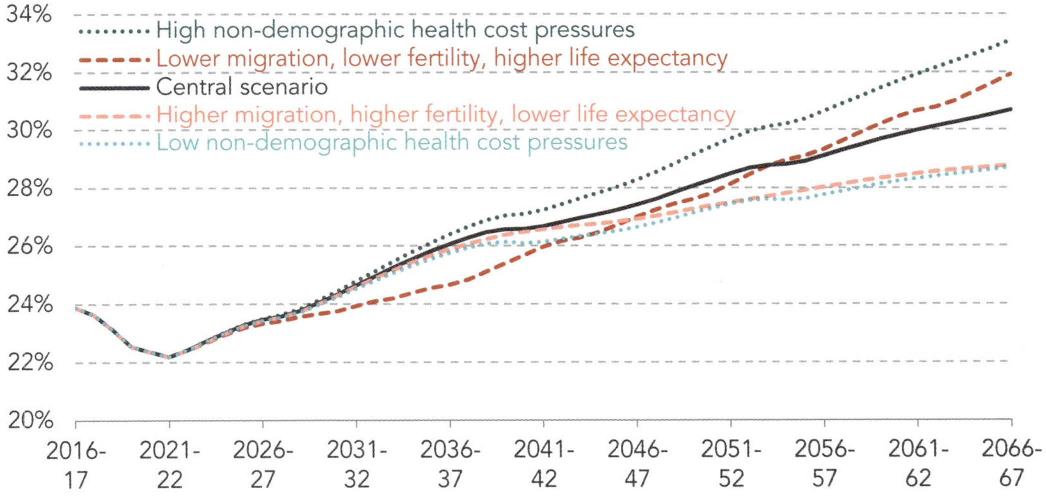

Notes: Projections are based on 2014-based population projections and do not account for out-turn or policy change since January 2017.
Source: OBR, *Fiscal sustainability report – January 2017*, January 2017

9 Figures are GDP-adjusted to 2017 prices, i.e. expressed in relation to the size of the economy in 2017.
10 Office for Budget Responsibility, *Fiscal sustainability report – January 2017*, January 2017

Whatever the precise path, costs are clearly set to rise if the welfare state in its current form is to continue. For the strength of the intergenerational contract, how we deal with those cost pressures is crucial. Whether we decide to meet those costs will determine whether older generations will receive health services when their need is greatest. And on top of that there are huge generational issues in terms of who pays.

Passing rising costs onto future generations is a strategy that will run out of road at some point

If this additional spending pressure is met through borrowing, it pushes the national debt above 100 per cent of GDP by 2040 and above 230 per cent of GDP by 2066. Figure 5.5 shows that this would lift debt interest payments to 9 per cent of GDP, from 1.8 per cent today. Such a path may be possible for a time, but is not politically and financially sustainable in the long run. We cannot pass costs on this scale onto future generations who will already bear the higher debt burden that the financial crisis has left us with. The only circumstances when national debt on this scale has been accumulated have been after world wars, and even then the national debt was not as high as at the end of this projection.

Figure 5.5: Long-term spending projections with no tax changes suggest our debt-to-GDP ratio is set to treble in four decades

Long-run path of spending, revenue and debt: UK

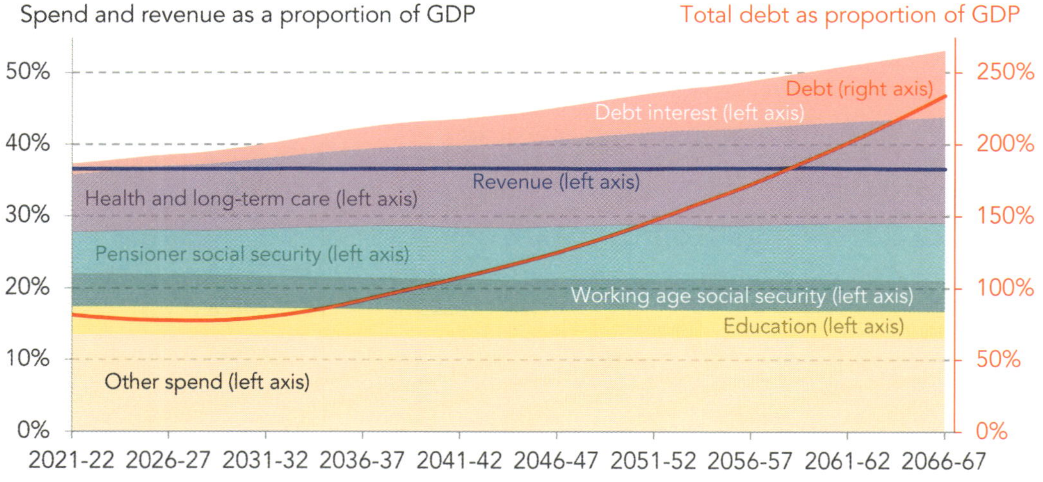

Notes: Projections are based on 2014-based population projections and do not account for out-turn or policy change since January 2017.
Source: OBR, *Fiscal sustainability report – January 2017*, January 2017

Looking over the nearer term, public debt remains higher than pre-crisis levels. And, while projections are for it to fall, this path could easily be disrupted by future shocks.[11]

11 M Whittaker, *A man for all seasons? What the Chancellor can expect in the OBR's Spring outlook*, Resolution Foundation, March 2018

Reducing the generosity of the welfare state would hit the health and care services the baby boomers need in the coming decades

An alternative approach would be to rein in public spending, by reducing the effective generosity of the welfare state in future. If cuts were focused on the big and growing programmes, such as health and social care, it would be older generations that are hit first.

However, the effects would not stop there. We can consider the long-term generational implications of this using an approach first adopted by Professor John Hills in his seminal research on life-cycle welfare transfers between generations.[12] This incorporates detailed histories of tax and welfare spending by age with the spending projections described above, and assumes future tax revenues rise – maintaining the current age profile of taxation – in order to match spending requirements.[13] This approach enables us to summarise each cohort's average lifetime welfare position, expressed in terms of a 'net lifetime withdrawal rate' – the value of benefits, health and care and education received by each cohort, less taxes paid.[14]

To assess how a reduction in the generosity of the welfare state would affect each cohort's long-term position, we hold back health cost increases such that the additional

Figure 5.6: If welfare spending does not rise in future, younger cohorts will record lower average 'net lifetime withdrawals' than their predecessors

Average cumulative net lifetime withdrawal from the welfare state in 'welfare spending held constant' scenario, by birth year: UK

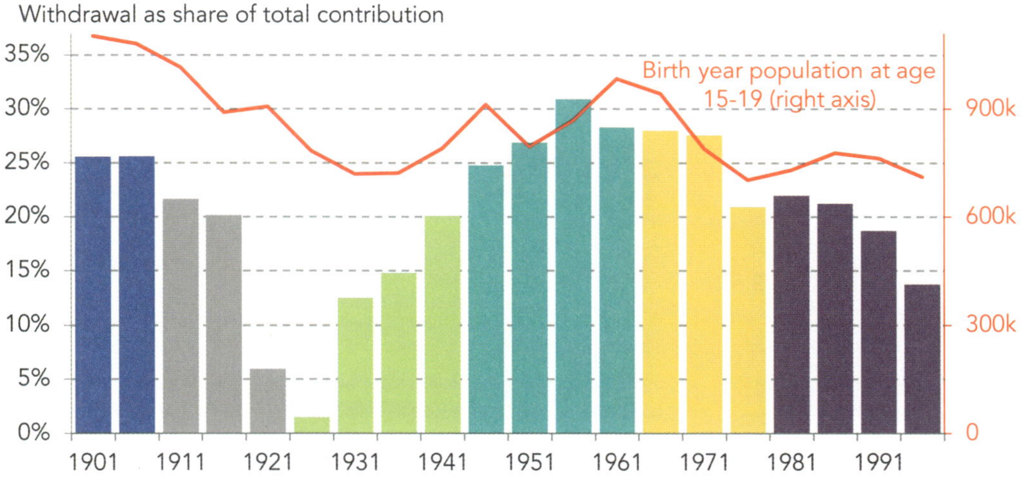

Notes: Net lifetime withdrawal is the average withdrawal within each cohort as a share of the average contribution. Net lifetime withdrawal measured relative to GDP per capita.

Source: RF analysis of OBR, *Fiscal sustainability report – January 2017*, January 2017; HMT, *Public Expenditure Statistical Analyses*; ONS, *2016-based mid-year population estimates*; ONS, *2016-based population projections*; J Hills, *Inequality and the State*, Oxford University Press, October 2004

12 J Hills, *Inequality and the State*, Oxford University Press, October 2004

13 For more details on the method used here and the underpinning assumptions, see: *A welfare generation* (Intergenerational Commission report 14)

14 This method presents the average position of different cohorts which says nothing about the distribution of tax revenues and welfare state spending within them. In the following chapter, we assess intra-cohort differences, and consider how they interact with inter-cohort divergence.

spending requirement mentioned above falls from £24 billion to just £6 billion in 2030.[15] A similar scale of decreases then feeds through beyond 2030. The results of this exercise are shown in Figure 5.6.[16]

Overall, all cohorts have positive net withdrawal rates, because the long-term trend over the entire period is of rising public service spending due to the expansion of the welfare state and the effects of longevity. As they broadly have in the past, taxes in future are projected to rise to meet these requirements in each given year, with the bill always falling most heavily on future cohorts. Within this overall picture, however, the differences between cohorts are illuminating.

Of those cohorts now past or near the end of lives, the older members of the silent generation (born in the late 1920s) do least well. This is because they were mostly in early working age during the establishment of the modern welfare state from the late 1940s onwards. The result was that they paid taxes to fund increased spending on education for subsequent cohorts that they did not benefit from themselves when young.

Younger baby boomers are the big winners – those born in the early 1960s have a net withdrawal from the welfare state around twice as large as that of the late 1990s millennial cohort. It is notable that under this assumption of falling per-head welfare generosity, levels of net withdrawal from the welfare state closely match fluctuations in cohort size, highlighting the all-else-equal advantage of being born into a big generation from a welfare state perspective. As Box 5.2 discusses, this logic – the opposite of what demographers had traditionally assumed about birth cohort ups and downs – has broader implications than just direct interactions with the welfare state itself.

Box 5.2 Big cohorts versus small cohorts

The dominant view among demographers such as Richard Easterlin has been that it was better to be born in a small cohort than a big cohort, due to less competition for jobs when entering the labour market, for example.[1] However, David Willetts in *The Pinch* argues that the evidence from the baby boomers suggests that being a big cohort is proving to be advantageous – perhaps because of their power in the market place and in a modern democracy.[2] In addition, because big

1 R Easterlin, *Birth and Fortune: The Impact of Numbers on Personal Welfare*, Basic Books, 1980

2 D Willetts, *The Pinch: How the baby boomers took their children's future – and why they should give it back*, Atlantic, 2010

15 We do this by holding per-head welfare state spending constant relative to GDP in future, which entails much-reduced services given the projections for rising non-demographic health costs discussed in Box 5.1.

16 As we discussed at the start of this chapter, governments have recently tried to cut the welfare state by focusing on reducing working-age welfare. Persisting with such an approach would produce similar lifetime net withdrawal rates across cohorts to those shown in Figure 5.6, a clearly generationally unfair outcome.

generations tend to be followed by smaller ones, there seems an explicit benefit to being in a large cohort. The following account of the life cycle for a big cohort demonstrates how.

In working age, when people are most productive and therefore tend to pay most tax, big cohorts find themselves in the middle of a demographic sweet spot in their families and nation states, with relatively fewer children and older people to support. Life feels prosperous, creating a strong temptation to pay less in taxes in favour of building up personal wealth. It takes a state with a particularly sophisticated and long budgeting time-horizon (and one that cannot be overly swayed by the democratic weight of this big cohort in the middle), to predict and plan for a reversal in this situation.

But the reversal comes as the big cohort moves into retirement. Dependency rises as they begin to rely on the smaller cohorts coming behind them for support, members of which end up paying relatively more tax as a result. And because they retain democratic weight, the big cohort has some ability to ensure that the productivity of the new working-age generations is used to support them. Indeed, coupled with the greater propensity to vote in older age groups, cohort size gave the baby boomers a 33 per cent numbers advantage over the millennials in the 2015 General Election.[3]

3 *Votey McVoteface* (Intergenerational Commission report 2)

Reshaping the NHS in the way implied by the restricted welfare spending scenario we've set out here would appear to be politically impossible, as well as an undesirable breach of the intergenerational contract at the point at which baby boomers will rely on state support the most.

Turning to the usual taxes to meet these costs puts pressure on generation X and millennials in the medium term

The third option for dealing with the looming fiscal challenge is to raise taxes. Sticking with John Hills's method, we can assess what this would mean for cohorts' lifetime welfare state position; this time using the OBR's central projection, rather than the 'declining health service generosity' scenario set out above. Importantly, to raise the required amount of revenue to fund increased future spending, this method assumes that the age profile of taxation remains as it is now. Any additional spending requirement is therefore met via income and consumption taxes according to their current age distribution and in proportion to their current size.[17]

17 Inheritance tax also takes the strain, but accounts for just 1 per cent of the total.

Focusing first on the next two decades, Figure 5.7 sets out what raising the additional £24 billion annually required by 2030, and £63 billion required by 2040, in this way would equate to in terms of individuals' cumulative additional tax burden. Because they are at peak earning and tax-paying age, those in millennial cohorts bear the biggest tax increases, with those born in the late 1980s facing a cumulative additional tax bill of around £14,000 each on average over these two decades.[18] The £63 billion in-year requirement in 2040 would translate into a 15p increase in the basic rate if it were funded entirely from income tax today. These figures underscore the heavy pressure that these revenue requirements would put on working-age cohorts over the next two decades if the usual taxes are turned to.

Figure 5.7: Raising income and consumption taxes over the next two decades weighs on millennials

Cumulative additional tax revenue (GDP-adjusted to 2017 values) required per person in 'rising welfare spending' scenario, by birth year and generation: UK, 2021-40

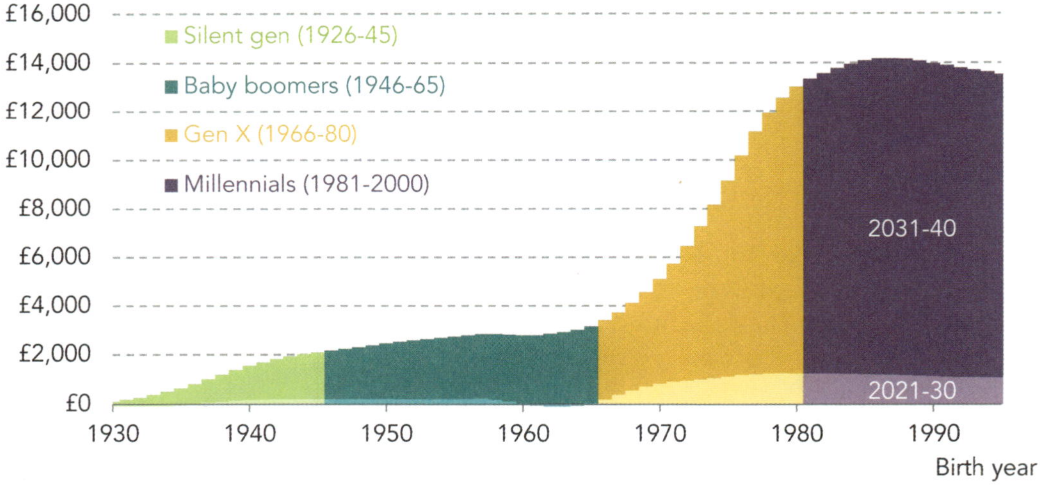

Source: RF analysis of OBR, *Fiscal sustainability report – January 2017*, January 2017; HMT, *Public Expenditure Statistical Analyses*; ONS, *2016-based mid-year population estimates*; ONS, *2016-based population projections*; J Hills, *Inequality and the State*, Oxford University Press, October 2004

However, in the long run these greater tax contributions by today's working-age cohorts are more than offset by the gain they receive from rising spending on the welfare state in their own old age, which future cohorts then pay for. This is shown in Figure 5.8, which replicates the picture shown in Figure 5.6 in this alternative scenario in which public spending rises to maintain generosity across cohorts. Under these assumptions, millennial cohorts in fact have slightly higher net lifetime withdrawal rates than baby boomer cohorts. The ratchet effect on health spending benefits them in the distant future more than enough to offset the challenges of funding the welfare state for the baby boomers in the nearer future.

18 This figure is expressed in current-GDP terms.

Figure 5.8: Ever-rising taxation would compensate the millennials eventually, if sustained

Average cumulative net lifetime withdrawal from the welfare state in 'rising welfare spending' scenario, by birth year: UK

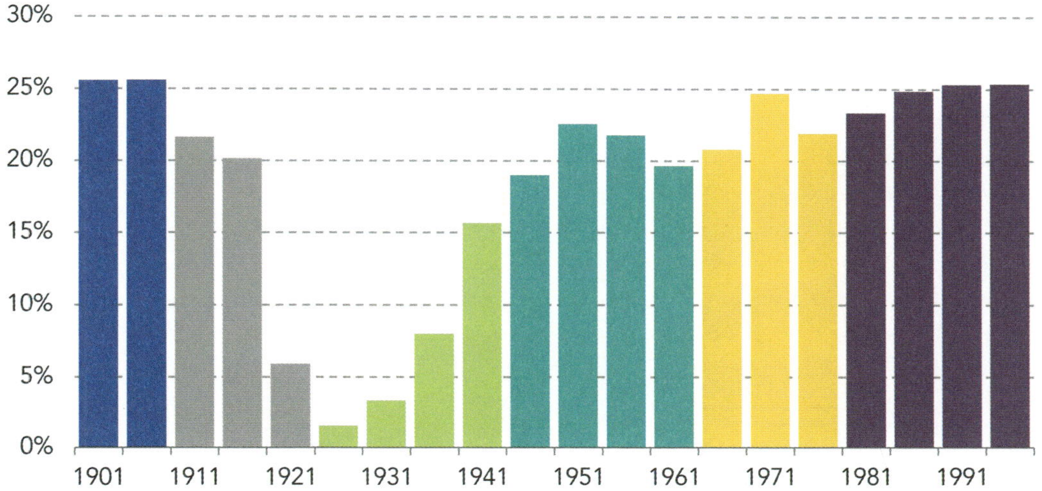

Notes: Net lifetime withdrawal is the average withdrawal within each cohort as a share of the average contribution. Net lifetime withdrawal measured relative to GDP per capita.

Source: RF analysis of OBR, *Fiscal sustainability report – January 2017*, January 2017; HMT, *Public Expenditure Statistical Analyses*; ONS, *2016-based mid-year population estimates*; ONS, *2016-based population projections*; J Hills, *Inequality and the State*, Oxford University Press, October 2004

Like ever-rising government borrowing, the implication here is that future younger cohorts always bear the burden of rising spending for those who came before them, with taxes taking up an ever-growing share of the economy as a result. OBR projections imply that taxes as a share of GDP would need to rise 7 percentage points to nearly 45 per cent by the 2060s to satisfy these assumptions.

Such a position is not impossible – it would put the UK on a par with Germany for example – but, like the option of pushing up debt, it essentially passes the burden onto future generations forever more. Eventually, this approach would run out of road. Moreover millennials, whose experience is that welfare state services available to previous generations have not been made available to them, may think it unlikely that these other services will be maintained for them as they age. Indeed, consistent with this pattern of behaviour is a scenario in which health service financing shifts, such that boomers continue to get healthcare free at the point of use but younger generations coming after them are told they have to pay.

A different but comparable exercise to the one set out here is an approach known as *generational accounting*, which suggests that a much greater fiscal burden is being placed on the unborn than on those alive today. Box 5.3 summarises this novel approach to bringing a focus on intergenerational equity to estimates of fiscal sustainability.

Box 5.3 Generational accounting

Generational accounts show the net discounted lifetime contribution, positive or negative, that people of different ages are expected to make to the Exchequer. First calculated in the US by Laurence Kotlikoff, estimates for the UK by the National Institute of Economic and Social Research show that the current fiscal position implies a required contribution from the unborn more than double the size of that from those being born today. The authors estimate that taxes would need to increase by 6 per cent to 7 per cent of GDP today in order to correct away from this unsustainable path for future generations and deliver both intergenerational and intertemporal budget balance.[1]

More recently, analysis has expanded on this method to capture transfers between generations that do not flow through the public sector, occurring instead within families or capital markets. These 'generational wealth accounts' set as their exam question whether the UK's consumption patterns (relative to GDP) can be sustained through future cohorts. The private sector is estimated to be in surplus from an intergenerational perspective because wealth held today is far greater than what is required to support consumption, giving rise to bequests and gifts sufficient to sustain consumption paths for the unborn (on average – this approach says nothing about intra-generational distributions). However the deficit in the public sector set out by the generational accounting work described above more than offsets this surplus, implying that, in aggregate, today's consumption plans are unsustainable for future generations.[2]

1 D McCarthy, J Sefton & M Weale, *Generational accounts for the United Kingdom*, National Institute of Economic and Social Research, January 2011

2 D McCarthy et al., Generational Wealth Accounts, October 2017

The three scenarios we've outlined – rising debt, cutting the welfare state and increasing taxes on the working-age population – are all politically very difficult and impose unfair burdens on younger or not-yet-born generations. They would also undermine rather than strengthen the intergenerational contract. Projections, of course, carry a high degree of uncertainty. Future growth and technological advances may substantially change our view on spending requirements, but a path that includes some measure of additional tax revenues is almost certainly necessary.

One way of addressing some of the generational implications of tax rises would be to change the age profile that these additional revenues are drawn from. Further increases in employment at older ages – building on the progress documented in Chapter 2 – would help. But we also have to look at the tax treatment of the property and pension wealth that older generations have amassed. This is addressed in our assessment of policy in Section 4.

In considering the country we pass on to future generations, it is not just debt that matters but the wider 'social inheritance' we leave

So far in this chapter we've considered the welfare state – education, health and care, and social security – and the balance of contributions and withdrawals between today's generations, and those not yet born. But to assess the country we will pass on to future generations, we should also take a broader view of the overall resources we leave for future generations, given how important these can be for their living standards. The Victorians, for example, left future generations railway and water networks that helped underpin future economic activity.

At first glance, the news is good. The overall net worth of the UK – that is, the total value of the country's assets less its liabilities – has grown markedly as a share of national income over the past 70 years. As of 2015, our net worth stood at 610 per cent of net national income; a level not recorded since 1913. Yet beneath this headline, the split between private and public net worth has shifted significantly. Figure 5.9 shows that *all* of the growth in net worth recorded in recent decades has come from the private sector. In contrast, public sector net worth has *fallen*.

Having topped 100 per cent of net national income at the start of the 1980s, the programme of privatisations and council house sales that marked the subsequent decade helped to push the UK's public sector net worth down to around 20 per cent by the mid 1990s. It fell further still following the financial crisis, reflecting the more than doubling of government's net debt in this period. It has been *negative* since 2012.

Figure 5.9: The private sector accounts for the entirety of the UK's net worth

Net private and public net worth as a proportion of net national income: UK

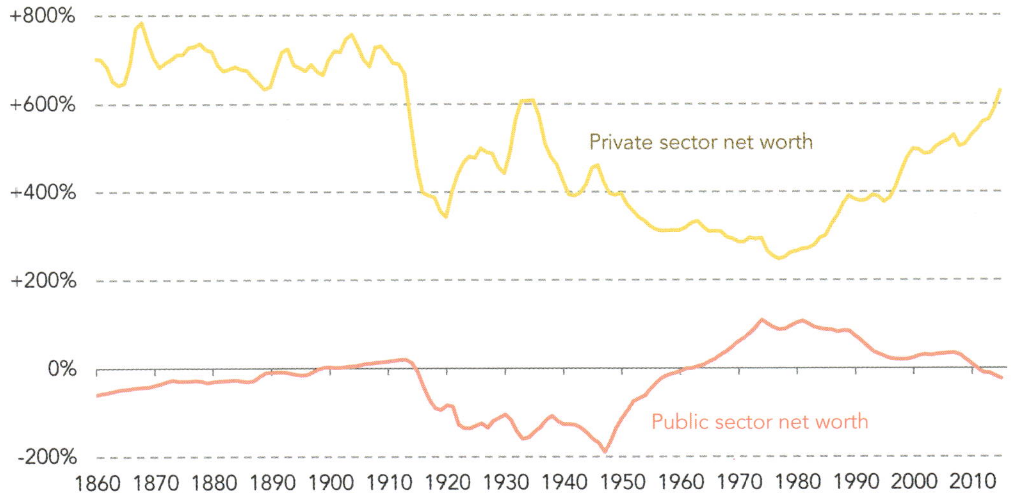

Source: *World Wealth & Income Database*

This figure does not tell the whole story: it fails to account for the net present value of any *future* liabilities incurred from past activities. Such an approach is instead provided by the Whole of Government Accounts (WGA), which cover the future costs associated with existing commitments in relation to student loans, public service pensions, PFI deals, nuclear decommissioning and oil and gas decommissioning. Interpretation of the WGA should be treated with some caution,[19] but they do provide a fuller account of the liabilities that future cohorts will need to deal with as a result of activity already undertaken. The latest WGA figures relate to 2015-16, and put net liabilities roughly one-quarter (24 per cent) higher than implied by the public sector net debt figure.[20] The implication is that there are significant costs coming down the line which future generations will be asked to pay for.

Of course, we might be less concerned about negative net worth in the public sector given the backdrop of huge increases in private sector net worth over the past 40 years. As Figure 5.9 shows, this increase has been very rapid, and the private sector total is now back where it was before World War I. But as the *World Inequality Report 2018* argues, irrespective of what's going on in the private sector, negative public sector net worth potentially "limits government ability to regulate the economy, redistribute income and mitigate rising inequality".[21] The increased concentration of net worth in the private sector also raises questions about how household wealth will be passed down through the generations – an issue we turn to in Chapter 11.

Alongside *who* holds the country's net worth, we might also be concerned by the *form* it takes. Of the large increase in UK net worth recorded between 1995 and 2016, 92 per cent was associated with just one asset: land. But while that value has increased significantly it does not represent any additional productive assets that can be passed on to future generations. If we strip land out of the equation, the overall trend looks very different. While the value of dwellings and other buildings also grew relative to national income between 1995 and 2016, the worth of financial assets and other non-financial assets (such as transport equipment, ICT equipment and intellectual property rights) declined. Given that we might expect such assets to be crucial to the future productive capacity of the country, this is a concerning finding from an inter-generational standpoint.

UK investment has been falling for some time, but the state is trying to do better

The 'social inheritance' facing future cohorts will be driven not just by today's stock of assets and liabilities, but by the level and type of investment being made in the UK. On this, the picture is again discouraging for future generations.

19 For example, it is not a projection of the future – it provides no present value estimate of future *assets* such as tax revenues – and it is very sensitive to discount rate changes.

20 Net liabilities of £1,986 billion compare with reported public sector net debt in 2015-16 of £1,606 billion. See: HM Treasury, *Whole of Government Accounts: year ended 31 March 2016*, July 2017

21 F Alvaredo et al., *World Inequality Report 2018*, World Inequality Lab, 2017

The UK invests relatively little by international standards. As a share of GDP, its average across the two decades from 1997 of 16.7 per cent is 2.9 percentage points lower than Italy's – the next lowest-placed-country. The UK figure contrasts with 20-year averages of 20.8 per cent in the US, 21.7 per cent in France, 26.5 per cent in Australia and 30.8 per cent in South Korea.[22] As an advanced, services-based economy, the UK might be expected to be investing less than economies with larger manufacturing bases. And the country fares better internationally in relation to investment in intangibles – such as research and development, brand and design. But even after allowing for this, overall the UK's investment deficit relative to other countries remains marked.[23]

Investment in the UK has been on a downward trend for much of the last 45 years: as a share of GDP it has fallen by more than a quarter since 1973. Falling public sector investment in the 1970s – associated with the ending of the programme of mass social housing construction by local government[24] – kick-started the decline. But it is the trend in the private sector which has dominated from the 1980s onwards. For example, corporate investment accounted for 84 per cent of the decline in total investment as a share of GDP recorded between 1987 and 2016.[25]

According to the World Economic Forum, the UK sits ninth in the world in terms of its access to infrastructure.[26] But its score has trended downwards over recent years, and the country ranks much lower on some individual aspects: it is 27th on the "quality of roads" for instance. Moreover, the Organisation for Economic Co-operation and Development (OECD) has argued that the UK has for some time under-invested in its infrastructure relative to other countries,[27] suggesting that its international ranking will come under threat in years to come with obvious generational implications. The implication is that the UK population has for a number of decades enjoyed the benefits of past investment in infrastructure without paying its way to ensure further improvements are available to support younger generations.

The government has set out plans for significantly increasing public investment over the coming years. It has also set a target for increasing (public and private) R&D spending to 2.4 per cent of GDP in 2027. Both measures are very welcome, but may be challenging to deliver. Alongside maintaining commitment to such targets across governments, it is important that this increased investment does not come solely at the expense of lower spending on services and support that benefit younger groups. In seeking to support the future quality of the UK's infrastructure, environmental issues are crucial too. Such concerns are outside of the scope of the Intergenerational

22 E Woolcott, *An international comparison of gross fixed capital formation*, Office for National Statistics, November 2017

23 J Haskel & S Westlake, *Capitalism Without Capital – the Rise of the Intangible Economy*, Princeton University Press, 2017

24 The sale of social housing to the private sector also has the effect of lowering recorded investment because the gross fixed capital formation figure deducts for asset sales. This is not 'disinvestment' however, with the assets simply transferred to the private sector instead.

25 Source: ONS, *National Accounts*

26 World Economic Forum, *The Global Competitiveness Report 2016-17*, September 2016

27 M Pisu, B Pels & N Bottini, *Improving Infrastructure in the United Kingdom*, Organisation for Economic Co-operation and Development, July 2015

Commission, but are clearly a vital part of both the economic and social inheritance being left to future generations.

Generational equity must factor into future tax and spending decisions

We've highlighted that spending decisions have tilted the welfare state away from younger generations during the post-crisis deficit-reduction phase. We have also looked at longer-term trends, and the large fiscal challenge coming down the track. Rising to this challenge will not be easy.

There is rightly a strong political consensus in favour of the basic provision of the welfare state, notably in healthcare and pensions. These are the very services where the costs pressures from the ageing of the baby boomers are most intense. It is therefore not credible that the boomers will support cutting back these services just when they most need them. Nor can we just borrow the money. That puts tax firmly on the agenda. How to raise the tax to fund these services in ways that are fair across the generations is the question we turn to in Section 4. In particular, we consider the benefits of extending revenue-raising later into lives via continued improvements in older employment (Chapter 8) and how wealth is taxed (Chapter 11).

The future path of productivity and growth will have a substantial bearing on the nature of the fiscal challenge in the coming decades. As well as reflecting on this path, the next chapter brings together the discussion in this section of the component parts of living standards – jobs, houses, pensions, tax and welfare – by considering generations' net positions in incomes, consumption and wealth. It also addresses the important question of differences *within* cohorts – both young and old.

SECTION 3

REVISITING THE GENERATIONAL SETTLEMENT

CHAPTER 6

Living standards across the generations – progress on pause

Chapter summary

The trends in housing, jobs and pay, and the welfare state can be brought together to analyse disposable incomes and hence living standards. Far from showing significant generational progress, millennials' incomes have broadly tracked those of generation X to date.

The financial crisis also significantly reduced income progress for generation X, albeit only after they enjoyed 15 years of much higher disposable incomes than the boomers had in their late-20s and 30s. Older baby boomers have maintained significant generational income progress compared to the silent generation.

Consumption levels are a direct measure of living standards, and popular narratives sometimes imply that millennials are particularly high spenders. But the evidence on spending reinforces that on incomes. In 2001 young adults were spending the same as 55-64-year-olds; they are now spending 15 per cent less.

Household wealth is growing rapidly overall, but despite this, cohorts born after 1960 are not accumulating more assets than their predecessors. Unexpected house price and pension windfalls have largely benefitted older cohorts with existing wealth, and are unlikely to be repeated in future.

Inequalities of income within generations are higher for younger people today than for their predecessors. Looking ahead, there is a risk that the growing importance of inheritances means intergenerational gaps combine with intra-generational inequalities to hold back social mobility.

Bringing together earnings, housing and the welfare state, younger adults are achieving little income progress

We have seen a clear divergence in outcomes between generations in the labour market, the housing market, pension saving and interactions with the state. We now put them together to assess generational trends in the best measures of current living standards – household incomes and consumption. We also look at longer-term resources – wealth and intergenerational wealth transfers.

Disposable household income after housing costs brings together employment within households, pay trends, the impact of direct taxes, benefits, private pension contributions and the cost of housing. Figure 6.1 summarises income differences between generations at each age and shows that, far from experiencing big generational progress, millennials have broadly tracked the incomes of generation X throughout their 20s. Those who have already reached age 30 have incomes no higher than generation X at the same age.

Figure 6.1: Millennials have so far made no income progress on generation X

Median real household annual net income after housing costs (CPI-AHC-adjusted to 2017 prices), by generation: GB, 1961-2016

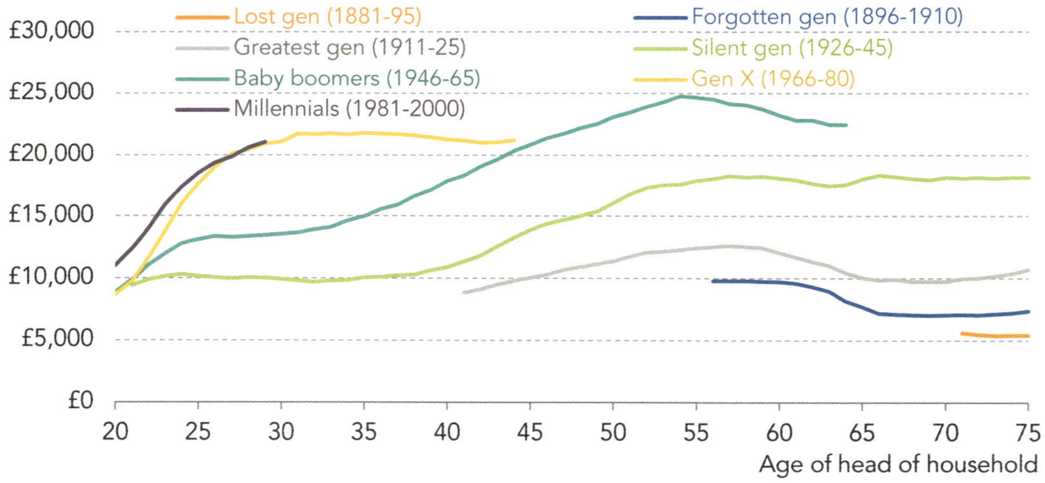

Notes: Incomes are equivalised to account for differences in household size. See notes to Figure 2 in: *As time goes by* (Intergenerational Commission report 4)

Source: RF analysis of IFS, *Households Below Average Income*; DWP, *Family Resources Survey*

Generation X has also experienced a big reduction in its income progress compared to baby boomers, but that unhappy outcome does at least come on the back of having recorded large income gains on the baby boomers during their late-20s and 30s. The financial crisis has also had an effect on the baby boomers, but they have still maintained significant generational income progress compared to the silent generation.

These outcomes stand in contrast to historically large generation-on-generation income gains throughout the second half of the 20th century: at age 30 the baby boomers had incomes over one-third higher than the silent generation did at that age. And progress has been maintained for older generations even through the crisis period. Overall, while the lack of generational progress is striking, the picture on incomes is not as bad as the trends on pay we've already seen. This is because the incomes of younger households have been bolstered by high employment and, to some extent, welfare support.[1]

Figure 6.1 shows generations when not all members have reached each age. Coupled with generations of different widths, this means that these generational gaps capture slightly different time spans and will be likely to change in future as younger members of generations progress through their lives. To get beyond these challenges, we can look at trends for narrower and consistent birth cohorts. These are shown in Figure 6.2, including the Resolution Foundation's projections of working-age incomes over the remainder of this parliament.[2]

Figure 6.2: Income progress has faltered for younger cohorts in particular

Median real household annual net income after housing costs (CPI-AHC-adjusted to 2017 prices), by cohort: GB, 1961-2023

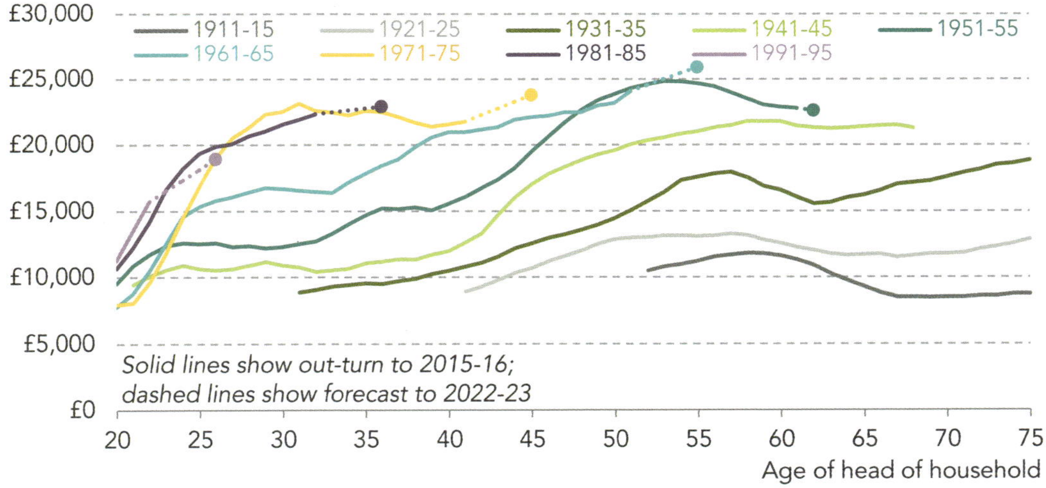

Notes: Incomes are equivalised to account for differences in household size. Figures for each cohort are derived from a weighted average of estimates by single year of age for each single birth year; cohorts are only included if all five birth years are present in the data. Data is smoothed using three-year rolling averages. Incomes are only forecast for working-age households; for details on the approach to forecasting household incomes, see: A Corlett, G Bangham & D Finch, *The Living Standards Outlook 2018*, Resolution Foundation, February 2018

Source: RF analysis of IFS, *Households Below Average Income*; DWP, *Family Resources Survey*; RF nowcast & forecast

The financial crisis dampened both income progress as cohorts age, and cohort-on-cohort income gains for all working-age adults. Those born in the first half of the 1960s, 1970s, 1980s and 1990s have similar household incomes to those born 10 years before them when they were the same age. This is not the case for older cohorts because of the strong performance of pension incomes discussed in Chapter 4.

1 In addition, incomes are measured by the age of the head of the household, so young adults living with their parents are not included, for example.

2 For further details, see: A Corlett, G Bangham & D Finch, *The Living Standards Outlook 2018*, Resolution Foundation, February 2018

Incorporating income projections over the current parliament shows that the youngest cohorts face the most severe stalling of progress. While baby boomer cohorts in 2022-23 are projected to have made modest (5-6 per cent) income gains on those born 10 years before them, households headed by those born in the early 1990s are expected to have incomes on a par with those born 20 years before them when they were the same age.

Stalling generational income progress tilted against the young – and in some cases substantial declines compared to predecessors – is a problem in many advanced economies. This helps to explain why the generational living standards pessimism discussed in Chapter 1 is so widespread. Indeed, the UK is actually doing better than the truly awful outcomes in Southern Europe because here millennial incomes have not actually fallen compared to generation X.[3] The unusual pattern of stalling income progress following very substantial gains for previous generations at each age is seen on incomes, as it was on pay and home ownership.

It is likely that this experience of having substantial generational progress but then losing it in living memory shapes attitudes towards the intergenerational living standards challenge in Britain. In contrast, Germany and the US have had limited or no generational progress for some time, with the financial crisis simply making a pre-existing challenge more acute.

In determining how worried we should be about this collapse of generational progress, two important points are worth exploring: variations around the average, and the possibility that strong future growth re-establishes generation-on-generation gains.

It is certainly true that averages mask very different experiences for certain groups, particularly disadvantaged groups for whom fast progress in recent years represents a process of catch-up, as significant barriers to equal opportunity are broken down. The stronger generational pay progress of women compared to men is one example. Although many groups continue to face significant disadvantages, incomes within certain ethnic groups have also grown much more rapidly than the average in recent decades. Between 2001-03 and 2014-16, typical incomes grew in real terms by 38 per cent for Bangladeshi households and 28 per cent for Pakistani households, compared with 13 per cent for the White British group.[4] These faster-than-average improvements for certain groups within British society sit alongside the improvements in freedoms and opportunities benefitting, for example, gay and transgender people, discussed in Chapter 1. In sum, significant generation-on-generation progress is still very much a fact of life for some people.

---

3 *Cross Countries* (Intergenerational Commission report 15)

4 A Corlett, *Diverse outcomes: Living standards by ethnicity*, Resolution Foundation, August 2017

But averages still matter a lot, not least because if some groups within society are having far better experiences than these averages suggest, others must be having worse experiences. As we discussed in Chapter 2, while the narrowing of the gender pay gap is something to be celebrated, this has happened partly due to a rise in lower-skilled jobs and involuntary part-time working for young men. Indeed, one group that has clearly not benefitted from generational progress is white working class males, with typical pay for men in Greater Manchester, for example, no higher than it was at the turn of the millennium.[5]

Box 6.1 Technology, productivity and generational living standards challenges

The role of technology in past and future living standards is a matter of some debate. One account – popularised in books such as *The Second Machine Age* and *The Rise of the Robots* – posits that the nature and transferability of current technological advances is such that many jobs will soon be made obsolete, with higher unemployment a consequence.[1] The Bank of England has raised concerns that up to 15 million UK jobs may be at risk of automation.[2] Technology is also sometimes targeted as having facilitated the rise of atypical employment forms – such as lower-skilled self-employment and zero-hours contracts discussed in Chapter 2 – to the benefit of firms more than workers. From this perspective, technologies that have expanded opportunities for younger generations are sometimes also seen as a headwind to their living standards.

These accounts underscore the need for policy to support those feeling the worst effects of rapid, technology-driven change. But in terms of the overall shape of change, robot-induced anxiety appears overplayed. The UK has record-high employment, and the reality is that jobs change and adapt to the influence of automation.[3] It may be that 'this time it's different', but such claims were also made during past waves of technological progress.[4]

An alternative viewpoint is that automation is exactly what the UK labour market needs, given our historically and internationally poor productivity growth. Indeed, we can partly attribute the UK's poor productivity performance to many years of low investment: gross capital formation in the UK has been consistently below that of comparable countries for many years, and has declined even more markedly after the financial crisis. Because productivity is the long-term driver of real wage growth, some technology-supported productivity growth would be a strong antidote to the stagnation of generational living standards progress.

1 E Brynjolfsson & A McAfee, *The Second Machine Age: Work, Progress, and Prosperity in a Time of Brilliant Technologies*, W. W. Norton & Company, 2014; M Ford, *The rise of the robots: Technology and the Threat of a Jobless Future*, Oneworld, 2015

2 A Haldane, *Labour's Share*, Bank of England, November 2015

3 M Arntz, T Gregory & U Zierhan, *The Risk of Automation for Jobs in OECD Countries: A Comparative Analysis*, Organisation for Economic Co-operation and Development, 2016

4 A Corlett, *Robot wars: Automation and the labour market*, Resolution Foundation, July 2016

5 S Clarke, *'A-typical' working day in Greater Manchester*, Resolution Foundation, October 2017

It is also true that strong income growth in future could wipe out today's poor outcomes on generational progress. For example, technology-induced productivity increases may (and hopefully will) leave millennials and all future generations substantially better off over their lifetimes than their predecessors – just as they did for older generations. The extent to which technological advances have boosted living standards and will do so in future is a matter of some debate, as explored in Box 6.1.

But, while no one knows what the future holds, it would take a major and sustained period of economic outcomes better than those currently forecast by the OBR and Bank of England to significantly restart progress in generational living standards. Figure 6.3 demonstrates this by showing cohort-on-cohort changes in cumulative real median earnings over lifetimes in two scenarios for future earnings growth. One is based on a strong earnings forecast that sees us maintaining an average annual real growth rate of 2.3 per cent right through to 2066, including through inevitable recessions. The alternative scenario shows a much lower average growth rate of 1.3 per cent, roughly matching the very poor pay performance of the 2000s and 2010s.

Figure 6.3: Even an optimistic wage growth scenario would deliver weaker cohort-on-cohort earnings progress than in the past

Cohort-on-cohort growth in cumulative median real lifetime earnings between ages 25 and 60 (CPIH-adjusted) under different scenarios: GB, 1965-2066

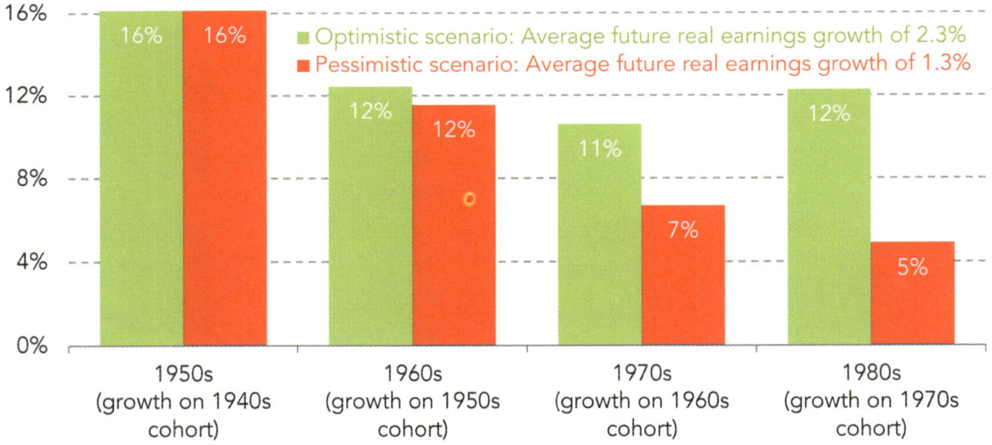

Notes: For details on the earnings projection methodology, see: *As good as it gets* (Intergenerational Commission report 12)
Source: RF analysis of ONS, *Annual Survey of Hours and* Earnings; ONS, New *Earnings Survey Panel Dataset*; RF lifetime model

Even in the optimistic scenario, the experience of the pre-crisis slowdown and post-crisis pay squeeze is such that those cohorts in prime age at the time experience less improvement than the 1950s cohort (who were in their 50s by the time of the crisis) did. And in the pessimistic scenario, lifetime cohort progress for those born in the 1970s and 1980s falls to less than half that of the 1950s cohort. Strong future growth feeding through to pay is hugely important and has the potential to improve the current meagre levels of generational progress. But even so it is not a panacea for all intergenerational challenges, such as access to housing or secure pensions.

The income squeeze is reflected in young adults' consumption, which has fallen back relative to those in their 50s and 60s

The earnings of today's younger generations have performed particularly badly. But some have suggested that this misses what is really going on. Millennials are said to be benefitting from the advent of smartphones and other new consumer technologies, perhaps suggesting their limited income goes further than it did for others at the same age.[6] Millennials have also been accused of living frivolously (excessive consumption of avocado toast is particularly shocking apparently), rather than saving for the future as previous generations did. Perhaps overwhelmed by the scale of their rent and the amounts required to put down a deposit on a house, they are said to be prioritising short-term spending over long-term saving.

Data on consumption – which can be viewed as the most direct measure of current living standards – can tell us whether this is the case by comparing relative spending levels of different age groups. While absolute changes over time should be interpreted with some caution,[7] Figure 6.4 shows that since the turn of the millennium the consumption of 25-34-year-olds has been pared back relative to that

Figure 6.4: A consumption gap has opened up between younger and older working-age households

Mean real weekly household non-housing consumption expenditure (CPIH-adjusted to 2017 prices), by age: UK

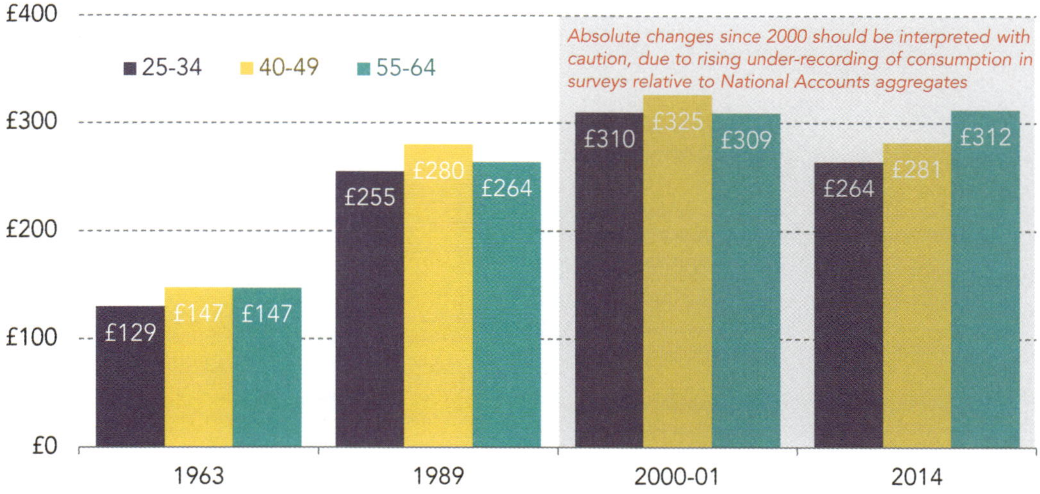

Notes: Household consumption expenditure is equivalised to account for differences in household size. All expenditures deflated using all-items CPIH (which has been indexed back to 1963 using historic trends in RPI), to give an indication of 'real' consumption expenditure changes over time.

Source: Loughborough University/RF analysis of ONS, *Family Expenditure Survey*; ONS, *Living Costs and Food Survey*

6 For a fuller summary of these arguments, see: *Consuming forces* (Intergenerational Commission report 10)

7 There are technical challenges to comparing consumption across time periods because of growing under-recording by surveys of consumption. See Box 1 in: *Consuming forces* (Intergenerational Commission report 10)

of 55-64-year-olds. In 2001 these two age groups had exactly the same after-housing spending; by 2014 however, 25-34-year-olds were spending 15 per cent less.

This pattern in the 21st century stands in contrast to consumption gains skewed towards younger working-age adults in the 1960s, 1970s and 1980s. As a result, the baby boomers have been on the right side of consumption improvements both when young and when older.

So patterns of consumption confirm that younger cohorts are having a tough time – reinforcing rather than challenging what other data shows on living standards.

Moreover, while technological progress means the goods and services millennials enjoy are far superior to those the baby boomers had when young, new technologies are not a new phenomenon. Nobody begrudges the baby boomers their pay progress when they grew up, simply because they were also able to benefit from the arrival of televisions and washing machines on a scale that the greatest generation could only have dreamed of. Indeed, as Box 6.1 discussed, these technological improvements are exactly what should underpin the cohort-on-cohort living standards progress the 20th century delivered. And all generations alive today are benefitting from new possibilities and living lives in more similar ways that many assume, as Box 6.2 sets out.

Box 6.2 Millennial myth-busting

In response to evidence of stagnating generational living standards progress, some have suggested that these conclusions miss some of what is really going on, because millennials are getting more for their incomes than previous generations.[1] However, a look at detailed consumption data for working-age adults provides little evidence to support this account:

- While young people have always spent more on eating out in restaurants and cafés and on takeaways than older people, the growth in eating out during the 21st century has been predominantly driven by better-off older working-age adults (aged 55-64). If anyone is eating more avocado toast in cafés it is this group.
- Older working-age adults spend the most on holidays and have experienced the strongest growth between 2000-01 and 2014, while holiday consumption for 25-34-year-olds has fallen.
- Spending on mobile phones is very similar across both age and income groups, suggesting that far from there being an iPhone generation, modern communications items have come to be regarded as essentials for the broad majority of working-age adults today.[2]

These findings go against the grain of the popular millennial narrative. Moreover there

1 For a summary of these accounts, see: *Consuming forces* (Intergenerational Commission report 10)

2 *Consuming forces* (Intergenerational Commission report 10)

is no evidence that they are lazier or more demanding at work; they do not trust institutions less; and they do not have a different relationship with brands than previous generations.[3] And as we showed in Chapter 2, the characterisation of millennials as disloyal job-hoppers is wrong: they move jobs less than their predecessors at the same age. Overall, we should be cautious of such myths distracting from the realities of what is happening to the living standards of younger generations.

3 B Duffy, H Shrimpton & M Clemence, *Millennial Myths and Realities*, Ipsos MORI, July 2017

Total wealth – which supports living standards over lifetimes and insulates from risk – is only improving for older cohorts

Household wealth has grown enormously in recent decades, increasing 2.5 times faster than GDP since the 1980s. Unlike earnings, wealth has continued growing strongly after the financial crisis. Earnings growth can drive both pay progress for each cohort as it ages and cohort-on-cohort progress, as younger cohorts see more years of that progress. But the same cannot be said for wealth, because wealth gains are not just about saving to build up assets but also include changes in asset prices for those things that households already hold. As Figure 6.5 shows, this crucial difference means that, compared to their predecessors, we are not seeing substantial progress in wealth accumulation for any cohorts born since 1960, despite big increases in overall household wealth levels over the past decade.

Figure 6.5: Only older cohorts have more wealth than predecessors

Median real family total net wealth per adult (CPIH-adjusted to 2017 prices), by cohort: GB, 2006-16

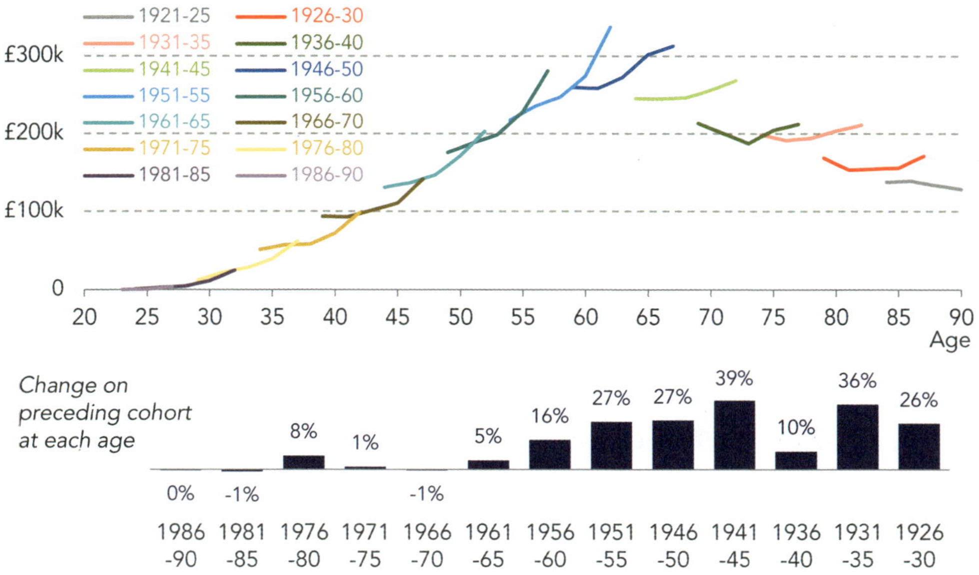

Notes: Excludes physical wealth.
Source: RF analysis of ONS, *Wealth and Assets Survey*

This pattern is reflected in trends among the different forms of wealth. For example, net financial wealth has fallen cohort-on-cohort for those born from the 1950s onwards. Pension wealth is keeping up to some extent: younger cohorts have roughly the same as their predecessors at the same age, but older cohorts have significantly more than their predecessors. And there are big declines in housing wealth among younger cohorts, reflecting both home ownership trends and the timing of house price increases.

As covered in Chapters 3 and 4, it is unexpected windfalls and valuation effects – rather than active savings behaviour – that explain the majority of families' wealth accumulation in recent decades. Such gains have predominantly accrued to cohorts born in the 1940s, 1950s and 1960s and are very unlikely to be repeated for younger cohorts, not least because interest rate falls cannot be repeated, underlining a clear reversal of generational progress on wealth accumulation.

Inheritances will help, but come too late and be too unequally shared to solve this problem

One effect of significant wealth increases among older cohorts is that inheritances and gifts will play a growing role in how younger cohorts accumulate assets. Having doubled in size over the last two decades, inheritances are projected to double again in the next two.[8] And high home ownership levels in older generations mean we might expect them to reach a larger group in the future than they have in the past.

Figure 6.6: The most common age of inheritance for millennials is expected to be 61

Proportion of adults aged 20-35 by age at which their parents have died or are expected to be deceased: UK, 2015-16

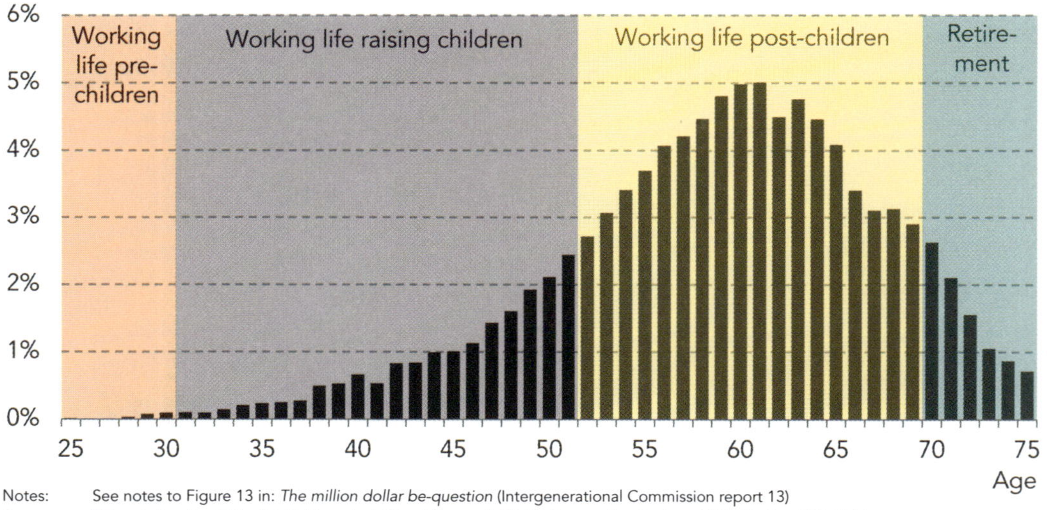

Notes: See notes to Figure 13 in: *The million dollar be-question* (Intergenerational Commission report 13)

Source: RF analysis using ISER, *British Household Panel* Survey; ISER, Understanding *Society*; ONS, *National Life Tables*

8 *The million dollar be-question* (Intergenerational Commission report 13)

However, inheritances are not a silver bullet when it comes to the living standards of younger generations. For many of those who might expect to receive them, inheritances will come too late to support living standards during the expensive child-rearing stage. The most common age at which 20-35-year-olds might inherit stands at 61, as Figure 6.6 shows. Of course gifts can bring these transfers forward (to the extent that wealth is not tied up in assets like main residences), and inheritances at this age would help in preparing for retirement, but relying on this windfall to support living standards appears far from optimal.

Despite looking set to be somewhat more widely shared than at present, inheritances will still reinforce intra-generational divides. The impact of inheritances on inequality is hotly debated, but focusing on lifetime consumption or incomes shows that in the past they have had a neutral or mildly inequality-increasing effect.[9] And crucially, given their sheer size they substantially increase absolute wealth gaps – making it harder still for members of the receiving generation to earn their way to being wealthy. With inheritances set to continue growing in size as well as number, these absolute effects will become more substantial.[10]

We can demonstrate this effect by simulating the unrealistic but illustrative scenario in which parental property wealth all flows down to young adults straight

Figure 6.7: Property inheritances look set to increase absolute wealth gaps among millennials

Median gross property wealth per adult of 20-35-year-olds not living with their parents excluding and including parental property wealth, by gross property wealth quintile: UK, 2015-16

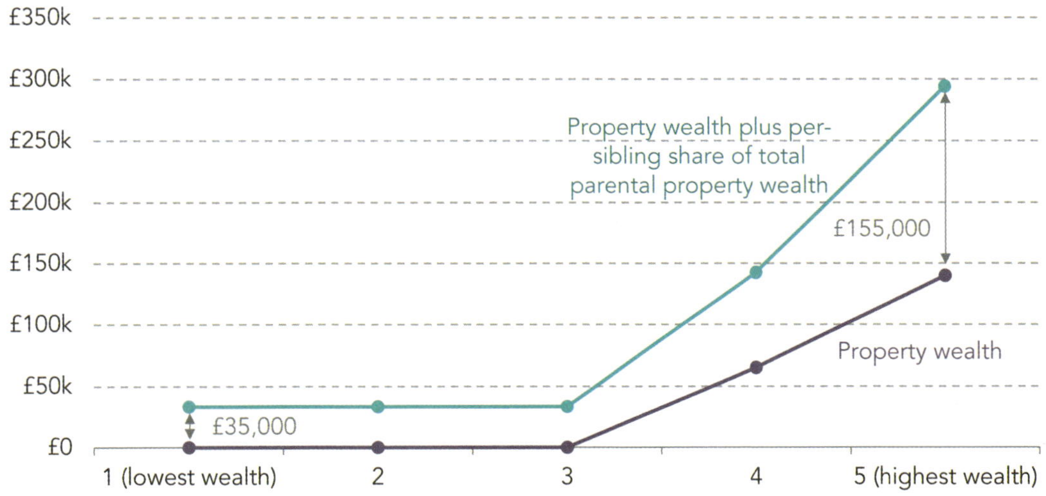

Notes: Data captures wealth in main residence only. For methodological details, see: *The million dollar be-question* (Intergenerational Commission report 13)

Source: RF analysis using ISER, *British Household Panel* Survey; ISER, *Understanding Society*

9 For a discussion of these debates, see: *The million dollar be-question* (Intergenerational Commission report 13)

10 *The million dollar be-question* (Intergenerational Commission report 13)

away, shown in Figure 6.7. The property wealth of those currently without any would typically increase by £35,000, whereas 20-35-year-olds in the top fifth of the property wealth distribution would see their property wealth increase by £155,000.

These outcomes at the individual level would be amplified by patterns of 'assortative mating', under which people couple up with those with similar inheritance expectations to their own. Those who expect to inherit nothing have partners with average expected inheritances of £25,000, compared to an inheritance expectation of £190,000 on average for partners of those who themselves expect to inherit £500,000 or more.

These effects mean the growing role of inheritances is a headwind to social mobility. It is the primary mechanism by which intergenerational differences in wealth accumulation can drive intra-cohort differences in younger cohorts.

The problem is even more acute because intra-cohort differences in incomes and wealth are already high and sometimes rising. Figure 6.8 shows those in each generation with incomes 25 per cent and 75 per cent of the way up within-generation distributions. Cross-generation patterns are similar at these two points in the distribution, but the growing gaps within generations following inequality increases in the 1980s mean that millennials and generation X have experienced the highest intra-generational inequality when young. Forecasts for rising inequality over the next five years suggest this situation could persist.[11]

Figure 6.8: Inequalities within generations are larger than those between generations

Percentiles of real household annual net income after housing costs (CPI-AHC-adjusted to 2017 prices), by generation: GB, 1961-2016

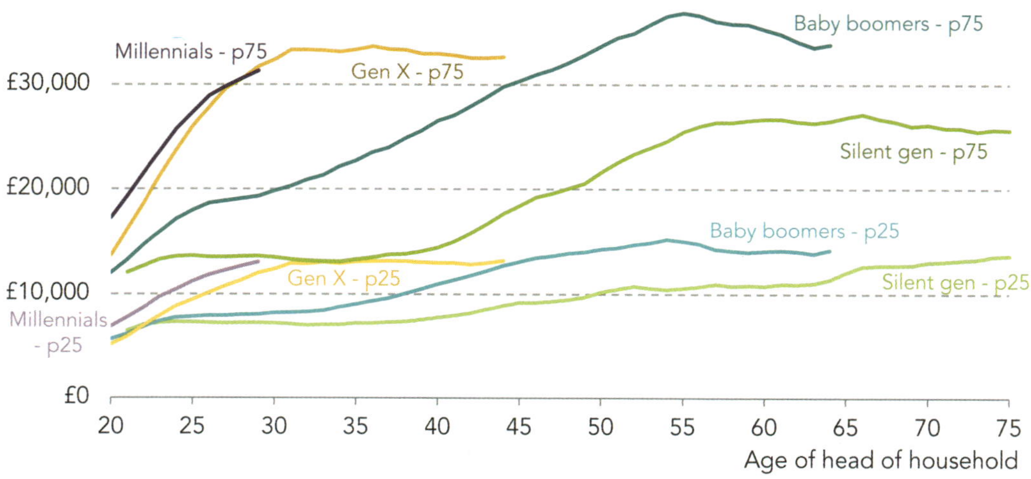

Notes: 'p25' refers to incomes at the 25th percentile within each generation; 'p75' refers to incomes at the 75th percentile within each generation. Incomes are equivalised to account for differences in household size. See notes to Figure 4 in: *As time goes by* (Intergenerational Commission report 4)

Source: RF analysis of IFS; *Households Below Average Income*; DWP, *Family Resources Survey*

11 A Corlett, G Bangham & D Finch, *The Living Standards Outlook 2018*, Resolution Foundation, February 2018

Intra-generational differences are laid similarly bare by a focus on wealth, as Figure 6.9 shows. And here there is evidence of wealthier members of cohorts pulling away from less wealthy ones. For each cohort born since 1956, wealth is higher at each age than it was in the preceding cohort for wealthier cohort members; yet for cohort members with fewer assets it is the same or lower than the preceding cohort at the same age. And it is not just inequalities within younger generations that should concern us – this presentation highlights just how large wealth differences are within older cohorts as well.

Figure 6.9: Wealth has grown cohort-on-cohort at the top of the distribution, but not at the bottom

Percentiles of real family total net wealth per adult (CPIH-adjusted to 2017 prices), by cohort: GB, 2006-16

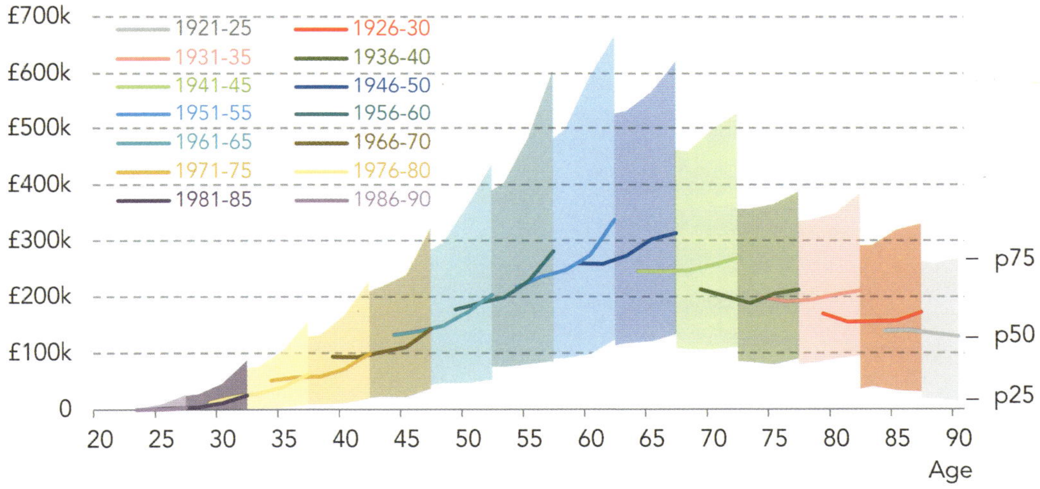

Notes: Excludes physical wealth. 'p25' refers to incomes at the 25th percentile within each cohort; 'p50' refers to incomes at the 50th percentile (the median) within each cohort; 'p75' refers to incomes at the 75th percentile within each cohort.

Source: RF analysis of ONS, *Wealth and Assets Survey*

The way forward

We've painted a picture of generational challenges threatening living standards now and in the future. We have shown real declines in progress across cohorts. This evidence stretches beyond just the recent crisis period or the current younger generation – a lack of generational progress started earlier on housing and earnings. And the decline in generational wealth progress affects even the youngest baby boomers.

But it is not all bad news. Unemployment is much lower than in the past, and auto-enrolment in pensions is promoting saving. And the good news is that there are clear examples of successful and patient policy interventions that have helped to tackle big, long-lasting problems. We turn next to our own blueprint for rising to today's intergenerational challenge.

CHAPTER 7

Renewing the generational contract – a blueprint for change

Chapter summary

The conclusion of the analysis conducted for the Intergenerational Commission is that Britain faces challenges to its intergenerational contract. These include a crisis of generational progress, but the challenges are about far more than the millennials or the financial crisis.

Renewing the intergenerational contract means delivering the health and care that older generations deserve, need and expect, and doing so in a generationally fair way.

Now is also the time to demonstrate to younger generations that we can make difficult changes so that Britain has as much to offer them as it did their predecessors. From housing to pensions and the labour market, we can reduce the challenges they face and the risks that they bear.

Our approach is to set out a policy agenda for renewing the intergenerational contract to achieve both a better Britain and a more united one.

The public is right – Britain has a crisis of intergenerational progress

Despite a widespread belief that each generation should do better than the last, British adults are overwhelmingly pessimistic about the prospects of today's young adults. The evidence we have compiled shows that this pessimism is rooted in very real experiences of stagnation or declines in generation-on-generation improvements. Millennial incomes have so far not improved on those of generation X, young adults are missing out on Britain's wealth boom and, crucially, they bear far more risk than their predecessors, from their jobs to the homes they increasingly rent.

This heightened risk poses a unique challenge for today's younger generations, with wide-reaching effects on their living standards. The rise in atypical working, the increase in renting in the private sector, and the decline of defined benefit pensions together add up to a burden on young people that hampers their own ability and appetite to take positive risks, like moving jobs.

The challenges reflect more than just the financial crisis and extend beyond the millennials themselves

It is clear that the financial crisis has played a large part in these trends, but they have deeper roots. Progress in the labour market had stalled before the crisis hit, changes in the pensions market began well before the late 2000s, and our housing failures date back decades.

These outcomes are not only affecting young adults. While millennials are clearly at the sharp end, there are areas of concern for older generations too. Housing costs have dragged on living standards progress for all generations alive today compared to their predecessors; and although the young are most affected by labour market insecurities, they extend across the age range. Additionally, large wealth divides within older generations highlight that while Britain's growing stock of wealth is increasingly concentrated in older generations, not all members benefit.

However, the biggest concern for older generations is likely to be the challenges facing the welfare state in delivering on its commitment to meet their health and care needs in the coming decades. The sums required to maintain these services are large. But cutting essential welfare support for older generations, or putting unsustainable costs on younger ones to pay for them, would undermine the intergenerational contract rather than help strengthen it. We need a different way forward.

Renewing the intergenerational contract means addressing the challenges facing both older and younger generations

While families are living with them day to day, society as a whole has neither fully recognised nor responded to the challenges of the 21st century: delivering the health and care that older generations deserve, need and expect in a generationally fair way; and demonstrating to younger generations that Britain can work for them as it did for their predecessors. Perhaps this is not surprising – finding a solution to these challenges is no easy task. But it can, and must, be done.

Some might contend that these problems will unwind of their own accord as the memory of the financial crisis fades. However, our analysis shows that labour market challenges for young adults are enduring in an era of record-high employment. Even if (and it is a big if) very strong productivity growth in the future were to feed through to restart significant generational pay improvements, the challenges in our housing market, and from riskier pensions, that younger adults face would remain. And the reality of an ageing society will be with us for decades to come.

Others might argue that the task of addressing these challenges is too tough. By characterising the issue as a 'generational war' and suggesting that the battle lines will remain drawn in favour of the relatively larger baby boomer generation, they might doubt the ability of our politics to rise to these challenges. But this view misses the fact that the intergenerational contract is something that adults across age groups recognise and support. This is demonstrated every day in our families – from the growing importance of the bank of mum and dad to the post-crisis rise in the number of young adults living with their parents. It is now the task of society as a whole to adapt too.

With fresh thinking and tough choices, the intergenerational contract can be renewed

With a recognition of the scale of the challenges, but a determination that they can – and must – be overcome, the following section sets out a package of policy recommendations intended to renew the intergenerational contract. We identify ways to give older generations the health and care they deserve. We focus on revenue-raising measures that harness Britain's growing stock of wealth in order to deliver equity both across and within generations.

We also set out how the challenges facing younger generations can be addressed. This means mitigating the lasting effects of the financial crisis; overturning long-term policy failures that are holding them back in areas like housing and technical education; reducing exposure to risk in jobs, housing and pensions; and recognising that asset ownership for young adults – no matter their background – must be part of the answer in a world in which wealth is a bigger deal than it has ever been.

Our approach

In a challenge as broad as the one we have set out, the options for policy are themselves varied. To limit our focus and prioritise areas for action in a way that does justice to the scale of the challenge, we have been selective, and focused on areas where significant change is needed.

Our policy recommendations target the major components of living standards discussed in the previous section: the labour market, the housing market, the pensions system and the role of the state. The following four chapters deal with each of these in turn. This means that we do not offer specific recommendations in relation to wider challenges and contextual factors that we have discussed, including levels of intergenerational mixing within our communities and the important task of supporting longer working lives. Instead, we highlight options suggested by others and promising approaches that could be replicated.

In the main, our policy recommendations are directed to government, particularly at the national level. However, we also signal actions we would like to see from local government, businesses, trade unions, and others. Renewing the intergenerational contract matters to all of us, and will require change for us all.

We pursue policies that are practical and implementable, but our view extends beyond what might be achieved in the current parliament. These are long-term challenges that will not fix themselves. We do not expect political parties to embrace them immediately – indeed they include proposals that will be difficult for all parties. But we hope that as the important issues we identify are increasingly recognised, our proposals can be a useful guide to action.

Our argument is about the state of the nation, both now and in the future – and our policy proposals have as their goal a more united Britain.

SECTION 4

A POLICY AGENDA FOR RENEWING THE GENERATIONAL CONTRACT

CHAPTER 8

Jobs and pay – progress in work

We recommend

A £1 billion 'Better Jobs Deal', offering practical support and funding for younger workers most affected by the financial crisis to train up or move jobs.

More secure work, with the right to a regular contract for those doing regular hours on a zero-hours contract; extended statutory rights for the self-employed; and minimum notice periods for shifts.

Strengthening technical education with £1.5 billion to tackle under-funding of further education colleges and improve technical education, paid for by cancelling 1p of the corporation tax cut planned for 2020.

Our approach to labour market policy

Relative to those who came before them, younger generations' qualifications are growing at a slower rate; they are more likely to be in low-skilled, atypical and sometimes insecure employment; and they have poorer prospects of moving on to better-paid jobs. The financial crisis played a large role, with its effects continuing to be felt, but the roots run deeper.

The task now is to update our labour market policy to respond to these new challenges, just as we did in response to the experience of high unemployment following the recessions of the 1980s and 1990s – a response that lies behind much of the good news on employment today. The risk if we do not is that long periods of low-paid work for today's young damage their earnings years after the financial crisis has passed.

This new approach should also recognise that many young workers now face greater risks, with lower job security and increased variability of hours. The danger is that these combine with risks deriving from less secure housing, less secure pension outcomes and lower asset safety nets, to hold young adults back from taking the *good* risks – like moving jobs – that are key to their progression.

The pay progress of younger generations is also being held back because their cohort-on-cohort gains in qualifications are not as great as those experienced by generation X following the higher education expansion of the 1990s. This is largely because the number of university and college places has not grown as fast as it did then, and because of the failure to provide clear and high-quality technical education routes outside university. Young people's jobs also appear less likely to boost their skills, whereas in the past workplace experiences helped compensate for weak educational outcomes for those who did not go to university.

We therefore focus on three key challenges: avoiding the potential 'scarring' effects of the financial crisis by getting the careers of those young adults most affected moving; reducing the worst insecurities in work; and addressing barriers to more investment in human capital.

Avoiding the potential 'scarring' effects of the crisis by restarting individuals' pay progression

For young people in low-paid work, moving jobs has long been a key route to higher pay. Job mobility is central to the future prospects of those who bore the brunt of the financial crisis by entering the labour market when it was taking place. But the job mobility of young people was declining even before the financial crisis, and has recovered only slowly from the precipitous drop that subsequently occurred. This is a key reason for their pay stagnation – they are more likely to be stuck in low-paid jobs than previous generations when they were young.

Why are young people not moving jobs? Our research suggests a mix of pessimism about new opportunities and satisfaction with existing jobs. As Figure 8.1 shows, when asked in 2017, satisfaction in their current position was the most common reason given for not changing jobs. However just over a quarter of millennials pointed to pessimism about the opportunities available to them.[1] Other aspects of their lives appear to play a role too. Rather surprisingly, young adults were the most likely to report that moving house or rearranging non-work responsibilities are barriers to moving jobs. In addition, of those who had moved jobs in the past two years, millennials were most likely to have done so to be closer to home.[2]

Figure 8.1: Pessimism and satisfaction are both keeping millennials and gen X-ers in their jobs

Reasons why people haven't left their job in the past two years, by generation: GB, 2017

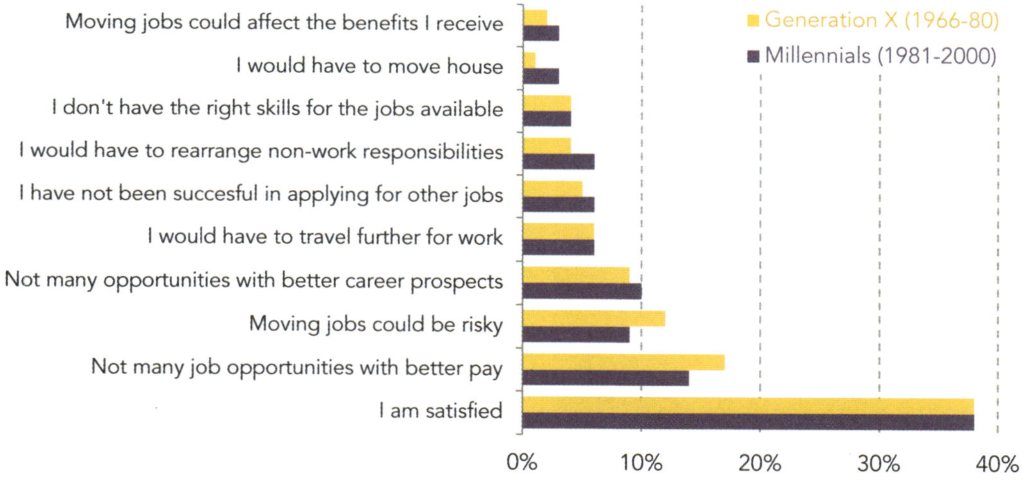

Notes: Multi-response question asked of adults who have remained in the same job over the past two years; 'other' and 'don't know' excluded. For full details, including question wording, see notes to Figure 14 in: *The kids aren't alright* (Intergenerational Commission report 17)

Source: Ipsos MORI

The fact that satisfaction features so prominently poses the question of whether there is actually a problem which needs tackling here. Our view is that there is.

First, aside from the fact that the data above cannot tell us if young adults are more satisfied than predecessors at their age, this satisfaction is strongly correlated with earnings, with lower earners much less likely to be satisfied.[3] Second, as we saw in Chapter 2, young adults are more likely to work in lower-paying occupations and are less likely to move out of them than predecessors at their age, so there is a real problem for their future earnings even if it is not always reflected in overt dissatisfaction.

1 This (27 per cent) is the proportion selecting at least one of the four answers "Not many opportunities with better pay", "Moving jobs could be risky", "Not many opportunities with better career prospects" and "I don't have the right skills for the jobs available".

2 *The kids aren't alright* (Intergenerational Commission report 17)

3 *The kids aren't alright* (Intergenerational Commission report 17)

Third, practical barriers to moving jobs appear to be playing a role, with high housing costs particularly standing out. And fourth, young adults' acceptance of the status quo may be shaped by only having experienced the post-crisis jobs market, in which insecurity and low pay are more common than in the past. Indeed, low expectations may be compounding the problems our analysis has uncovered.

The balance of labour market policy needs to change. The focus has been on unemployed young people and, while that remains important, more now needs to be done to support young people who are in work but face barriers to progression. The introduction of in-work conditionality for Universal Credit – although not without its concerns, including the narrow focus on increasing hours worked – potentially represents a step in this direction. But approaches limited to benefit recipients are not enough. We should build on initiatives like the Employment Retention and Advancement Demonstration and learn from successful mobility assistance programmes in Germany.[4] We propose the introduction of a new, targeted active labour market programme for those young people most affected by the financial crisis, to help more of them escape long periods in low-paid work.

Policy recommendation

Introduce a £1 billion 'Better Jobs Deal' – an active labour market programme offering practical support and funding for younger workers most affected by the financial crisis to take up opportunities to move jobs, change region for work, or train to progress.

- The programme should provide financial incentives and support to help with the upfront costs of taking up a new job, relocating for better work, and training for those who lack the skills to progress.
- The programme should be voluntary and it should be targeted at those most in need of support: those aged under 35 without degrees who are in low-skilled occupations and have remained so for a significant period. It should not just be aimed at benefit recipients. We estimate that up to 1.2 million workers in the UK could be eligible for the programme, with costs of around £1 billion, based on the unit costs of similar schemes.[1]
- Entry criteria should be based on evidence of a job interview, job offer, or a willingness to complete training.[2]

1 This is estimated based on an assumption that up to half of those eligible take up the scheme, and that it has costs towards the higher end of those recorded for comparable schemes in the UK and abroad. Our costings are for the UK as a whole and we recommend all parts of the country implement such a programme, but we recognise that Scotland and Northern Ireland have devolved powers in this policy area. For further details, see: *The kids aren't alright* (Intergenerational Commission report 17)

2 For further details on the group potentially eligible and other specifications, see: *The kids aren't alright* (Intergenerational Commission report 17)

4 For details on these programmes, see: *The kids aren't alright* (Intergenerational Commission report 17)

While our analysis has demonstrated the strong links between moving employers and individual (and economy-wide) pay progress, many workers will clearly remain with their current employer, or within the same sector. Around twice as many young people move jobs within sectors each year as move between them.[5] Even when job-to-job moves are at their strongest, around eight-in-ten workers stay put over a year.[6] We therefore need to improve progression within lower-paying sectors where young adults are most concentrated, especially because lower-paid industries in the UK invest less than lower-paid industries in other European countries.[7]

The government is already engaged with a number of key sectors as part of its industrial strategy. The current deals do not cover large, lower-paying sectors, however. And so far they have not explicitly focused on the nature of work and progression. We therefore hope to see further sector deals for the parts of the economy where low-paid young workers are concentrated: such deals would be an opportunity for an active labour market policy that focuses on firms not just individuals. The National Retraining Scheme, which brings together the CBI and TUC to help adults retrain and obtain new skills, provides an example of a promising collaborative approach. But it is small and, at present, undefined.

Young people are not just failing to make the job moves that would boost their pay. Returns to staying put in the same job are lower than they were. This may be connected in part to evidence that underestimating inflation and being unwilling to push for a pay increase have become increasingly common traits of younger workers.

Despite CPI inflation rising from 1.8 per cent to 3.1 per cent between January and November 2017, only a quarter of 15-24-year-olds thought that prices had been rising by 3 per cent or more when surveyed in the third quarter of 2017. Twice the proportion of 45-54-year-olds held this view. And the proportion of 15-34-year-olds who plan to push for a pay increase in light of expectations of price changes has not changed since 2012, despite slightly higher inflation and the much improved state of the labour market.[8] With collective pay bargaining becoming rarer and the fall in union coverage particularly pronounced for younger workers,[9] there is a case for giving employees (particularly younger ones) more information in pay negotiations.

---

5 Between 2014 and 2016 an average of 3.9 per cent of people aged 18 to 35 made a job-to-job move within the same sector each year, compared to 2 per cent who moved to another sector.

6 This figure has varied from 86 per cent to 79 per cent since 1998. Source: RF analysis of ONS, *Labour Force Survey*

7 S Thompson et al., *Boosting Britain's Low-Wage Sectors: A Strategy for Productivity and Growth*, Institute for Public Policy Research, May 2016

8 Source: RF analysis of Bank of England, *Inflation Attitudes Survey*

9 D Tomlinson & G Kelly, 'Act now or shrink later: trade unions and the generational challenge', *Resolution Foundation blog*, 25 September 2016

Policy recommendation

Boost pay progression via new sector deals in lower-paying sectors as part of the industrial strategy, and provide new guidance on pay review processes within businesses to improve transparency.

– There should be sector deals for social care, retail and hospitality. These should involve government, firms and worker representatives working together to design and publicise clear progression paths. There should also be a recognition that greater professionalisation and investment in staff is a way to boost productivity in these sectors.

– All firms should have formal pay review processes in place that are understood by employees. To promote this, the government should provide publicly available guidance outlining the standards a good pay review process needs to adhere to. At each review, staff should be provided with information on their current rate of pay, any pay increase they will receive (in cash and percentage terms) and how inflation has affected their pay in real terms since their last review.

Reducing insecurity as a basis for better careers over lifetimes

In Chapter 2, we demonstrated increasing insecurity and risk for young adults in the labour market. But younger individuals are also increasingly shouldering risks in the housing market and in relation to their pensions. Our view is that these multiple risks compound, limiting young adults' ability to take chances and make changes in their lives – particularly moving jobs and progressing in work. Subsequent chapters will address risks in these other domains. But there is also a clear need to tackle insecurity within the labour market itself, both to improve living standards in the short term and provide a more secure basis from which young adults can develop their careers.

Self-employment and atypical employment for younger workers increased after the financial crisis. But with employment now at record highs, a tightening labour market has led to a plateauing since 2016 in zero-hours contracts, self-employment and agency working, and a fall since 2012 in part-time working.[10] Nevertheless, the levels of such atypical work remain much higher than they were pre-crisis. The hope might be that younger workers had disproportionately benefited from recent falls. But the evidence suggests that unfortunately this is not the case. Figure 8.2 shows that only in part-time work is there a clear pattern of bigger proportional decreases for younger workers than for older ones. The situation is reversed for agency workers, and more mixed for ZHCs and self-employment.

10 *The kids aren't alright* (Intergenerational Commission report 17)

Figure 8.2: Declines in atypical work have not disproportionately benefited younger workers

Proportional change, from post-crisis peak, in share of people employed in various forms of atypical work, by age group: UK, 2012-17

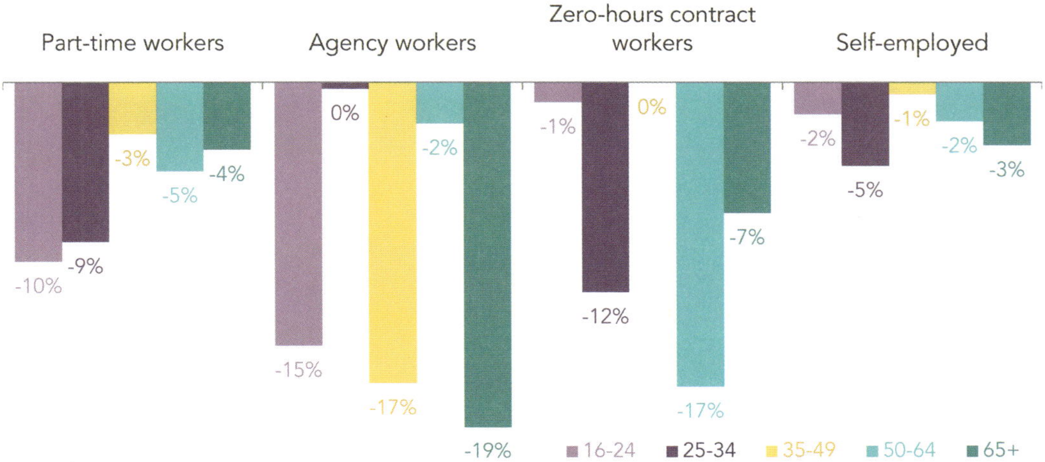

Source: RF analysis of ONS, *Labour Force Survey*

The initial evidence should therefore caution us against assuming that the rise in atypical work among younger workers will be fully reversed any time soon. This holds out the prospect that many of the current generation of young people may end up spending a significant proportion of their working lives in such roles. Policy makers should respond to this, rather than hoping it will go away.

As well as reducing the insecurity of work, we need to focus on particular problems facing younger workers in low-paid or insecure employment. For example, younger workers are less likely than older ones to receive a pay uplift when working overtime, which makes up 12 per cent of the hours worked by 16-24-year-olds compared to just 5 per cent of the hours worked by those aged 30-60. Virtually no 16-24-year-olds and only 15 per cent of those in their 30s benefit from enhanced overtime pay, compared to one-in-five across the population as a whole.[11] And while there are good arguments for some different minimum wage rates for younger workers, the introduction of the National Living Wage has resulted in a complicated system with five separate age-related bands, the logic of which is not at all clear.

We have to strike a balance between enhanced security for workers and the risk that tighter regulation hampers employment growth. We must value and maintain Britain's flexible labour market, which has in general served young workers better during the post-crisis years than the more rigid systems in parts of continental Europe.[12] But, with record-high employment and high levels of insecure work, now is the right time for measured steps to provide more security for those at the insecure and lower-paid end of the labour market.

11 *The kids aren't alright* (Intergenerational Commission report 17)

12 For details, see: *Cross countries* (Intergenerational Commission report 15)

Policy recommendation

Improve security for self-employed, atypical and the lowest-paid workers via extended statutory rights and greater certainty around working hours.

- After three months of employment, those on zero-hours contracts working regular hours should have the right to a fixed-hours contract guaranteeing them the average of their weekly hours over the previous three months.
- Workers should be explicitly protected when turning down non-guaranteed hours, and there should usually be minimum notification periods for shifts. In addition, the government should pilot different pay premia policies for non-guaranteed hours, building on the recommendation of a minimum wage premium for these hours put forward by the Taylor review of modern working practices.[1]
- Statutory parental pay and contributory Jobseeker's Allowance should be extended to the self-employed, at a cost of £100 million, funded by narrowing the difference in the National Insurance treatment of employees and self-employed workers.
- In 2020 – once the National Living Wage has reached its target value in relation to typical pay – minimum wage rates should be reviewed, with a view to including some younger workers in the National Living Wage and reducing the number of age-related rates below this.[2]

1 Department for Business, Energy & Industrial Strategy, *Good work: the Taylor review of modern working practices*, July 2017

2 For further details on these recommendations, see: *The kids aren't alright* (Intergenerational Commission report 17)

While we've highlighted that the insecurities of atypical employment forms are more common for younger workers, they exist across the workforce. Many of the recommendations we set out in this area will therefore have positive effects across the age range. Far from older workers being seen as part of the labour market problem for younger workers, maximising their employment opportunities is essential to successfully navigating the opportunities and challenges of an ageing population, including the fiscal challenge set out in Chapter 5. In Box 8.1, we set out the merits of a focus on boosting the quantity and quality of employment for older workers and some possible ways forward.

Box 8.1 Supporting longer working lives

We've highlighted the particular labour market challenges facing young adults, which might lead some to conclude that the relatively strong employment performance of older workers is part of the problem – blocking progression opportunities for younger workers, for example. But this view reflects a 'lump of labour' fallacy and the labour market rarely operates as a zero-sum game, especially outside of downturns. For example, in this century youth employment and the rate of job-to-job moves have grown most in regions and nations – including the North East and Scotland – where older employment has risen fastest.[1]

Indeed, reflecting on the fiscal challenge set out in Chapter 5, maintaining the tax base via supporting older working is essential to taking revenue pressure off younger generations. Modelling suggests that halving the employment gap between workers aged 50-to-State-Pension-age and those in their late 40s could boost nominal GDP by 1 per cent (up to £20 billion per year in 2017 prices).[2]

Half of people leave work before State Pension age. The onset of health problems and caring responsibilities is the main driver of this, although dismissal is more important in certain sectors including manufacturing, information and communications, and finance. Older workers also cite inflexibility in their hours and in the arrangements around retirement as a barrier to working longer

While we've said that younger workers are at the sharp end of insecurity, there are specific forms of insecurity that older workers are most exposed to, such as workplace restructuring. In addition, older workers report the greatest decline in perceived job security and are most likely to be stuck for long periods in low pay.[3] So our recommendations around security and progression will be beneficial across the life course.

Specific labour market policies to support older working should focus on the particular challenges of health and caring; rebalancing flexibility towards individuals; a tailored approach to back-to-work support; and the promotion of progression across the life course. Research for the Intergenerational Commission by the Centre for Ageing Better has suggested that a package might include:

- the right to request flexible working from day one in a job, rather than 26 weeks;
- supporting the development of options for flexible pensions drawdown; and
- a right to return to work following periods of absence for carers and those with health problems.[4]

1 Measuring between 2000 and 2017, the North East and Scotland had, respectively, the first- and fourth-fastest growth rates in the 50+ employment rate. They were also among the top three regions for growth in 18-29-year-old employment and job mobility rates. Source: ONS, *Labour Force Survey*

2 Department for Work and Pensions, *Fuller Working Lives: evidence base 2017*, February 2017

3 *A silver lining for the UK economy?* (Intergenerational Commission report 16)

4 For further details, see: *A silver lining for the UK economy?* (Intergenerational Commission report 16)

Improving the voice and collective bargaining power of young workers

Rights and regulations are not the only way in which security for younger workers can be improved. Although too often overlooked in discussions of how to achieve these goals, trade unions and other models of worker organising clearly have a potentially major role to play – albeit one that is limited in practice at present.

Union membership today is just 15 per cent among those aged 35-and-under, a rate that has fallen by a quarter since the early 2000s. In the private sector, membership for this age group is only 9 per cent.[13] These shifts have occurred despite young people being more positive about unions than older generations: just 8 per cent of millennials would not join a union because they do not agree with them in principle, compared to 11 per cent of generation X and 13 per cent of baby boomers. Only 13 per cent of millennials find the culture of unions off-putting, while the figures are 17 per cent and 22 per cent for generation X and baby boomers respectively.[14]

If younger workers are relatively well-disposed towards unions, then why are they not members? The evidence from our polling – summarised in Figure 8.3 – and focus group research is that this is down to two things. The first is a lack of access to, and awareness of, unions; the second is that some are unimpressed by the current union offer.

Figure 8.3: Young people want it to be easier for unions to recruit and cheaper to join one

Changes that would encourage 17-36-year-olds to join a union: GB, 2017

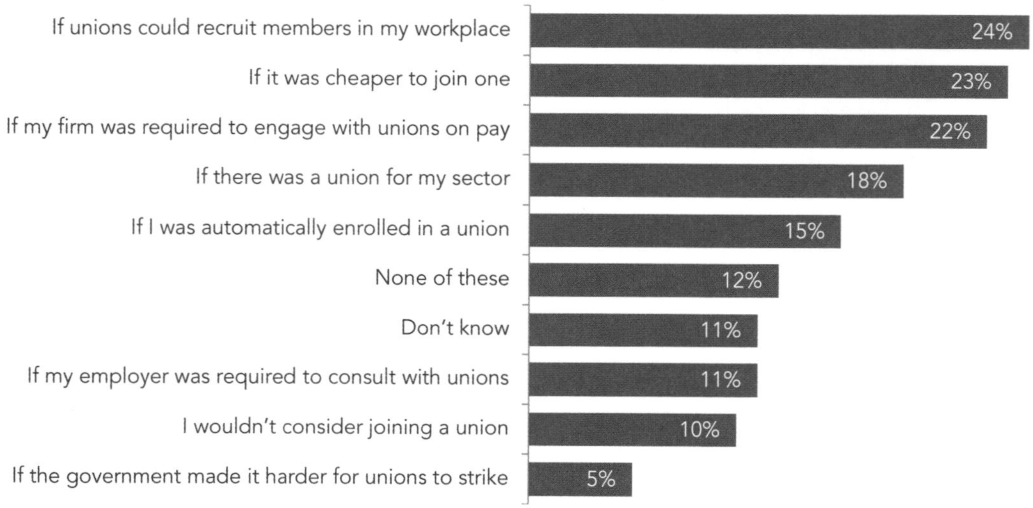

Notes: Multi-response question. For further details, including question wording, see Figure 12 in: *The kids aren't alright* (Intergenerational Commission report 17)

Source: Ipsos MORI

13 Source: RF analysis of ONS, *Labour Force Survey*

14 For further details, see: *The kids aren't alright* (Intergenerational Commission report 17)

On this basis – given their poor pay performance – there is a case for making it easier for younger workers to join unions. But reflecting the nature of the 21st century labour market and the potential that technological advances offer, our thinking should stretch beyond the old ways of organising. Indeed, in the UK and abroad a range of initiatives inside and outside traditional unions are currently underway to explore new, technology-inspired forms of worker organising. These are summarised in Box 8.2.

Box 8.2 New ways of backing workers

Recently a number of initiatives, both in the UK and elsewhere, have sprung up to represent workers. These initiatives have a wide range of goals, but they all focus on placing more power and control in the hands of workers. Many use new technologies to overcome some of the difficulties of traditional organising. Some of these UK-based 'WorkerTech' initiatives have been backed by the Resolution Trust, in partnership with Bethnal Green Ventures. Examples include:

- **Organise:** A UK start-up that has developed an online petitioning tool making clever use of targeted advertising to reach people about the issues affecting them at work. It has been running for little over a year and has already won improved pay and rights for a small number of workers at some of Britain's best-known employers, including ITV, Tesco and McDonald's.
- **Labour Xchange:** A platform that seeks to match workers who want additional hours with businesses in need of short-term labour. It is unique in so far as work carried out through the platform must be paid at least the 'real' living wage, and it is the workers who first express their availability before businesses are matched with them.
- **Co-worker:** An established start-up based in the US, Co-worker runs petitions to galvanize workplace campaigns much like Organise in the UK. Successes include securing paid parental leave at Netflix and changes to the uniform policy at Starbucks. One-in-ten Starbucks employees worldwide have interacted with this platform.
- **Shyft:** A US-based shift-swapping platform. Shyft takes some control over when, and how much, people work away from managers and puts it in the hands of the workers themselves. Instead of having to go through managers to swap shifts, employees can post shifts they can no longer work on the app to be picked up directly by their colleagues.

A renewed focus on the representation of younger workers that is flexible to the challenges and opportunities of the 21st century labour market would help them play a greater role in discussions around pay, terms and conditions.

Policy recommendation

Enhance the rights of unions to speak to employees in their workplace and encourage innovation in models of worker organising, including reduced union membership rates for the young and better use of technology.

- Unions should be permitted to access workplaces, with the objective of better-informing younger workers of the role they can play.
- In exchange for these rights, unions should consider a range of innovations to make it easier and more economical for younger workers to join. These could include longer introductory rates for new members, or cheaper fees for younger workers.
- Large foundations and trusts should support the development of new models of worker organising and information-sharing that harness technology to improve the voice of young workers.

Addressing structural challenges in human capital accumulation with a focus on technical routes

As we identified in Chapter 2, a key factor underpinning the recent poor pay performance of younger groups is the slowdown in cohort-on-cohort human capital accumulation from generation X to the millennials. Clearly, marginal gains become harder to achieve the higher the starting point, but there is space to do significantly better. After all, young adults in England who have not been to university have literacy and numeracy levels that are significantly below the OECD average – with this gap only opening up *after* the age of 15.[15] While much of the focus in intergenerational debates recently is on the funding of higher education, this misses the point that the biggest challenge facing young people in education today is our woeful educational offer for those not aiming for university.

This relative underperformance is a deep problem arising from the lack of a broad secondary school curriculum after the age of 16, or a school leaving exam at age 18 other than A Levels. It has been compounded by poor levels of funding for technical routes in further education.

The good news is that the government has already advanced a series of reforms designed to improve technical opportunities. The recent introduction of the apprenticeship levy places a charge on large employers' wage bills, with the receipts then put into an apprenticeship training account for each levy-paying firm. It has also

15 A Green & N Pensiero, 'The effects of upper-secondary education and training systems on skills inequality. A quasi-cohort analysis using PISA 2000 and the OECD survey of adult skills', *British Educational Research Journal*, 42(5), October 2016

introduced tighter quality controls for apprenticeships. More efforts may be needed here though: of the 189 apprenticeship training providers that Ofsted managed to inspect during 2016/17, more than half were judged as either "'inadequate" (11 per cent) or "requiring improvement" (40 per cent). Such providers are unlikely to drive progress on skills.

Since 2015, the government has had a target to achieve three million apprenticeship starts by 2020. In practice, the immediate period following the introduction of the new levy has coincided with a fall in the number of apprenticeships, likely driven by the challenges of transitioning to the new system. It is important that the levy works in a way that ensures employer involvement and commitment, and the government should monitor those falls given the welcome aim to boost provision. But we should not focus only on crude numbers at the exclusion of wider questions about apprenticeship quality, skills development and outcomes.

There are also less developed, but equally crucial, plans for an ambitious new system of technical education at Level 3 (A Level equivalent). 'T Levels' are expected to come online from 2020, and largely replace the current Level 3 college-based technical system. Under the new system, many students who do not do A Levels will instead choose from a series of 15 streamlined, two-year technical routes. Beyond college-based learning, each T Level student will also be required to undergo a work placement that lasts a minimum of 45 days. While we are still four years from when most T Levels come online, delivering these work placements represents a big challenge. It will require a step-change in college engagement with employers and a willingness among firms to take on a new educational role with 16-18-year-olds.

At the beginning of 2018, 73 per cent of businesses reported being unaware of T Levels. And more firms reported that their workplace is unsuitable for 16-18-year-olds (25 per cent) than said they would be willing or already set up to provide placements (18 per cent),[16] with this finding fairly consistent across sectors, as Figure 8.4 shows. Moreover, not all T Level students will have easy access to employers for work placements in their sector of choice – particularly those in rural or economically deprived areas.

16 *Technical fault* (Intergenerational Commission report 20)

Figure 8.4: The majority of businesses are unready to provide work placements

Business views on T level work placements, by industry: GB: 2018

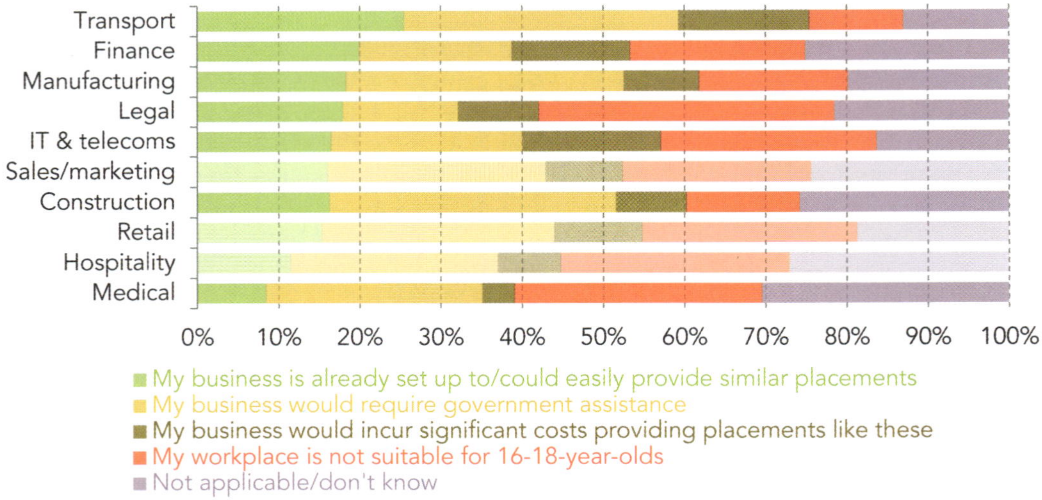

Notes: Bolded bars indicate sectors involved in T level routes. For further details, including question wording, see: *Technical fault* (Intergenerational Commission report 20)

Source: YouGov

In light of these challenges around employer engagement, employer preparedness for work placements and location, it is important that the government considers how T Level work placements can be delivered. For example, for those students unable to access employers in their sector of choice, elements of work placements could be delivered 'virtually', harnessing the latest simulation and remote-working technology.

While T Levels represent an ambitious overhaul of the system, the range of specialist technical qualifications currently offered will not all fit neatly into the 15 T Level routes. At the same time as efforts to make a success of the new system, there is a strong case for keeping some established specialist qualifications outside of T Levels in order not to limit student choice.

Policy recommendation

Ensure that apprenticeships are underpinned by rigorous regulation of quality; engage with employers flexibly on T Levels to ensure that the targeted volume of work placements can be delivered; and maintain high-quality specialist technical provision that does not fit neatly within these routes.

- The government should maintain its requirement that apprenticeships now include 20 per cent off-the-job training; firms who do not provide this should face sanctions. Ofsted should step up inspection of apprenticeship providers.
- The government should replace the numerical target of achieving three million apprenticeship starts by 2020 with three directional targets for growth: on starts, starts at more advanced levels, and progression onto higher-level apprenticeships.
- The Department for Education should set in train a significant employer engagement process as we approach the start of T Levels in 2020, to try to ensure a sufficient number of work placements are available.
- The government should assess where T Level work placement gaps exist and build in flexibility for those students who wish to pursue a course even where there are no related employers locally, for example by encouraging use of virtual-working technology.
- Successful specialist provision that does not fit well within the 15 T Level routes should be maintained alongside them.

Driving human capital progress for those already in work

Fixing our education system for the future will help to restart generational human capital progress. But these steps will come too late for a considerable number of young people who have already entered into and lived with a labour market with fewer opportunities for skills development and progression in the aftermath of the financial crisis.

In previous decades, the deficiencies of the technical education route have been offset by opportunities for lower-qualified young adults to catch up in the world of work. As a result, the skills gap with similarly aged contemporaries abroad has been significantly narrowed by the time adults reach their mid 30s.[17] However, the changing experiences of young adults in the labour market suggest that this positive role that work plays in upskilling people may not be as strong as it was in the past. Insecure and part-time employment offers fewer opportunities for skills development.

In addition, while unemployment for younger adults has not been the major concern in recent years, this hides divergence by qualification level. Among those with no more than GCSE-equivalent qualifications, unemployment at ages 25-34 rose from an average of 5 per cent for those born 1961-80 to an average of 7.9 per cent among millennials born 1981-90.[18] This matters because unemployment clearly removes the opportunity to develop human capital through work and work-related training.

17 A Green & N Pensiero, 'The effects of upper-secondary education and training systems on skills inequality. A quasi-cohort analysis using PISA 2000 and the OECD survey of adult skills', *British Educational Research Journal*, 42(5), October 2016

18 *Technical fault* (Intergenerational Commission report 20)

The provision of work-related training for those young people who do have jobs is also falling. The proportion of 25-year-olds reporting having 'recently' received work-related training fell from 35 per cent among those born 1976-80 (the youngest members of generation X), to less than 30 per cent of those born 1986-90, as Figure 8.5 shows. This is a trend that appears to hold across all occupations and job types, not just those lower-skilled and less-secure ones that younger people increasingly find themselves in. And lower-skilled people are less likely to receive training than higher-skilled workers, even if they are in a firm that *does* train.[19]

Figure 8.5: Each cohort is receiving less in-work training than predecessors at the same age

Proportion of workers receiving work-related training in the past 13 weeks, by age and cohort: UK, 1996-2017

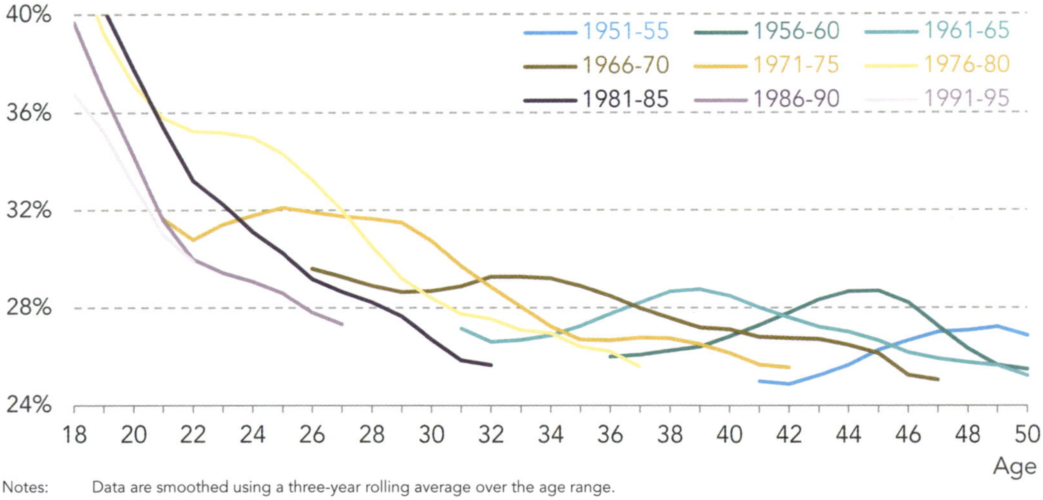

Notes: Data are smoothed using a three-year rolling average over the age range.
Source: RF analysis of ONS, *Labour Force Survey*

Given the labour market they have experienced thus far, there is clearly a case to address the skills-development opportunities of young adults already in work. This will need to be properly funded with demand coming from individuals. In Chapter 11 we return to the question of how these funds might be provided when we consider opportunities and resources available to young people for capital and human capital accumulation in the round. Alongside such an education endowment, there are other steps that the government should prioritise to boost human capital accumulation for those in work.

19 *Technical fault* (Intergenerational Commission report 20)

Policy recommendation

Ensure lifelong learning options are available to lower-qualified young people who will not benefit from post-16 technical reforms but who are struggling in today's labour market.

- The 'Better Jobs Deal' programme should include specific help for career 'switchers' to upskill, including brokerage of appropriate training opportunities and support with the costs associated with undertaking training.
- The Department for Education should review barriers to adult learning and consider whether a system of credit transfer would boost educational participation among lower-qualified adults.
- The government should support the development of high-quality but flexible lifelong learning via online courses and 'Open University'-style qualifications.

Funding technical education and labour market support

Making a success of the technical education reforms described in this chapter will not come cheap: moving to a system of high-quality technical educational routes requires high-quality educational institutions. In a report on long-term trends in education expenditure, the Institute for Fiscal Studies found that spending on further education "fell faster during the 1990s, grew more slowly in the 2000s, and has been the only major area of education spending to see cuts since 2010".[20] The relative level of underfunding that exists today – both by historical standards and in comparison to secondary school and higher education funding as shown in Figure 8.6 – will not suffice.

20 C Belfield, C Crawford & L Sibieta, *Long-run comparisons of spending per pupil across different stages of education*, Institute for Fiscal Studies, February 2017

Figure 8.6: Further education spending has fallen relative to spending on other types of education

Real per-pupil spending in further education compared to secondary and higher education (CPIH-adjusted to 2017 prices): UK

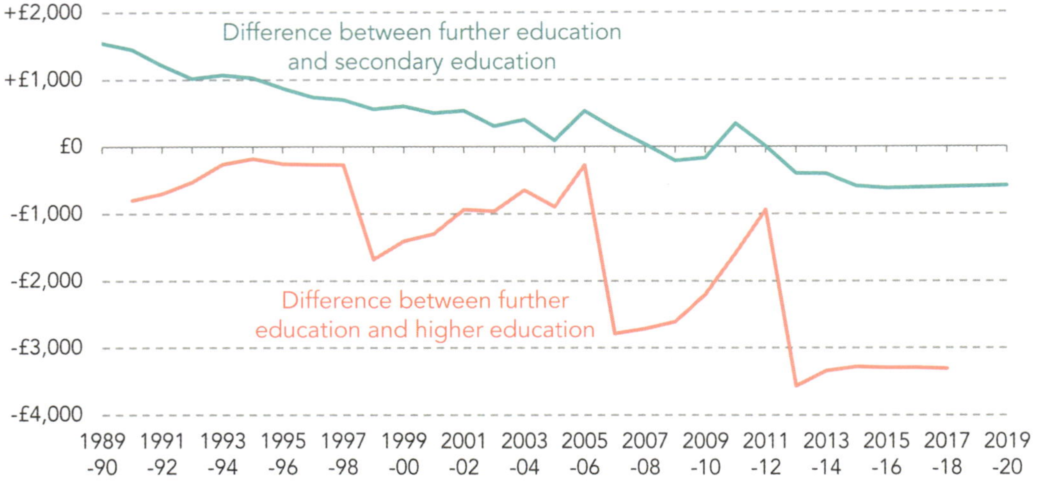

Source: C Belfield, C Crawford & L Sibieta, *Long-run comparisons of spending per pupil across different stages of education*, Institute for Fiscal Studies, February 2017

The apprenticeship levy has directed funding to employer-based training, but this funding gap for training not linked to an employer stands out – with big implications for the quality of further education colleges and other providers. There is also a need to provide financing for the steps outlined previously in this chapter in relation to T levels and the 'Better Jobs Deal'. Given a ready supply of highly-skilled candidates is a priority for UK businesses – particularly following our exit from the EU – we believe the government should re-consider current plans to reduce corporation tax to levels far below international averages, in order to deliver the workforce that businesses need and want.[21]

Policy recommendation

Boost the funding of technical education provision and underpin the 'Better Jobs Deal' by cancelling 1p of the corporation tax cut planned for 2020.

- The rate of corporation tax should fall to 18 per cent rather than 17 per cent in 2020. By 2022 the cancelled cut would raise £2.9 billion.[1]

1 HM Treasury's costings at the Autumn Budget 2017. See: HM Treasury, Table 22, *Autumn Budget 2017*, November 2017

21 For details on the UK's corporation tax position, see: M Whittaker, *Changing Tax: pressing reset on the UK's tax policy*, Resolution Foundation, November 2016

- This funding should support the £1 billion required for the 'Better Jobs Deal', with £1.5 billion allocated to improving technical education provision and better-funding further education colleges in England, with proportional allocations to other parts of the UK. This would reverse the decline in funding for further education colleges since the financial crisis, as well as specifically supporting the promotion of employer engagement in T Level work placements and rigorous inspection of apprenticeship providers.

With a much tighter labour market today than at any point in the past decade, now is the ideal moment for a renewed approach that will support progression, reduce insecurity and address structural problems in human capital accumulation. However, the labour market cannot be seen in isolation. Many of the risks we have identified as sitting increasingly on the shoulders of younger individuals – which may reduce their ability to take chances in the labour market – derive from other domains. These risks may themselves be contributing to the labour market outcomes younger cohorts are experiencing. The following chapters pick up this challenge, turning first to housing.

CHAPTER 9

Houses – renovating the market

We recommend

Indeterminate tenancies for those renting in the private rented sector, with light-touch, three-year rent stabilisation and a new housing tribunal.

Replacing council tax with a progressive property tax paid by the property owner, with surcharges on second and empty properties.

Halving stamp duty rates to encourage moving, and a time-limited capital gains tax cut to incentivise owners of additional properties to sell to first-time buyers.

Piloting community land auctions so local authorities can bring more land forward for house building, underpinned by stronger compulsory purchase powers.

A £1.7 billion building precept to allow local authorities to fund house building in their area.

Our approach to housing policy

Families want to own a home because of what it offers: a sense of security and control; the ability to reduce housing costs over time (especially in retirement); and the opportunity to build up an asset that can be drawn on in later life or bequeathed after death. It is not only the drop in home ownership among younger generations that is a cause for concern. Young people today spend more of their income on housing than previous generations at the same age, but they get less in return when it comes to security and quality of life.

If policy makers truly wish to tackle the housing crisis, action on three fronts is required. In the short term, it is essential to improve the lot of private renters. In the medium term, we should rebalance demand so young first-time buyers are in a stronger position compared to those buying second or subsequent homes. And in the long run, reducing housing costs requires building more homes, year in, year out, in areas of strong housing demand, alongside increasing the number of affordable homes. All this adds up to a new intergenerational contract on housing.

Shifting the private rented sector towards longer tenancies and greater security

As with so many other aspects of their lives, millennials find themselves exposed to more risk than their predecessors on housing, not least because they increasingly live long term in the private rented sector (PRS). This type of tenure has significant

Figure 9.1: **Households with children increasingly live in the private rented sector**

Proportion of households with children in owner occupation and in the private rented sector: England

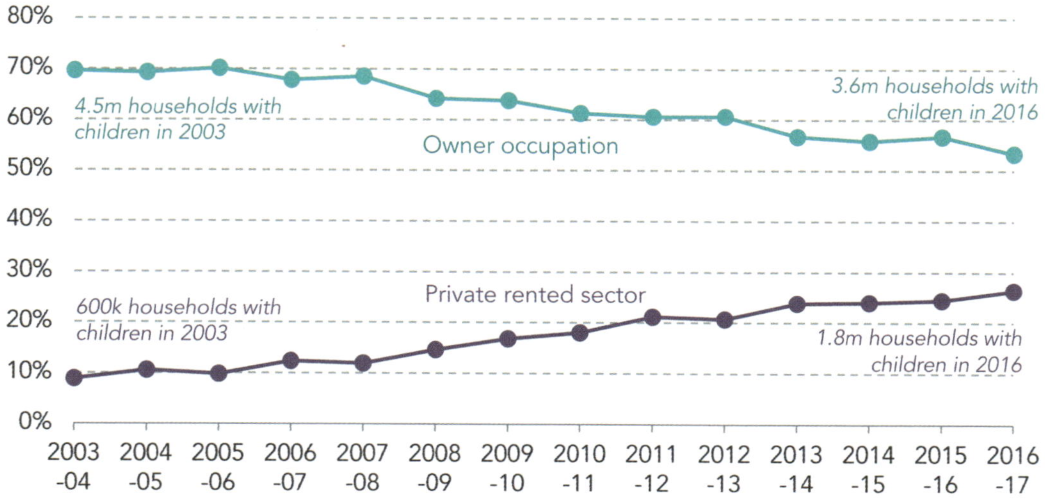

Source: RF analysis of MHCLG, *English Housing Survey*

potential downsides: losing one's home at short notice; housing costs increasing sharply with little warning; and problems with the property left unaddressed by the landlord.

This issue of risk in the PRS has taken on added urgency because many young people who have been unable to move on from the tenure are now having children. The number of households with children renting privately in England has tripled in the last 13 years, from 600,000 to 1.8 million, as Figure 9.1 shows. In the early 2000s, there were eight households with children in owner-occupied houses for every one household with children in the PRS; today that ratio is two-to-one.

To improve stability for young families in the PRS, we need to reform the standard tenancy. The majority of private tenants in England and Wales rent their homes on an assured shorthold tenancy (AST). Introduced in 1988 and the default lease since 1997, an AST gives tenants an initial term of typically six or twelve months during which they can only be asked to leave if they fail to pay the rent or breach other statutory terms. Once the fixed term expires, however, the lease continues on a month-by-month, or week-by-week, basis. From this point on the landlord can give two months' notice to tenants to vacate, and critically does not need to give a reason for this decision.

Longer leases are, in principle, possible in England and Wales via the use of assured tenancies (ATs) but these comprise only 3 per cent of all private sector leases.[1] The government has tried to nudge landlords to offer longer leases in recent years – most notably with the introduction of the 'Model Tenancy' in 2014 – but there is little to suggest this has had any effect on the average tenancy term.

Among landlords there is considerable resistance to tenancy reform that is perceived to tilt power in favour of tenants.[2] In practice, fewer than one-in-ten tenancies are currently ended at the landlord's request, with more than 60 per cent of these because the landlord wishes to sell.[3] In addition, many landlords appreciate the lower turnover associated with long-staying tenants.[4] Nevertheless, longer tenancies would clearly go hand in hand with a more demanding burden of proof on the landlord if and when they wished to break the lease.

Genuine though some landlord concerns are, however, on balance we do not believe the problems that longer tenancies could represent for a small proportion should prevail over the urgent need for a growing number of tenants to be able to create a stable home.

---

1 *Home Affront* (Intergenerational Commission report 9)

2 For example, see: Communities and Local Government Committee, *Written evidence submitted by the Residential Landlords Association*, January 2013

3 Ministry of Housing, Communities and Local Government, *English Housing Survey 2015 to 2016: private rented sector*, July 2017

4 For example, see: J Rugg & D Rhodes, *The private sector: its contribution and potential*, University of York, 2008

Policy recommendation

Introduce indeterminate tenancies as the sole form of private rental contract available in England and Wales, following Scotland's lead.

- A sensible set of break clauses should be included in order to allow landlords to repossess with a minimum of three months' notice, as is the case in other countries with a similar rental regime. These would apply if the landlord wishes to sell or occupy the property, if tenants fail to pay the rent or mistreat the home, and in other reasonable circumstances.
- To ensure reciprocity, tenants should be required to give their landlord three months' notice of intent to leave.

Introducing longer leases would be a huge step towards improving security for today's young people, but other changes are needed to reduce the risks of renting. In the long run and on average, rents rise quite smoothly, but rent spikes are not uncommon. Such spikes, whether driven by market movements or by a landlord putting up rents so high as to undermine the purpose of an indeterminate tenancy, are part of the insecurity of renting. There is, therefore, a need also to consider some form of rent stabilisation.

The issue is too often depicted as a stark choice between stringent controls on rents that depress the long-run equilibrium and an entirely unregulated market-based approach. Yet most countries avoid both horns of this dilemma by instead putting in place modest smoothing mechanisms to protect tenants from dramatic rental spikes, while allowing market rents to prevail with a pressure valve.

We therefore propose providing tenants with medium-term stability by linking rent rises to inflation for a set period, after which landlords can re-negotiate the appropriate rent level with reference to prevailing market prices.

Policy recommendation

Introduce light-touch rent stabilisation that limits rent rises to CPI inflation for set three-year periods.

- New tenants should have their annual rent rises limited to a maximum of CPI inflation for three years, after which a rent review can be undertaken. The landlord must give six months' notice of any subsequent change in rent, and must provide evidence showing that the new proposed rent is in line with market norms and/or reflects significant improvements made to the property.

Improving standards for renters via a new tribunal system and landlord registration

Indeterminate leases and light-touch rent stabilisation could increase demand for adjudication, on either the landlord's side (for example to evict a recalcitrant tenant or move back into a property) or the tenant's (for example to contest a rent rise). In England and Wales, there is currently no nimble or inexpensive forum to which both parties can take such matters. Instead, the majority of cases that are presently actionable have to be taken through the county court with substantial costs and delays.[5]

In Scotland, the introduction of indeterminate tenancies in 2017 was accompanied by transferring jurisdiction for possession proceedings in the PRS from the sheriff's court to the first-tier tribunal. In many countries and municipalities that have rent stabilisation, tenants can file a petition with a board for a decision if they believe their rent has breached any limit.

The government has indicated that it is interested in better resolution mechanisms, consulting on options for strengthening consumer redress in the housing market, and exploring the case for a new 'Housing Court'.[6] Transferring housing disputes from the county courts to a dedicated housing tribunal need not be a radical departure from current practice, and it could result in more consistent and expert decisions for all. Its success would depend on a number of factors, however. Critically, it would need to:

- Be cheap – in the Netherlands, for example, a tenant can challenge a new rent for just €25.
- Be fast – to ensure that landlords could reassert control over their property efficiently and tenants could nip any egregious rent rises in the bud.
- Be effective – for example by being able to make possession orders or require landlords to refund excess rent they have charged.
- Be underpinned by clear information for landlords and tenants on their rights and responsibilities – ensuring that all parties know both what actions they could bring to the tribunal, and what actions could be brought against them.

---

5 For further details, see: Ministry of Justice, *Mortgage and Landlord Possession Statistics: October to December 2017*, February 2018

6 Ministry of Housing, Communities and Local Government, *Strengthening consumer redress in housing*, February 2018

Policy recommendation

Establish a housing tribunal system which has powers to adjudicate on possession applications and challenges to rent rises.

- The new tribunal should be cheap, easy to access, speedy and offer effective remedy for tenants and landlords alike.
- The government should run an information campaign for both tenants and landlords that draws attention to their new rights and responsibilities.

Another major gap in the English system is that there is no official information held on landlords, making communication with them ad-hoc and unreliable. This is not the case in Scotland, Wales or Northern Ireland, however, where landlords are required to register with their local authority and provide basic information on their holdings. A similar approach in England would deliver many benefits.

By holding a comprehensive record of rented properties, local authorities could keep landlords better apprised of relevant changes, with which the vast majority are keen to comply. Registration would also make it easier for the government to identify landlords who were not abiding by the rules, by failing to declare rental income to HMRC, for example. Finally, local authorities could then undertake quality checks and have the power to strike landlords off the register – ending their ability to lawfully rent property – in cases of rogue behaviour.

Policy recommendation

Bring England into line with the rest of the UK by requiring landlords to register with their local authority.

- Local authorities should have the power to inspect properties and to remove landlords from the register in the event of a serious breach of standards, thereby barring them from continuing to operate.

Rethinking housing benefit to tackle rental affordability for those on low-to-middle incomes

While rent stabilisation will protect tenants from the sharpest rent spikes, it is not designed to address the overall problem of affordability in the PRS. In the long term this can only be resolved by bringing supply and demand into better balance (the topic we turn to below). But in the short term, housing benefit (HB) is best placed to do the job.

The rules that govern both HB eligibility and generosity have changed significantly over time, not least because a rapidly expanding PRS has resulted in an HB bill of over £25 billion today. But today's young private renters are doubly disadvantaged when it comes to housing support. They are at the sharp end of policies that have eroded the value of HB for all over time – such as uprating local housing allowance (LHA) in line with CPI in 2013-14, and by 1 per cent in 2014-15 and 2015-16, before freezing its value for the next four years. Young people are also subject to age-specific restrictions, such as the extension of the shared accommodation rate to under 35s in 2012.[7]

The outcome of these reforms, as Figure 9.2 shows, is that private renting millennials with incomes low enough to be eligible for support have just 13 per cent of their rent covered by HB on average at age 25; compared with a figure of 20 per cent among their generation X counterparts. While the expectation was that lower LHA rates would lead to lower rents, studies suggest that private landlords have absorbed only a small part of the cuts to HB, leaving tenants to take a major hit to living standards as a result of the shortfall.[8]

Figure 9.2: Millennials have less of their rent covered by housing benefit than predecessors

Proportion of housing costs covered by housing benefit – private renters in receipt of some housing benefit only: UK, 1994-2015

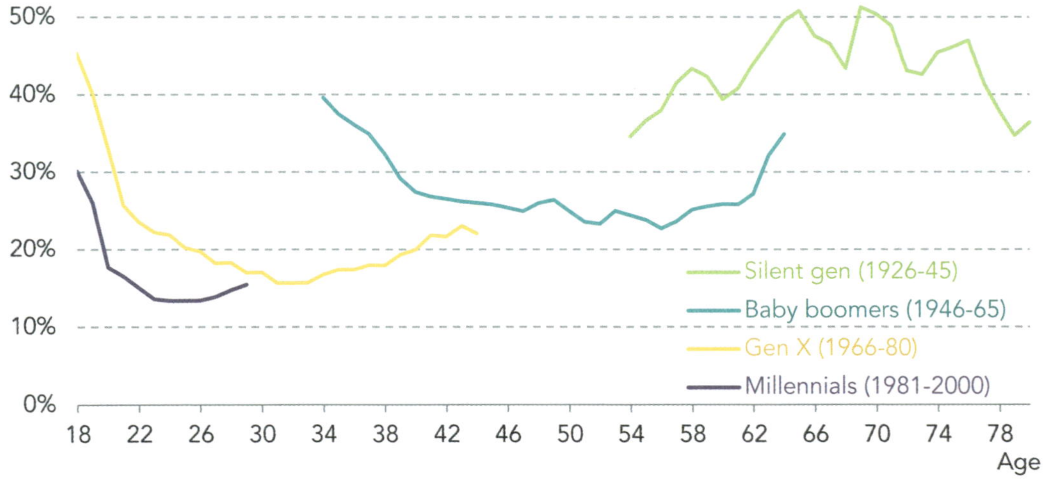

Notes: Data are smoothed using a three-year rolling average over the age range.
Source: RF analyis of DWP, *Family Resources Survey*

7 It is worth noting that while sharing a home is quite common for individuals in their 20s, by the age of 30-31 less than one-third of single, childless private renters who do not claim housing benefit are living in this way. For further details, see: *Home improvements* (Intergenerational Commission report 19)

8 For example, evaluation evidence suggests that 89 per cent of the incidence of reduced LHA entitlements fell on tenants and 11 per cent on landlords. See: M Brewer et al., *Econometric analysis of the impacts of Local Housing Allowance reforms on existing claimants*, Department for Work and Pensions, July 2014

Policy recommendation

Revisit housing benefit rules to improve support for younger families on low-to-middle incomes.

- The government should reduce the age at which young people can only claim the shared accommodation rate from under 35 to under 30, at a cost of less than £100 million annually.[1]

- In the medium term, the government should link local housing allowance levels back to real rents.

1 This is estimated by taking the government's savings accruing in 2014-15 as a result of the extension of the shared accommodation rate to under 35s rolled forward based on housing benefit caseloads, then apportioned according to the share of single, childless private renters in receipt of HB aged between 25-29 and 30-34.

Targeting support for young people to get into home ownership

De-risking the PRS could significantly improve the lives of many young people, both now and in years to come. But housing policy reform must also consider the aspirations of the majority of renters who continue to say they would prefer to own their home.[9] Their ability to fulfil this ambition has been constrained in recent years, not least because credit has become harder to access (see Box 9.1).

As lending criteria have tightened, successive governments have introduced a variety of 'Help to Buy' (HTB) interventions in order to facilitate house purchases by largely younger buyers. The most enduring of these schemes has been the HTB equity loan programme. Introduced in 2013, this allows buyers to borrow up to 20 per cent of the purchase price of a new-build property from the government (since February 2016, HTB equity loans have been available for up to 40 per cent of the value of a new-build property in London). The scheme is limited to properties worth £600,000 and under, but there is no cap on the income of potential applicants. While no interest is charged on an equity loan for the first five years, from year six onwards a 'fee', which increases annually, is levied.[10]

The scheme has helped over 140,000 households buy a property in England to date, but it has some significant flaws. Figure 9.3 shows that the scheme is poorly targeted. One-quarter of those who have purchased a home with an HTB equity loan

9 65 per cent of 18-40-year-olds who do not own hope to do so in the future. For further details, see: L Marshall & N Smith, *First-time buyers, An early life crisis: Britain's homeownership aspirations*, NatCen, March 2016

10 In all instances, the buyer must separately put down a deposit of at least 5 per cent, obtaining a mortgage for the remainder of the purchase. The government loan is repayable when the property is sold, with its value shifting in line with the property price. That is, if the buyer has taken out a loan worth 20 per cent of the initial property price, then their repayment should be 20 per cent of the sale price when they come to move. The fee is set at 1.75 per cent of the loan from year six and then rises by RPI + 1 per cent in every subsequent year.

to date have an annual household income of £60,000 or more: that compares with just one-tenth of the total population of households in England headed by someone aged under 40. The government's own evaluation of the scheme also highlighted a significant deadweight inherent in the scheme, with 35 per cent of HTB recipients indicating they could have bought a home in the absence of the subsidy (albeit perhaps a smaller property or one in a less desirable neighbourhood).[11]

Box 9.1 Credit and the younger generation

While rising house prices are a key reason why upfront costs have increased so rapidly in recent years, as discussed in Chapter 3, tighter credit conditions have also played a significant role. A key feature of this has been the Mortgage Market Review of 2014, which aimed to end the loose lending practices that had characterised the 2000s. The MMR banned self-certification mortgages; tightened the rules around interest-only mortgages; and demanded more stringent affordability checks by lenders, including 'stress testing' a potential buyer's ability to cope with future interest rate rises.

While there have been some offsetting developments in lending policy – for example, younger buyers today can get mortgages for much longer terms than were standard in the past – today's young people face tighter credit conditions than their recent predecessors. For example, the median first-time buyer in 1997 needed only to find 5 per cent of the purchase price for a deposit; today, the equivalent buyer finds an average of 16 per cent.[1]

While some argue that the MMR has overshot, there is limited scope to liberalise the credit regime today, given its important macro-prudential function. But as a minimum, lenders should operate in ways more in tune with the modern labour market. For example, with many more young people today working on short-term contracts or as self-employed, evidencing a steady income to lenders can be difficult. Given this, we very much welcome initiatives such as the Rental Recognition Challenge, in which the government tasked FinTech companies to come up with ways to enable a borrower's record of regular rental payments to be taken into account by lenders when applying for a mortgage.[2]

1 Source: UK Finance, *Industry data Table ML2*

2 HM Treasury, *Rent Recognition Challenge: Using FinTech to help renters*, December 2017

11 Ministry of Housing, Communities and Local Government, *Evaluation of the Help to Buy Equity Loan Scheme*, February 2016

Figure 9.3: Receipt of Help to Buy loans is skewed towards higher-income households

Proportion of households headed by under 40s and Help to Buy equity loan recipient households, by net household income: England, 2013-17

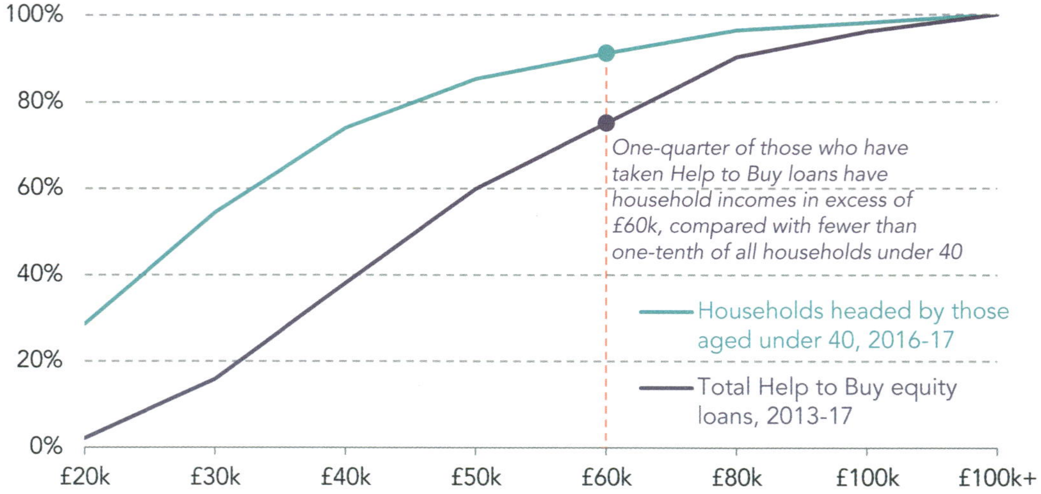

Notes: Incomes are measured before housing costs, and are equivalised to account for differences in household size.

Source: RF analysis of DWP, *Households Below Average Income*; MHCLG, *Help to Buy (Equity Loan scheme)*; MHCLG, *Help to Buy: NewBuy*

With the government's announcement of additional funding to maintain the HTB programme to 2021, the scheme looks here to stay. There is, therefore, a strong case for better targeting the support it provides, not least because there are costs attached to running the scheme,[12] and a net cash requirement for the government of £10 billion over the next three years alone. This may not add to the deficit, but it will increase national debt in the coming years.[13] The income cap for the HTB equity loan's predecessor scheme of £60,000 a year would be a sensible point to apply a restriction.

Policy recommendation

Limit future Help to Buy equity loans to those with an annual household income of less than £60,000 a year.

Addressing the inequities and inefficiencies of property taxation

We have focused so far on directly helping 'under-housed' younger generations. Given that supply is likely to be constrained for years to come, there is also a case for rebalancing effective housing demand by examining the position of the 'over-housed' older generations.

12 National Audit Office, *The Help to Buy equity loan scheme*, March 2014

13 The OBR forecasts, for example, that over the final three years of the scheme the net cost of the equity loans, in terms of the government's cash requirement, will be just under £10 billion. For further details, see: Office for Budget Responsibility, *Economic and Fiscal Outlook*, March 2018

How much housing we consume is ultimately a matter of personal choice within the financial constraints we face. However, the fact that housing is more lightly taxed than other forms of consumption may shift the balance of what we spend our money on. Moreover, if supply is constrained, increased consumption comes at a cost for someone else. Table 9.1 explores some key patterns of home ownership and shows that, even if we exclude those properties held by individuals but rented out to others, close to one-third of housing stock is held by those we might consider 'over-housed'. There is also a strong generational angle: baby boomers in particular are more likely to have already accumulated wealth and are able to leverage this in order to purchase additional property as well as to afford larger homes.

Table 9.1: The distribution of housing today: GB, 2014-16

Type of 'over-housing'	Estimated number of properties	Proportion of total housing stock	Proportion owned by baby boomers
Second homes	0.6m	2%	61%
Empty properties	0.3m	1%	42%
Under-occupied owner-occupied homes	7.9m	29%	44%
Sub-total	**8.8m**	**32%**	
Rented properties	5.3m	19%	n/a
Total	**14.1m**	**51%**	

Notes: Data on second homes and empty properties comes from the *Wealth and Assets Survey* and refers to 2014-16; data on properties rented out to others and under-occupied properties comes from the *Family Resources Survey* and refers to 2015-16. Under-occupied properties are defined here as all those with more than one spare bedroom. Studies suggest approximately 2 per cent of rented properties are owned by institutional investors.

Scurce: RF analysis of ONS, *Wealth and Assets Survey*; DWP, *Family Resources Survey*

We recognise that it is natural for families to want better and bigger housing as their incomes increase, and there are all sorts of wholly legitimate reasons why people can become 'over-housed'. There may be practical requirements, such as working away from the primary residence, or a couple working far apart; or it can be the product of happenstance, such as when individuals inherit a property or children depart from a large family home. But these individual decisions add up to very large inequities between the generations. That is why the time has come to look at whether these forms of housing consumption are taxed equitably.

An ideal property tax would be both equitable and efficient, yet council tax – Britain's main recurrent property tax which is collected by councils and used to fund their services – manages to be neither of these things. It is a highly regressive, regionally imbalanced, complex tax that is not fit for the 21st century.

Council tax started off as a compromise between a progressive property tax increasing as values rose and a regressive poll tax levied at the same rate for everyone. It has always had regressive features – such as flat tax bills within bands and small differences between them – but this distortion has increased over time. That's due to out-of-date property valuations and because higher-value areas (in which a greater share of properties are in top bands) can set council tax lower in order to fund a given level of local services.

As a result, council tax is significantly higher as a proportion of property value for those living in lower-value properties. For example, someone living in a property worth £100,000 in 2015-16 faced around five times the effective tax rate of someone living in a property worth £1 million. A tax designed to replace the poll tax has come to look increasingly like it.[14]

Council tax falls particularly heavily on younger generations. Young adults are more likely than their predecessors to live in the lowest (most regressive) council tax bands. As Figure 9.4 shows, 85 per cent of households in their 20s in Great Britain lived in the bottom three council tax bands in 2015-16, compared to 79 per cent 19 years earlier. The result is that council tax has become most generous to older households and most onerous for younger generations when measured as a proportion of property value – even more so as a proportion of property *wealth* (given low home ownership among younger cohorts).

As well as being inequitable, council tax is also inefficient. Second homes and empty properties are more likely to receive a discount than face a surcharge; consumption of large houses is under-taxed relative to consumption of smaller ones; and property is under-taxed relative to other investments. In addition, under-occupation is subsidised through the single person discount. These and other features have boosted house prices and led to inefficient stock allocation. Younger generations have been affected in particular in terms of entry into home ownership and the fact they have less space than predecessors.

Figure 9.4: Younger households have shifted down to more highly-taxed council tax bands

Proportion of households in each council tax band, by average age of adults: GB

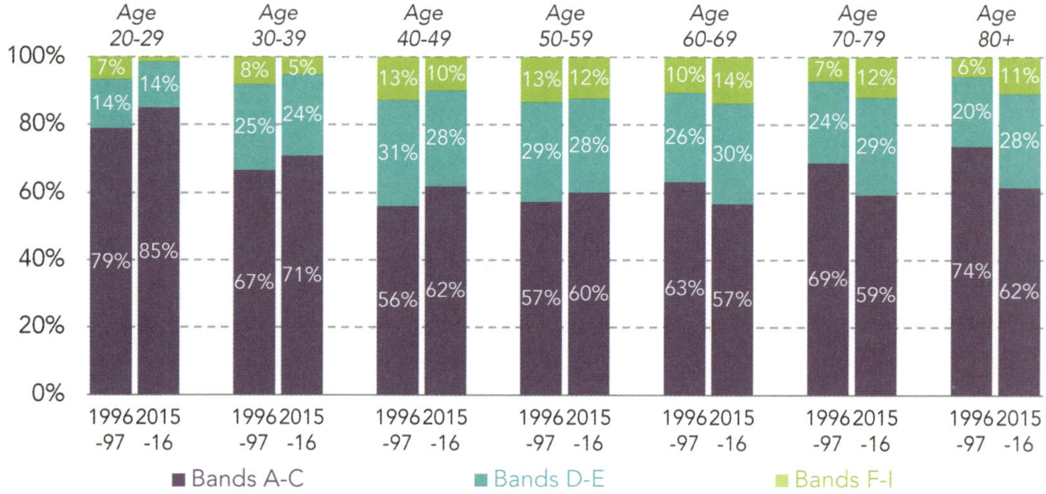

Notes: This analysis covers primary residences only. For further details, see: *Home affairs* (Intergenerational Commission report 18)
Source: RF analysis of DWP, *Family Resources Survey*

14 *Home affairs* (Intergenerational Commission report 18)

We favour the replacement of council tax with a progressive property tax that is directly linked to up-to-date property values. This would be more in line with the structure of recurrent property taxes in many other countries and, if designed well, could eliminate a number of the inefficiencies present in the current council tax system.[15] While the need for frequent valuations has long been considered a barrier to reform, new technology and mechanisms for feedback from taxpayers used in other countries mean that revaluation is now nothing like the barrier to reform it might have been in the 20th century.

There would of course be challenges in the transition to this new form of property tax. Council tax is principally used to fund local services, and the ability for local councils to vary it is a key pillar of local democracy. This is wrapped up with the local government finance settlement process and the level of redistribution between authorities, which would need to increase under a more progressive residential property tax system. This need not be an insurmountable barrier, however: national government could play the lead role in setting the initial rates of property tax, with local decisions to vary tax rates made within limits. The responsibility for managing the increased or reduced revenues resulting from rates that deviate from the central assumption would then sit with local councils outside of the national redistribution process. And of course, the different nations of Britain have the ability to implement their own systems, and could target their own revenue needs.

Reforms would also be needed to address households' ability to pay, particularly asset-rich, income-poor households facing higher tax bills than under the current system. Cuts to council tax reduction schemes in recent years, associated with their localisation, have accentuated this problem. We favour a return to the more substantial levels of support provided before 2013. Alongside this, an essential step would be the option for lower-income households – particularly older ones – to defer payment or pay in the form of an equity stake. Local government revenues could be protected by giving councils the power to borrow against these commitments.

There is also a case for transferring the direct burden of tax from occupiers to property owners. A tax on owners is the usual approach in other countries, and the potential administrative savings (both for individuals and councils) could be significant. Owners change less frequently than tenants and social and private landlords could streamline the payment of taxes that are currently made separately by millions of people and which result in excessive numbers of cases of arrears and court actions.

---

15 For details of international approaches to recurrent property taxation, see Box 5 in: *Home affairs* (Intergenerational Commission report 18)

Policy recommendation

Replace council tax with a progressive property tax – including a tax-free allowance and multiple tax bands – that is related to up-to-date values.

- It should be introduced in each nation of Great Britain by the relevant administration, with a regionally specific tax-free allowance set such that the lowest-value 10 per cent of properties in each region face no tax; with a tax rate of 0.85 per cent above this; and with an additional 1.7 per cent rate on marginal values above £600,000 (encompassing the highest-value 10 per cent of properties nationally). These new rates could be phased in.
- Combined with a reversion to pre-2013 levels of council tax reduction for those on the lowest incomes, this structure would boost revenues by £5 billion initially compared to council tax.[1] This revenue should fund stamp duty reductions and help meet wider public spending pressures in coming years (see later in this chapter and Chapter 11).
- A deferral or equity payment system should be introduced in order that asset-rich, income-poor individuals do not face unreasonable requirements to pay up front.
- Local authority funding should remain linked to property taxation, with an element of local discretion over the rates charged, coupled with greater revenue redistribution between authorities.
- Property tax should be levied on owners rather than renters. To discourage 'over-housing', owners with multiple properties for personal use – second and empty homes rather than those being rented out by landlords, for example – should be taxed on the full value of these additional properties, with no additional tax-free allowance.[2]

1 Revenue estimates are for 2020-21.

2 For further details on this recommendation, see: *Home affairs* (Intergenerational Commission report 18)

This represents a substantial overhaul of a major tax that is the primary mechanism for funding local authorities, but would confer many advantages. It would leave more than 72 per cent of households better off, including 78 per cent of households headed by those in their 20s. In addition, all those not able to own their own home could be taken out of the system of making property taxation payments entirely. Where necessary, taxes could be deferred until death leaving many lower income households with no annual tax payment. A tax based on timely valuations would dampen changes in property prices, and provide an improved link between tax revenues and new public investments that boost property values. It would help achieve a property tax system that was fairer across the generations and across the regions. It would also make the housing market more efficient and less volatile.

Improving the matching of supply with demand through taxing transactions differently

Stamp duty is the UK's property tax paid at the point of transaction.[16] While highly progressive, it also impedes the proper functioning of the housing market by reducing the incentive for individuals to move for work, to downsize or simply to buy a home that more closely matches their preferences.

Complete abolition of stamp duty – if done independently of other changes to housing taxation – would be expensive and provide a large benefit to higher-income households, largely in London and the South East. For that reason, and because of its ease of collection and the need for a broad tax base, we favour scaling it back very significantly, rather than outright abolition. Reducing stamp duty rates will, in isolation, increase property prices. However, from the perspective of affordability for new purchasers, this would make little difference: increased property prices would be offset by lower stamp duty. In addition, because mortgages can be used to cover the cost of houses but not associated taxes, such a change would reduce the amount of the overall cost of the purchase that would need to be found up front.

Replacing stamp duty also presents an opportunity to rebalance demand away from those seeking to purchase additional properties. Government policy has already started moving in this direction in recent years. In April 2016 the government introduced a 3 per cent stamp duty surcharge for purchasers of additional property, including those already owning a home overseas. This surcharge of 3 per cent applies to all 'slices' of the tax schedule and is intended to dis-incentivise the purchase of additional property. This was a sensible reform. The higher tax levels created by it should be maintained even as standard rates are cut, so that property transaction taxes moderate demand still further from those seeking additional property, by increasing their relative disadvantage in the market.

In addition to stamp duty reform there have also been a number of tax changes introduced of late – including changes to mortgage interest tax relief and the ending of the 'wear and tear' allowance – which have acted to reduce the returns on buy-to-let investing, tilting the balance of effective demand towards first-time buyers and movers.

16 Stamp duty is paid on a 'slice' system. If a household is purchasing a main property then they pay no tax on the first £125,000, and a higher rate on additional slices of the property's value up to 12 per cent on the portion of the value above £1.5 million.

Policy recommendation

Halve stamp duty so it supports property purchases by first-time buyers and movers and retain a higher tax rate on the purchase of additional properties.

- Rates of stamp duty on first properties should be halved (from their current levels of 2, 5, 10 and 12 per cent), at a cost of £2.7 billion if implemented across Great Britain, paid for from the additional revenues raised by reformed property taxation.[1]
- The existing first-time buyer relief should be retained, in the form of a higher threshold of £300,000.
- Existing levels of stamp duty on additional property should be retained (at 3, 5, 8, 13 and 15 per cent).

1 Cost estimates are for 2020-21: costed using the HMRC ready reckoner, with costs for England scaled up to Great Britain (not accounting for differences in stamp duty systems in Wales and Scotland) using OBR forecasts for devolved property transaction tax revenues in 2020-21.

These reforms to stamp duty would lead to a more efficient housing market with lower taxes on the majority of property transactions. They would also act to significantly tilt the advantage towards first-time buyers and main residence movers by opening up a very large difference in tax rates between them and the 'over-housed'. The flat rate 3 per cent surcharge would increase to a surcharge of 5.5 per cent on the average-priced house, and 9 per cent on the marginal value of the most expensive properties.

Overseas buyers are a special case also worthy of consideration, with research suggesting that in some high-demand areas they have accounted for as much as 20 per cent of transactions.[17] Outside of the UK, national and regional governments have also used either (or sometimes both) higher property transaction taxes or targeted regulations to dis-incentivise overseas buyers.[18] Some local leaders in the UK may wish to introduce similar sorts of restriction on overseas purchases in areas of intense housing pressure.

Policy recommendation

Give city and city-region mayors the authority to limit residential property purchases in housing hot-spots to those resident in the UK.

17 Estimates indicate that 7 per cent of all properties in Greater London and 20 per cent in Inner London are sold to an overseas buyer. For further details, see: A Wallace, D Rhodes & R Webber, *Overseas Investors in London's New Build Housing Market*, University of York, June 2017; Knight Frank, *International buyers in London*, October 2013

18 For more detail on approaches to overseas buyers taken in other countries, see: *Home improvements* (Intergenerational Commission report 19)

Alongside changes to the cost of purchasing property, we must also consider the extent to which the tax treatment of those who *sell* additional property helps orient the market towards younger, less wealthy, buyers. Currently, owners of additional property are also liable for capital gains tax at the point of sale, set at 18 per cent for basic-rate taxpayers and 28 per cent for higher-rate payers. It is right that the gains from the accumulation in value of additional property are taxed in this way – and the tightening of rules around 'flipping' properties from a second home to primary residence in 2013, to limit avoidance, was welcome.[19] Indeed, some advocate extending capital gains tax to primary residences too – an approach that has a certain logic but might be a step too far, adding complexity and dis-incentivising moving in the same way that stamp duty currently does.[20]

Instead, we believe the introduction of the new progressive property tax that no longer incentivises multiple property ownership should allow for time-limited *cuts* to capital gains tax for those selling additional properties to first-time buyers. Individuals have an annual capital gains tax allowance, set at £11,700 in 2018-19, which cannot be rolled-up over the years during which an asset accumulates in value. Increasing this allowance for a time-limited period in this way should incentivise exit from multiple ownership and facilitate an increase in home-ownership rates. At the same time, it cannot be right to continue with a system in which capital gains tax is forgiven upon death, incentivising holding on to properties.

Policy recommendation

Introduce a time-limited cut to capital gains tax for owners of additional properties selling to first-time buyers.

- The capital gains tax allowance associated with the sale of an additional property to non-owners should be tripled for two years, providing a maximum gain of £6,900 in 2020-21.
- Capital gains on additional properties should be taxed when passed on to anyone other than a spouse or civil partner at death.

Any temporary increase in the capital gains allowance for the sale of additional property would benefit from quick implementation – a large lag between announcement and tax change would act to stall sales of additional property as owners wait for lower taxes. If the policy was announced later this year for implementation in the 2019-20 tax year then it would provide a maximum tax cut, to higher-rate payers, of £6,700 in 2019-20 and £6,900 in 2020-21 (if allowances

19 In the Autumn Statement of 2013 private residence relief was cut from 36 months to 18 months. See: HM Treasury, *Autumn Statement 2013*, December 2013

20 For further details, see Box 3 in: *Home affairs* (Intergenerational Commission report 18)

continue to be uprated in line with current government policy). Owners of additional property disposing of their assets would be relieved of a 28 per cent tax on any gains between the normal allowance (£12,300 in 2020-21) and the temporary higher allowance (£36,900 in 2020-21).

This tax cut would likely have a large dynamic effect, bringing forward disposals that would otherwise have happened in the years ahead. As a result, though likely to act as a revenue raiser in the short term, it would reduce the tax take in the years after the temporary tax cut. However, the ending of the forgiveness of capital gains tax at death will increase revenues now and in the future. It will mean that disposals of property might happen earlier than otherwise – because there would no longer be a tax advantage from holding on to properties until death. The value of estates would be reduced by the amount of capital gains tax paid before being subject to inheritance tax in the normal way.[21]

Rebalancing the housing economy via a focus on additional supply

While the measures outlined so far would improve life in the private rented sector and level the playing field for first-time buyers, building more homes is critical if we are to bring down the market cost of housing over the longer term. While some accounts have minimised the role that supply has played in exacerbating the housing

Figure 9.5: The UK has far fewer dwellings relative to its population than most comparable countries

Housing stock per 1,000 inhabitants aged 20+

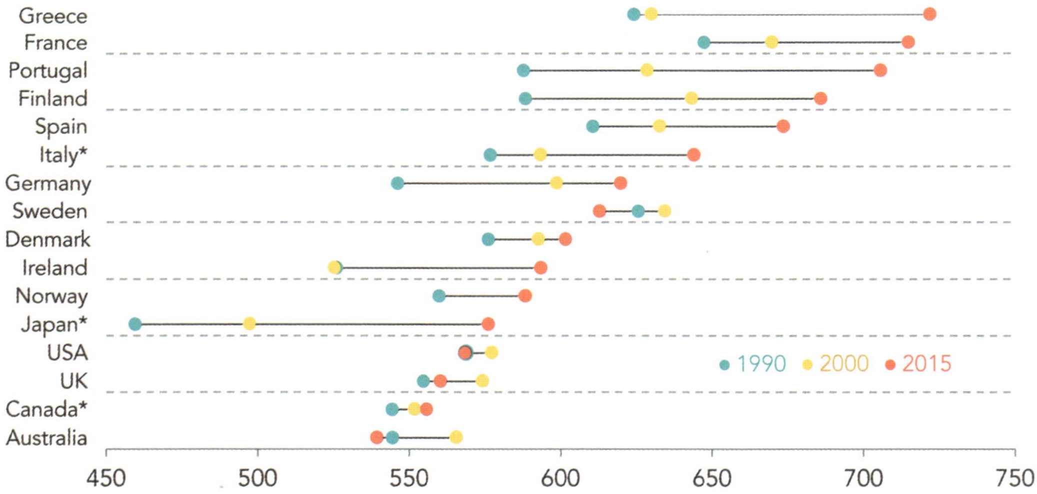

Notes: Countries with asterisks are those for which 2015 data has been imputed based on 2010 results.
Source: RF analysis of OECD, *Questionnaire on Affordable and Social Housing*; EMF, *Hypostat*; UN, *Population Prospects*

21 *Home improvements* (Intergenerational Commission report 19)

challenges of young people,[22] a rise in multi-family households suggests constrained supply.[23] And when we look cross-nationally, as we do in Figure 9.5, we can see that the UK has a far lower housing-stock-to-population ratio than most comparable countries *and* has been far less successful at increasing that ratio in recent years.

Building homes at a faster rate than the adult population is growing is essential if supply and demand are to be rebalanced. The government's target for England of getting 300,000 new homes built a year, significantly above the projected rate of population change, is a good place to start.

The strategy for making this happen has focused mainly on getting tough with councils – insisting they produce a local plan or lose their planning powers for example, or requiring them to use a prescribed formula when assessing local need. But there are further steps the government could take to deliver on its housing ambitions.

There have been a substantial number of changes to planning rules and powers in recent years, all with the intention of making the system more nimble and efficient. This has had a beneficial impact, with a higher proportion of planning permissions being granted today than in the past.[24] But while there may still be scope to streamline rules further, developers today are just as likely to point to lack of *capacity* in planning departments as a hindrance. Research has suggested that planning departments lost one-third of their staff across the UK between 2010 and 2015.[25]

A central resource of planning experts could help local authorities keen to play their part in delivering on building 300,000 homes a year. Available to give expert advice and training to planning departments and elected representatives, this would increase the quality of planning and unlock local logjams, enabling substantial building programmes to be delivered in a way that commands public support.

Policy recommendation

Create a unit of highly skilled planners in central government to support local authorities in areas of high housing need, and with a full five-year land supply, to deliver high-quality developments.

22 For example, see: I Mulheirn, 'Two housing crises', *Medium*, 27 March 2018

23 *Home Affront* (Intergenerational Commission report 9)

24 For example, 88 per cent of applications were granted in 2017, compared with 83 per cent in 2006-07 and 2007-08. Source: MCHLG, *Live tables on planning application statistics*

25 Royal Town Planning Institute & Arup, *Investing in Delivery: How we can respond to the pressures on local authority planning?*, October 2015

Moving to the higher-volume, lower-cost house-building equilibrium we need requires more than just efficient processes and improved capacity, however. It also demands our taking a close look at the cost of the inputs and the processes needed to build more homes. We take a specific look at modular building in Box 9.2.

Box 9.2 Building the homes of the future

Building homes at volume is a significant challenge, but one that has motivated creative thinking in many quarters. One idea that is often advanced is modular building, where homes are largely built (or indeed 3D printed) off site and simply assembled on site. A much more common building method in countries such as Germany,[1] modular homes are – relative to the classic build – quicker to complete (with average build times cut by six months or more),[2] cheaper both to produce and assemble (with construction costs of around a third less)[3] and less prone to defects.[4]

Today's modular builds could be especially attractive to those making moves in later life. Research shows that older people particularly prize homes that are easy to manage and maintain, and hence have a stronger preference for new builds than other age groups.[5] The good design and state-of-the-art materials associated with modular building mean that homes built using this method could be particularly suitable for older movers.

There are other issues when it comes to future proofing our housing stock, however. Much of the debate about housing in later life has focused on facilitating downsizing, but evidence shows that many older people move to homes of a similar if not larger size as they age. Rather than second-guessing the number of rooms that older families may need, a more useful question for policy makers to consider is whether today's new builds should all be built to certain accessibility standards. Delivering easy-to-maintain new builds that are sufficiently spacious to allow adaptations to be made in the future – enabling ageing owners to live in their own homes for as long as desired – could be a very attractive proposition.

1 Statistics on building permits issued in Germany for new builds suggest around 15-20 per cent of homes have at least a prefabricated element. Source: *Destatis (Germany)*

2 G Robinson, *Modular Construction in UK Housing: An Overview of the Market, the Players and the Issues*, Pinsent Masons, February 2017

3 For example, see: O Storbeck, 'Vonovia looks to prefabs to build growth', *Financial Times*, 7 March 2018

4 W Wilson & C Rhodes, *New-build housing: construction defects – issues and solutions (England)*, House of Commons Library, December 2017

5 For example, see: B Beach, *Generation Stuck: Exploring the Reality of Downsizing in Later Life*, International Longevity Centre UK, January 2016

Looking beyond the costs of labour and raw materials (and the way they are combined), it is the cost of the land on which houses are being built that has risen most rapidly over time. One way of both bringing more land forward for development and reducing the price is via community land auctions (CLAs). Under this model, local authorities put out calls to landowners asking for the reserve price at which they would be prepared to sell their land in a specific window of time (usually 18 months). If the plots are fit for local purpose and suitably priced, the council can then grant planning permission on the land and offer it for sale to developers, keeping any difference between the reserve and the price paid.[26]

The scheme has much to recommend it. Cash-strapped councils do not need to purchase the land themselves but instead simply play the role of honest broker. However, there are some additional features the CLA system requires to make it work in practice. To begin, it needs to be the only mechanism through which landowners can sell their land to avoid a parallel market. Second, it needs to be backed up by the credible threat that a local authority could issue a compulsory purchase order (CPO) if land was not brought forward in the volumes required.

Although it is legally permissible to hold a CLA (section 154 of the *Housing and Planning Act 2016* allows local authorities to apply to the Secretary of State for 'planning freedoms' which would allow this), to date not a single council has trialled the model. The risks of being the first mover for an innovative scheme such as this are considerable: alienating large and important lobbies, for example, or exposing the council to judicial review.

Policy recommendation

Homes England should support five local authorities that are prepared to pilot community land auctions by 2020.

- Given the challenges landowners face when seeking to establish the value of their land, agricultural landowners should be offered a standard rate per hectare, which they could then deviate from if they wished.
- Pilot areas should only allow land to be brought forward via community land auctions, to avoid landowners seeking a higher price outside the system.
- Local authorities piloting the scheme should be given sufficient resource to make the threat of compulsory purchase credible.
- Pilot areas should be backed by expert guidance from Homes England, along with legal support as required.

Homes of all types are important if we are to solve the intergenerational housing challenge, but there are certain types of building that it makes sense to privilege.

26 For example, see: T Leunig, *In my back yard: unlocking the planning system*, Centre Forum, 2007

First, despite a great deal of discussion about its many virtues and some recent growth, the build-to-rent (BTR) sector remains small in the UK. With slimmer margins than build-to-sell (at least in the short term), there is a case for at least some type of preferential policy treatment if government wishes to increase BTR volumes.

Policy recommendation

Support the development of the build-to-rent sector by exempting from the stamp duty surcharge on additional properties any institutional investors that either construct build-to-rent properties or buy them within five years of construction.

- In return for this exemption, build-to-rent providers should be expected to deliver fully on affordable homes requirements.

Second, policy makers have aimed for many years to ensure that private developers build a certain proportion of affordable homes through section 106 requirements. However, this system has both inherent and deliberate limitations. To begin, while it may deliver well in buoyant times, in downturns developers both build fewer properties of all types and find requirements to deliver affordable homes more onerous. In recognition of this, since 2012, developers have been able to negotiate down the number of affordable homes they are required to build if such requirements are found

Figure 9.6: The proportion of affordable homes built by the private sector has fallen in recent years

Affordable homes by type of builder: England

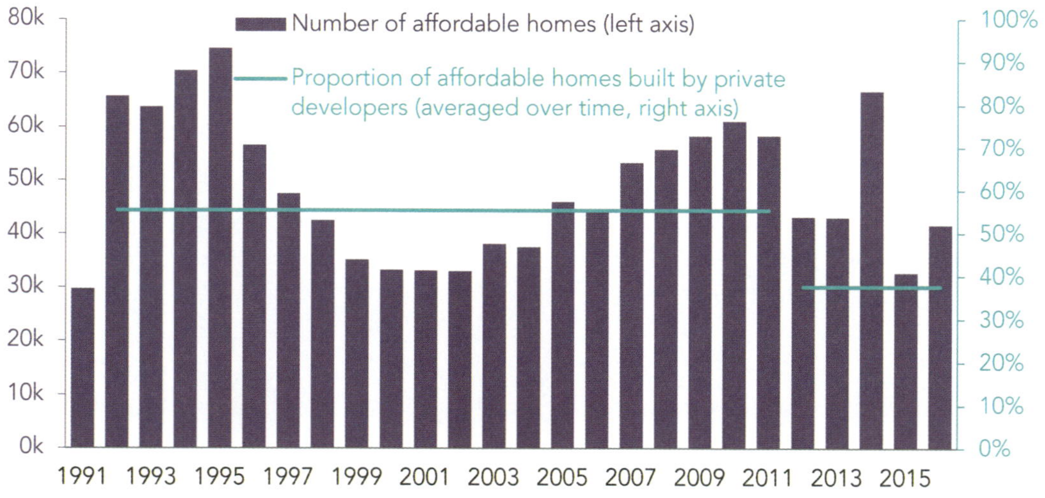

Source: MHCLG, *Live tables on dwelling stock (including vacants)*

to make the development 'unviable'.[27] Moreover, since 2010, developers can be charged the community infrastructure levy in lieu of an affordable homes requirement.

These pressures have led to a sharp decline in the share of affordable homes built by market rather than by registered providers in recent years. Figure 9.6 shows how private developers built on average 55 per cent of new affordable supply each year between 1991 and 2011; yet since 2012, this figure has dropped to 38 per cent.

It is unrealistic to expect private developers to deliver on all our needs for affordable homes, especially given how vulnerable they are to downturns. However, a better, more reliable system does need to be found.

Policy recommendation

Reform the viability process to ensure that builders deliver on their up front affordable homes commitments except in exceptional circumstances.

- The norm that develops will only be able to reopen affordable housing commitments in circumstances of significant market shifts should be reset.
- Where developers have negotiated down the number of affordable homes during the building phase on viability grounds, the financial outcome of that development should be examined at the end of the process and the equivalent of any affordable homes reduction clawed back where it is shown to have been unwarranted.
- Builders who are deemed to have unreasonably reduced their affordable homes contribution on the grounds of viability should also be subject to a penalty to ensure developers do not use this mechanism simply to avoid integrating affordable homes within the development.

Bringing the state back into the house-building business

While the changes we call for in this chapter would incentivise the private sector to move to a higher-volume, lower-cost model of housing supply, it is questionable whether private developers on their own will deliver the number of properties – and especially affordable homes – we desire. Historically there is no precedent for private developers delivering anything close to 300,000 homes a year in England. In fact, since 1946 there have only been two years when the number of new dwellings built by the private sector surpassed the 200,000 mark (1964 when 200,600 were built, and 1968 when 203,300 units were completed).[28]

27 Ministry of Housing, Communities and Local Government, *National Planning Policy Framework*, March 2012

28 Source: MCHLG, *Live tables on dwelling stock (including vacants)*

There are, of course, good reasons why this might be the case. As the independent reviewer of Build Out, Sir Oliver Letwin, has said, developers will not build homes more quickly than the market can absorb as this risks new-build house prices falling.[29] For private developers who owe a duty to their shareholders, this is an entirely logical approach.

Central government has shown some signs of being interested in directly commissioning building in recent years and, while there are a range of constraints that currently inhibit councils from building, the proliferation of local authority housing companies and growth of some housing associations shows that both an appetite and a capacity for construction still exists. So what would help central and local government to commission building at scale once again?

Borrowing is an important consideration: central government could borrow at record low interest rates and distribute additional funds to local authorities or housing associations to support their building activities, or the borrowing rules for local authorities could be loosened. But there are other sources of finance that are worth exploring too.

In particular, the social care precept on council tax in England provides a useful model. This precept has allowed councils to raise tax bills between 2016 and 2019 faster than would normally be allowed, in order to provide funds specifically for social care services. While funding for social care was sorely required when this precept was brought in, its revenue-raising potential mapped very poorly onto the areas with the greatest social care needs.[30] A precept designed to raise funds for local authorities to build new homes would not suffer from this tension, however, particularly after the reforms to recurrent property taxation we set out above. Instead, those areas with the highest housing wealth (and therefore the highest property tax base) are also those with the highest demand for new homes.

In Chapter 11 we return to the issues of social care funding. But with the social care precept flexibilities coming to an end after 2019 and incorporated into budgets from then on,[31] now is an opportunity to consider what better-targeted flexibilities around local taxation might look like.Said flexibility could be introduced by devolved administrations as well as for England.

29 As documented in a letter from Sir Oliver Letwin to Philip Hammond MP and Sajid Javid MP regarding the gap between planning permissions granted and housing completions, dated 9 March 2018.

30 N Amin-Smith, P Johnson & D Phillips, *How far do today's social care announcements address social care funding concerns?*, Institute for Fiscal Studies, December 2016

31 Because our modelling of a new progressive property tax system set out earlier in this chapter is based on 2020 council tax levels, the revenue raised for social care via the precept is included in our baseline assessment. In other words, we do not propose that the additional funding that the precept has delivered to social care in England be unwound.

Policy recommendation

Allow local authorities to raise additional money to build new homes via a property tax building precept and new borrowing flexibilities.

- The social care precept in England should be repurposed into a Britain-wide 'building precept' alongside the introduction of a new property tax. This would provide the flexibility for local authorities to vary their property tax rates beyond the usual constraints in order to raise additional funds specifically for building new homes. For example, a flexibility to add up to 0.04 percentage points to the rates of property tax applied above tax-free allowances would raise an additional £1.7 billion in 2020 if used in full across Great Britain.

- City and city-region mayors should be given greater flexibility to borrow for housing as part of city deals.

While local authorities could use the building precept to fund any aspect of house building to accelerate supply, full use of the £1.7 billion across Britain could bring forward additional stock of over 21,000 homes a year for full social rent, or more than 48,000 shared ownership or affordable rent properties.[32] In combination with borrowing flexibilities, reinvigorated affordability requirements, improved planning capacity, and a renewed focus on BTR and community land auctions, such an approach can help deliver the homes that Britain needs for long-term affordability.

Addressing Britain's housing costs challenge is one of the main ways to de-risk long-term living standards for all generations and for today's young adults in particular. In the following chapter, we turn to policies that address the other significant area in which lifetime living standards appear at risk: pensions.

32 Estimated on the basis that each new social rent property requires £80,000 of investment from government, in line with the announcement made at the Conservative Party Conference 2017 that £2 billion of new funds would enable 25,000 full social rent properties to be built. We assume that each shared ownership or affordable rent unit requires £35,000 of support, in line with the additional £1.4 billion announced for the Shared Ownership and Affordable Homes Programme in Autumn Statement 2016, to enable 40,000 of these types of homes to be built.

CHAPTER 10

Pensions – saving for tomorrow

We recommend

Raising the value of the new State Pension relative to median earnings and replacing the triple lock with a new 'double lock'.

Extending auto-enrolment to lower earners and the self-employed, alongside a new flatter system of pensions tax relief benefiting the majority of pension savers.

Reforming pension freedoms to offer pensioners protection from the uncertainty of how long they will live, and re-energising the debate about a risk-reducing middle-ground between defined benefit and defined contribution pensions.

Our approach to pensions policy

There are reasons for some optimism about pensions in the UK – with State Pension reforms lifting the minimum that will be paid to future pensioners and auto-enrolment dramatically increasing occupational pension coverage. If more favourable economic conditions returned (and with the simplifying assumption of constant investment returns), today's younger generations have the potential to achieve broadly similar outcomes in later life to recent retirees.

There is, however, one key difference between the outlook for today's and tomorrow's pensioners: namely, risk. Changes to the UK's pension's landscape in recent years have systematically shifted risk onto the shoulders of younger pension savers, making this one of the most pressing issues of generational fairness for policy makers today.

In this chapter we take further the best features of recent successful reforms and tackle this crucial issue of risk. We focus on three issues in particular: the future trajectory of the State Pension and its relationship with earnings; the evolution of auto-enrolment during the critical next phase in which minimum contributions are raised; and the broader pension reforms needed to mitigate risk in a world dominated by defined contribution pensions rather than defined benefit schemes.

Delivering a fairer State Pension across generations

The State Pension is a core part of our generational contract, providing pensioners with an income in retirement that is funded from taxes paid by the workers of the day. Those workers must be confident they can enjoy a pension funded in a similar way in future. Reforms in recent years have covered two key features of this contract: the age at which people can access the pension and the amount they are entitled to. The reforms have much to recommend them, but they have also produced potential intergenerational inequities which we need to tackle.

The appropriate *level* of the State Pension has been at the centre of discussions of intergenerational fairness in recent years. The triple lock for uprating the State Pension was put in place, in striking contrast to cuts in working-age benefits. However, the policy shift that raises even more acute issues of intergenerational fairness is actually the new State Pension – which transfers greater support to baby boomers while reducing that planned for millennials.

From the early 1980s the basic State Pension was increased in line with inflation and fell behind earnings. Since 2011 the triple lock ensures that it, and the new flat-rate State Pension, rise by the highest of growth in earnings, prices and 2.5 per cent. As a result, the State Pension has increased in value relative to earnings, and the level of the new State Pension is very close to the historic high reached in 1979. It is good news that pensioners enjoy improved living standards. This success has, however, come at a cost: per-head spending on benefits for working-age households is set to fall by 7.9 per cent between 2015-16 and 2022-23, compared to a rise of 1.8 per cent for pensioners over the same time period.

Looking ahead, if (and it is a big if, judging by the historical experience) these higher levels of the State Pension relative to earnings are maintained, today's younger groups would benefit when they reach retirement too. On the flipside, if the State Pension permanently kept growing faster than working-age incomes, funding it would place an ever-greater burden on taxpayers. The government's answer to this trade-off is to maintain the triple lock until 2022, before moving to earnings uprating.[1] Projections by the OBR show that an extreme alternative of keeping the triple lock in place in the very long term would cost 0.9 per cent of GDP by 2066-67.[2]

Setting the State Pension involves debate about the formula for raising it each year. But behind that, there is the fundamental issue, often ignored, of what its value should be relative to the incomes of the working-age population.

It is important to maintain a link between the State Pension and earnings growth over the longer term. If the State Pension were instead increased by inflation from 2022, by 2060 it would be worth around two-fifths of its value today relative to earnings – with more pensioners in poverty. But that does not mean that a simple earnings uprating in every year is the best way to deliver the link. Providing some additional protection for future periods of weak wage growth or fast price rises – as the triple lock has done recently – is also desirable. To achieve that, the State Pension should maintain its peg to earnings in the medium term, but could be uprated by more than earnings in years when prices rise faster, with the gap then subsequently being closed by increases less than earnings.[3] Such a 'double lock' would have much in common with the current approach to setting the National Living Wage.

But while maintaining the level of the State Pension relative to earnings should remain a core part of the intergenerational contract, the outstanding question remains what proportion of median earnings the State Pension should be pegged to. Some argue that it has risen enough, as the value of the new State Pension currently represents around 32 per cent of median earnings – equivalent to the 1979 peak (see Chapter 4). But 32 per cent falls a little short of providing half the 67 per cent replacement rate targeted by the Pensions Commission.[4] Reasonable people will differ on whether further increases are warranted in pursuit of this ratio.

From the perspective of fairness between generations, our view is that, having asked current working-age cohorts to pay for returning the State Pension towards historic

1 Current government policy is to end the commitment to the triple lock at the end of this parliament.

2 Office for Budget Responsibility, *Fiscal sustainability report – January 2017*, January 2017

3 For further details on this approach, see: Work and Pensions Select Committee, *Intergenerational fairness: Third Report of Session 2016–17*, November 2016

4 Pensions Commission, *A New Pension Settlement for the Twenty-First Century: The Second Report of the Pensions Commission*, November 2005

highs, it should not then be reduced relative to earnings. The new State Pension should also be reformed given that some cohorts of future pensioners are set to do better than others from its introduction, with the first cohorts retiring into the new system (roughly the middle of the baby boomer generation) on average receiving a greater level of support than generation X and millennials. This is because the new State Pension abolishes earnings-related top-ups to the basic State Pension in favour of a higher flat-rate payment for almost everyone in future cohorts. However, those starting to receive their pension now get the best of both worlds: access to the higher new State Pension, alongside the remnants of the earnings-related system via what are known as 'protected payments'.[5]

This helps in part to explain why, as Figure 10.1 shows, the first cohorts retiring on the new State Pension will overwhelmingly do better than they would have done under the old system. Of baby boomers born in 1954, reaching State Pension age in 2020, around 85 per cent are expected to gain over their lifetime in retirement, while around 15 per cent will lose out. But the reverse is true for millennials born in 1991: they will on average be worse off under the new regime than the one it replaces. This is a vivid example of how easily intergenerational unfairness can be exacerbated by failing to consider properly the interests of different generations when a reform is implemented.

To ensure that the State Pension remains fair for future cohorts, these differentials should be narrowed. Therefore, rather than simply settling for the share of earnings

Figure 10.1: Younger cohorts are more likely to have lost out from the new State Pension reforms

Impact of the new State Pension reforms compared to the system they replaced across life in retirement, by year of birth: UK, 2020-60

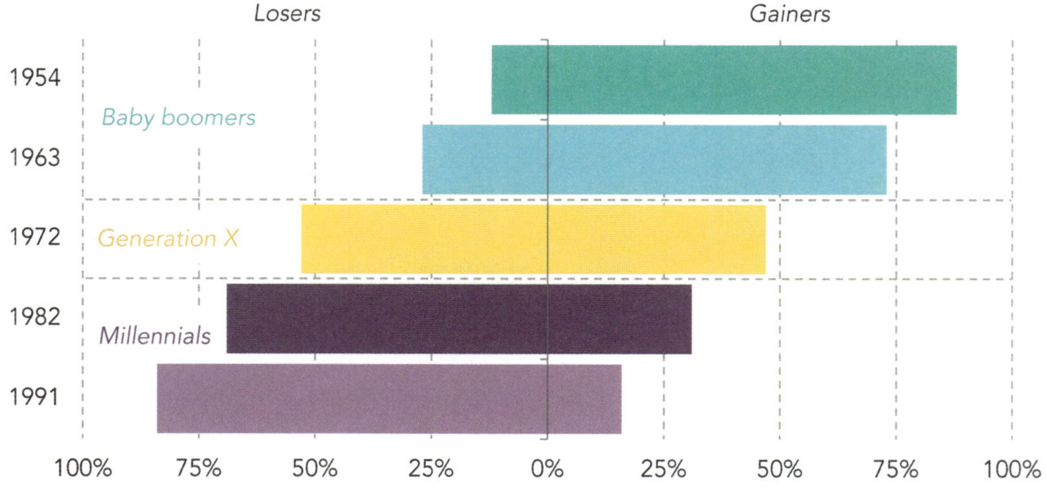

Source: RF analysis of DWP, *Impact of new State Pension (nSP) on an individual's pension entitlement – longer term effects of nSP*, January 2016

5 These 'protected payments' are earnings-related entitlements accrued under the pension system in place before April 2016 that, combined with basic State Pension entitlement, exceed the new State Pension rate. These 'excess' entitlements are CPI-uprated and paid on top of the main new State Pension rate.

reached at the end of this parliament, a higher level for the new State Pension should be reached, so that future cohorts receive a broadly similar level of generosity as those reaching pension age today.[6]

This could be funded by freezing protected payments and using the funds to increase the new State Pension faster than earnings in the short term.

Policy recommendation

Maintain the value of the new State Pension relative to earnings at a slightly higher level than the current position, funded by freezing 'protected payments'.

- The government should increase the value of new State Pension relative to earnings between 2022 and 2035 by 1 per cent above average earnings growth, to reach 32.5 per cent of median earnings.
- Beyond this, the long-term uprating mechanism for the State Pension should be a 'double lock', which maintains a peg to median earnings over the medium term but allows short-term deviation during periods of weak wage, or fast price, growth.

This policy would boost the average value of the new State Pension by a further 0.5 percentage points relative to median earnings by 2035-36, from 32 per cent to 32.5 per cent. This policy redistributes within the new State Pension population, narrowing the gap in entitlements between the first and subsequent cohorts receiving it and weighting reallocated spending towards younger cohorts. The cumulative savings from freezing protected payments that are used to fund this approach amount to £4 billion by 2035. By 2067-68, this approach would cost 0.1 per cent of GDP more than a simple earnings link from 2022, but the cost would be 0.8 per cent of GDP lower than a 45-year continuation of the triple lock.

This approach achieves a balance of maintaining better relative levels of generosity between successive cohorts, while avoiding a permanent ratchet on the costs of the State Pension that future generations of workers would need to fund.

6 Here we focus on *intergenerational* fairness for future cohorts. Of course, there remain big questions of *intra-generational* fairness for the current pensioner population. Historical accruals and the earnings-related system of Additional Pension leave some with high amounts of State Pension and others, mostly the oldest single female pensioners, with far less. While important, these issues are not our focus.

Ensuring a fair share of life in retirement

Alongside rises in the generosity of the State Pension, a key reform has been the decision to link the age at which it starts to be paid to cohort life expectancy. The approach rests on the proposition that future cohorts should spend the same share of adult life in retirement as current cohorts – established as 'up to one-third' of adult life by the government in 2013. The consequence is a State Pension age (SPA) set to rise to 66 by 2020 and 67 by 2028, with an expectation of a further rise to 68 by 2039 (though this last increase is yet to be legislated for).

This broad principle reduces pressures to always ask younger cohorts to pick up the bill for increases in longevity, or to cut the generosity of payments to those who have already retired (many of whom cannot expect to live as long as future retirees). It also reassures future retirees that the pension age will not simply be increased to meet wider financial pressures.

We welcome this. Implementing this sensible policy is, however, quite difficult in practice. Setting a pension age which delivers a similar share of life in which people are entitled to the State Pension depends on projections of life expectancy, and these change. For example, current government plans for SPA rises provided for about 33 per cent of adult life in retirement on the Office for National Statistics' (ONS's) 2014-based longevity projections, shown in Figure 10.2. But just two years later there was a *reduction* in ONS longevity projections because of a slowing of the improvement in mortality among the oldest age groups.[7] Because the path of State

Figure 10.2: Reduced longevity projections have implications for the share of life spent in retirement

Median share of adult life in retirement for cohort reaching State Pension age in each year, by longevity projection: UK

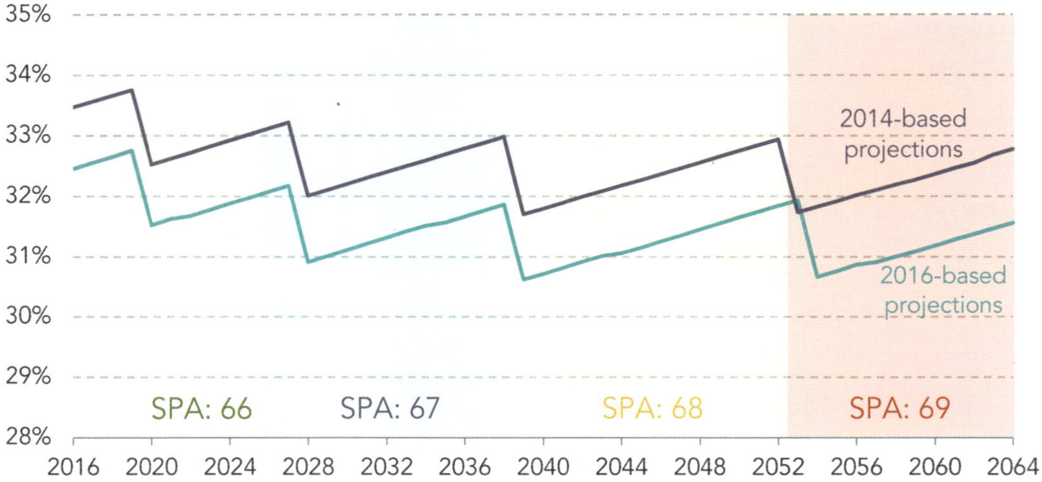

Notes: Share of adult life in retirement is calculated as years of life above State Pension age divided by State Pension age minus 20. Life expectancy is based on an average of median expected years of life for men and women.

Source: RF analysis of ONS, *Life expectancy projections* (2014-based); ONS, *Life expectancy projections* (2016-based)

7 V Raleigh, 'Why have improvements in mortality slowed down?', *The King's Fund blog*, 29 November 2017

Pension age rises has not changed in response, the result is that we are now on course for people to spend less (up to 32 per cent) of their adult life with a State Pension.

We cannot eliminate the uncertainties of making such longevity projections, but this experience highlights the need for transparency in decision-taking if future generations are to believe they are being treated as fairly as the principled policy position implies. John Cridland's recent report for the government is a good example of such transparency.[8]

There are also big questions about the extent to which the improvements in overall life expectancy are felt by all. Given that rises in the SPA affect those with shorter life expectancies the most, it is important to note that socio-economic and regional longevity disparities remain wide. Life expectancy in some areas is lower today than it was in other parts of the UK two decades ago.[9]

Ultimately we do not consider that such disparity is purely a matter for SPA policy, but it should play a part in considerations of any future changes to the SPA. Similarly, policy makers will also want to recognise the possibility that even if successive generations are able to spend the same share of their adult life in retirement, the duration of *healthy* life may differ on average between cohorts. Overall life expectancy among those aged 65-plus has risen more quickly since 2000-02 than has the number of years of expected good health (men at age 65 in 2009-11 were expected to live for an additional 2.1 years compared to the 2000-02 estimates, but only enjoy an extra 1.2 years of good health).[10] For all these reasons it is important that a better understanding of both the recent mortality improvement slowdown and projections of life expectancy inequities is prioritised.

Policy recommendation

To maintain fairness between generations, continue to link the State Pension age to longevity, aiming to provide a broadly consistent share of adult life in retirement on average to each cohort.

- Changes to the State Pension age should aim to affect all working-age generations as equally as possible.
- The Office for National Statistics should improve measurement and projections of inequalities in life expectancy, particularly when considering variations in life expectancy by region, socio-economic status or health, and the extent to which these track overall improvements in life expectancy.

8 Department for Work and Pensions, *Independent Review of the State Pension Age: Smoothing the Transition*, March 2017

9 Office for National Statistics, *Life Expectancy at Birth and at Age 65 by Local Areas in England and Wales: 2012 to 2014*, November 2015

10 C Jagger, *Trends in life expectancy and healthy life expectancy*, Government Office for Science, March 2015

Building on auto-enrolment's successes to deliver higher pension saving

Alongside the benefits associated with the introduction of the new State Pension, the other cause for optimism in relation to the future pensions landscape is auto-enrolment. It has been a huge success with more than 9 million employees enrolled by the beginning of this year.[11] This surpasses initial expectations of coverage, and means that a greater share of millennial employees at age 30 has private pension coverage than baby boomers did at the same age. Not only are those gains providing a boost to the coverage of younger generations, they are being achieved predominantly among women and the lowest-paid – groups that have historically had the lowest pension coverage.

The task now is to build on that success in two ways: by spreading the benefits to groups that are at risk of remaining outside private pensions saving – including the very lowest earners and the self-employed – and by increasing how much is saved without large numbers of people dropping out of the new system.

For the self-employed, the good news is they are among the biggest beneficiaries from the new State Pension. But despite significant growth in self-employment in recent years, the number saving into a private pension has fallen.[12] Of particular concern is the higher share of self-employment at younger ages for those with fewer qualifications. Individuals in this group are likely to be in lower-paid and insecure forms of self-employment which, if they endure for a significant period of their working lives, will mean these individuals will build up very little by way of private pensions at current savings rates. The historical trend for higher-earning self-employed people to invest more in property than private pension saving is unlikely to be a route to building wealth for this group,[13] not least because, as discussed in Chapter 3, only three-in-ten millennials own their home at age 30.

To address these challenges, the self-employed should be brought into a form of auto-enrolment. This is not straightforward in practice, and the government is currently seeking to trial various savings mechanisms. That process of trialling and then implementing a mechanism needs to be pursued with more urgency, with a view to requiring contributions to be made by those contracting for self-employed labour.

11 The Pensions Regulator, *Automatic enrolment: Declaration of compliance report: July 2012 – end March 2018*, April 2018

12 HM Revenue and Customs, *Personal Pensions: contribution and tax relief statistics*, September 2017

13 C D'Arcy, *The self-employed and pensions*, Resolution Foundation, May 2015

Policy recommendation

Develop a system that places requirements on firms and individuals contracting self-employed people to make contributions to their pensions, and provide default routes via which the self-employed can save into pensions.

- Both the systems for those contracting self-employed labour to make pension contributions and default savings routes for the self-employed should initially be explored within the tax system.

A further barrier to saving is the threshold at which low-paid workers qualify to be auto-enrolled. At £10,000, the lowest earners are left out. Some argue this prevents the very lowest earners saving unnecessarily, given that it may make sense to prioritise current rather than future consumption because of a likely low private pension and the relatively high value of the State Pension. However, many people will have some period of low earnings at the start of their career and miss out on the gains from saving early. In the context of proposals below for better-supporting saving by low- and middle-earners – and in order for lower earners to benefit from employer contributions – the auto-enrolment threshold should be lowered.

Policy recommendation

Lower the auto-enrolment threshold to the equivalent of working 15 hours per week on the National Living Wage – currently just over £6,000 a year.

Alongside spreading private pension saving to other groups, we also need to maintain the marked success of increased coverage during a period in which minimum contribution rates are rising. In April 2018, minimum employee contribution rates under auto-enrolment rose to 3 per cent (from 1 per cent), and they are set to rise again to 5 per cent in April 2019. Clearly there is a risk that these increases will cause some employees to take greater notice of the immediate costs and stop saving for a pension. That risk is heightened by the weak wage growth anticipated in the coming years – especially following what has already been a bad decade for pay.

Figure 10.3 models the effect of increasing contributions on the take-home pay of a median-earning full-time employee. It highlights the very significant drag these contribution increases will constitute, with the increase in minimum contributions to 5 per cent equating to a drag of £945 per year by 2019-20.

Figure 10.3: Increases in the minimum contributions associated with auto-enrolment are set to act as a significant drag on take-home pay

Median real take-home pay for full-time employees (CPIH-adjusted to 2017-18 prices): UK

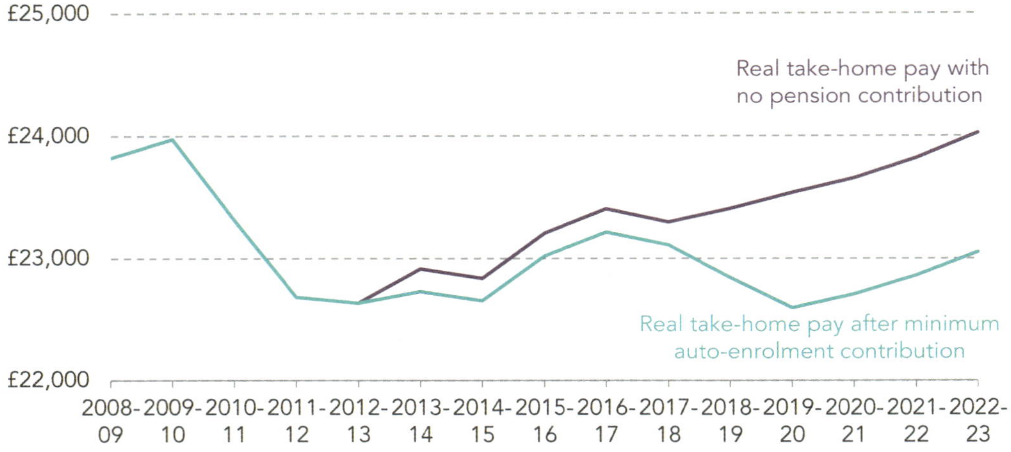

Notes: Our analysis assumes an employee pension contribution of 1 per cent from 2013-14, rising to 3 per cent in 2018-19 and 5 per cent in 2019-20. We account for changes to income tax and National Insurance thresholds.

Source: RF analysis of ONS, *Annual Survey of Hours and Earnings*; OBR, *Economic and Fiscal Outlook*

The government, reflecting the recommendations of a review of auto-enrolment,[14] is currently taking a 'wait and see' approach. It expects only small increases in opt-outs or cessations. In part this is due to the general inertia that appears to have underpinned the success of auto-enrolment to date, and which in the US appears to have remained despite rises in contribution rates.[15] There are also mechanisms to re-enrol after three years those who opt-out or cease contributions. How employees view their pay packets is also important. When combined with wider changes such as nominal pay increases and tax threshold changes, it is unlikely that large numbers of employees will experience a cash reduction in their take home pay. But they are likely to more generally feel a real-terms squeeze in income, and the risk associated with any reduction in scheme membership is large and should therefore be guarded against. A reduction in coverage could reduce replacement rates of middle and lower earning millennials by 5-8 percentage points.

Measuring the effect of rising contributions is likely to prove difficult in the short term. Data relating to employees' pay and pension contributions is published annually by the ONS, but there are significant timing issues. Data is collected in April and available for analysis the following October, meaning evidence on the impact of increased contributions over the next two years is unlikely to be available until October 2019. And given the prospect of a lag in employee behaviour, it may be later still before any warning signs can be observed.

14 Department for Work and Pensions, *Automatic enrolment review 2017: Maintaining the momentum*, December 2017

15 Department for Work and Pensions, *Automatic enrolment review 2017: Maintaining the momentum*, December 2017

The government could improve on this by using Real Time Information data (a monthly feed of PAYE records) and encouraging the Pensions Regulator to collect timely information from employers relating to initial opt-out rates and, more usefully, the numbers of employees reducing or cancelling contributions. The DWP could then report annually to the Work and Pensions Select Committee with an assessment of the impact of any shifts on future pension adequacy.

Given the consensus that we in fact need higher rates of saving than are currently planned for if Pensions Commission adequacy targets are to be reached, we believe the government should plan now to move in a sensible long-term direction to more actively support low- and middle-earners to save. This matters particularly for low-to-middle earners among generation X and millennials.

The recent review of auto-enrolment has set out one step on that path, suggesting that contributions should be taken from a greater span of employee earnings. Others have suggested further employee contribution rate increases to as high as 12 per cent of salary.[16] Both approaches have merits, but we should also be asking what further role there is for employers and the state. While, in the long run, pension contributions are part of their overall compensation package regardless of who pays them, greater employer contributions for those not opting-out can provide a stronger incentive to save for the employee.

Policy recommendation

Narrow the gap between minimum employee and employer auto-enrolment pension contribution over time.

There is a further actor that in aggregate already does much to boost private pension saving – the government. Tax reliefs currently provide a mixture of actual incentives to save and a necessary attempt to avoid double taxation on income when it is earned and then drawn down in retirement. The gross cost of these tax reliefs totalled £26.9 billion in 2015-16,[17] but as currently structured they offer the biggest incentives to save to those who are already most likely to do so – higher earners.

At its core our system of tax reliefs works by excluding occupational pension contributions when calculating a person's income tax liability, reflecting the principle that you are taxed on your income when you receive it. For income placed into a pension fund, and effectively deferred until retirement, tax is then applied when that income is finally drawn down. The highest earners receive up front tax relief of 45 per cent

16 Pensions and Lifetime Savings Association, *Hitting the target: Delivering better retirement outcomes*, October 2017

17 Source: HMRC, *Personal incomes statistics*

on pension contributions up to a lifetime limit, while basic-rate taxpayers have tax relief of 20 per cent. As Figure 10.4 shows, pensions tax relief overwhelmingly accrues to the very highest earners. The top 10 per cent of earners receives 52 per cent of the total tax relief, while the top 1 per cent alone receive 10 per cent. This raises a problem, not of intergenerational equity, but of *intra*-generational fairness.

Figure 10.4: Pensions tax relief overwhelmingly benefits the very highest-earning employees

Cumulative distribution of taxpayers and pensions tax relief, by gross individual income: UK, 2015-16

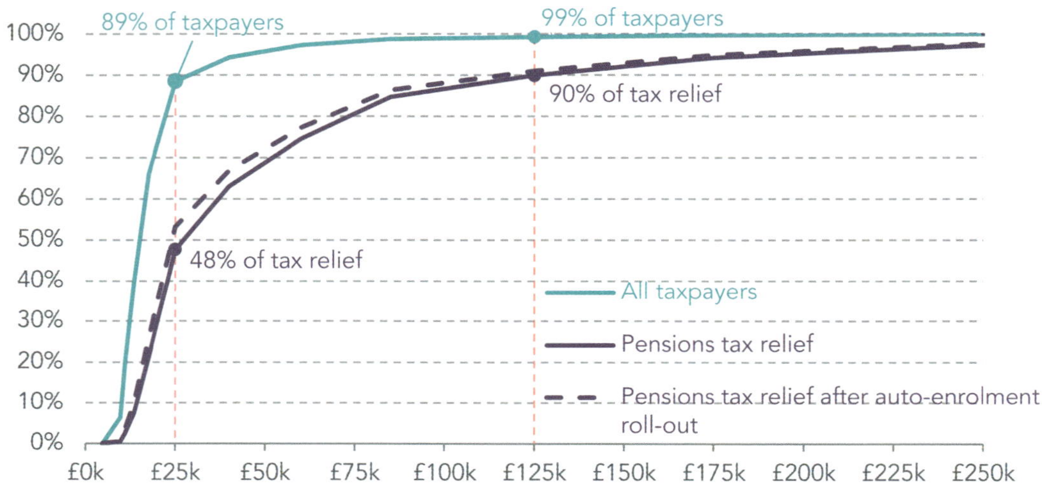

Notes: This analysis covers taxpayers only and so excludes the relief received by non-taxpayers who are paying into a pension and receiving relief-at-source at 20 per cent. It also excludes tax relief attached to lump sum payments from pension pots in retirement. The auto-enrolment scenario assumes current coverage rates and the 8 per cent contribution rates that will be required from April 2019 applied in 2015-16.

Source: RF analysis of HMRC, *Personal incomes statistics*; DWP, *Family Resources Survey*

The balance of tax reliefs is likely to shift a little in the coming years, as a growing number of low- and middle-earners are brought into private pensions – the likely shift is demonstrated by the dashed line in Figure 10.4. But the sheer scale of relief accruing to the highest earners means that the top 10 per cent will continue to receive almost half (46 per cent) of all relief.

To some degree this is to be expected in a system looking to avoid double taxation: after all, higher earners are likely on average to pay higher rates of tax in retirement. However, our current system of tax relief does more than simply allow individuals to smooth their income between working age and retirement without being tax disadvantaged. Higher earners are advantaged because they often pay a lower marginal rate of tax in retirement than when working and because they benefit most from the ability to take a tax-free lump sum of up to 25 per cent of their pension pot.

While providing a good incentive for people to save, because it is uncapped the lump sum does so in a very expensive and untargeted way. The typical lump sum taken is £20,000,[18] but the fact that some individuals are allowed to receive tax-free six-figure sums is very hard to justify and heavily skews tax relief expenditure towards a minority of high lifetime earners.

The regressive effect of the current tax relief system has led to a range of proposals for reform. Given the scale of funds involved, such proposals frequently include plans to release savings to help pay for rising costs of ageing, like the NHS or social care. However, taking such an approach would create a further inequity between generations, representing an effective tax rise for today's workers to pay for the health needs of older generations who benefitted from more generous pensions tax relief.

Instead, funds released from reforms to the current tax relief system should be recycled within the system to better support adequate private pension saving for working-age cohorts.

Policy recommendation

Support further progress on occupational pension saving among low- and middle-earners during a period of rising minimum pension contributions by providing a flat rate of income tax relief; and exempting employee pension contributions from employee National Insurance, funded by capping tax-relieved lump sums drawn at retirement to £40,000.

– The government should provide a flat rate of 'income tax relief' at 28 per cent. This will ensure that all pension contributions attract the same rate of tax relief regardless of earnings, providing an easy-to-understand increased incentive to save for low- and middle-earners. This measure would be self-funding, with reduced tax relief for higher earners offsetting gains for lower earners.

– The government should exempt employee pension contributions from employee National Insurance. This will have the effect of an additional 12 per cent of tax relief for all employees earning below the upper earnings limit (currently £46,350 per year) and 2 per cent above that level. It will also prevent a scheme of double taxation given recommendations in Chapter 11 to extend National Insurance to pensioner incomes. This measure would cost £2.2 billion.

18 *As good as it gets?* (Intergenerational Commission report 12)

– To fund these employee National Insurance exemptions, the government should cap tax-relieved lump sums at £42,000, leaving three-quarters of such drawdowns unaffected and raising over £2 billion in revenue.[1] This step promotes intergenerational fairness – it reflects the fact that future cohorts are unlikely to achieve the very highest pension pots, and therefore lump sums, that the luckiest current retirees benefit from.

1 RF analysis of Pensions Policy Institute, *Tax Relief for Pension Saving in the UK*, July 2013

Overall, this approach would significantly increase both the incentive to save and size of a pension pot for a given level of individual saving for most workers, with an increase in tax relief for 80 per cent of employees making pension contributions. Making this change rapidly would allow those in generation X at risk of failing to build an adequate pension income to benefit, as well as boosting the pension pots of younger cohorts. Returning once again to the distribution of tax relief, Figure 10.5 shows how tax relief under this policy would be distributed: relative to the current distribution this new approach would be much more beneficial to low- and middle-earners.

Figure 10.5: Our proposed pensions tax relief reform is targeted at low- and middle-earners

Cumulative distribution of taxpayers and pensions tax relief under different tax relief systems, by gross individual income: UK, 2015-16

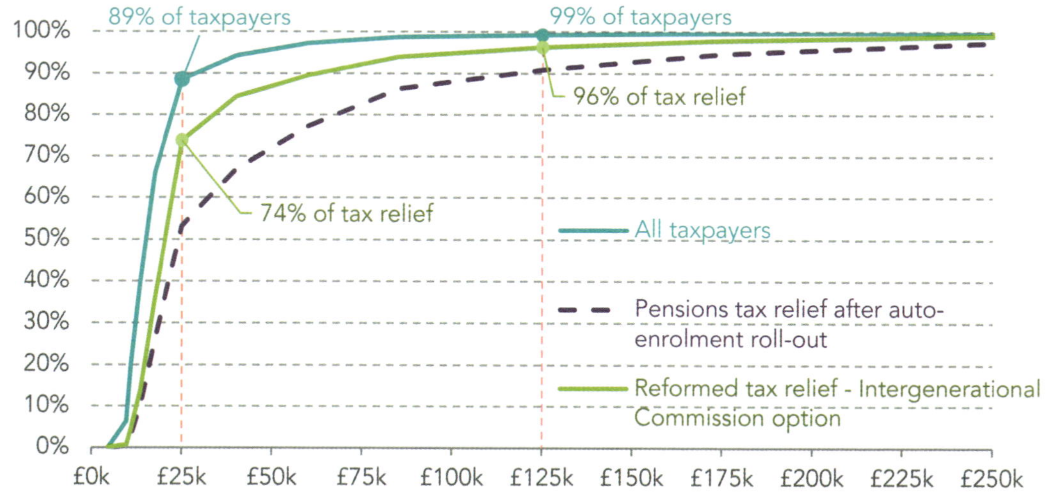

Notes: See notes to Figure 10.4. The reform option assumes current coverage rates and the 8 per cent contribution rates that will be required under auto-enrolment from April 2019 applied in 2015-16. It also excludes tax relief attached to lump sum payments from pension pots in retirement.

Source: RF analysis of HMRC, *Personal incomes statistics*; DWP, *Family Resources Survey*

Figure 10.6 shows the effect this approach would have on the lifetime tax relief and pension pots of different groups. Higher earners' tax relief would be reduced – but they would remain substantially higher than those of lower earners. A minimum wage earner from generation X could have an extra £5,000 in their pension pot (in 2017-earnings terms) at their retirement, while the equivalent millennial could build an extra £12,000.

Figure 10.6: **Pensions tax relief reform would lower savings among high earners, but boost them among low- and median-earners**

Change in lifetime tax relief and pension pots (earnings-adjusted to 2017 values) as a result of our proposed reforms (if introduced in 2020): UK, 2020-57

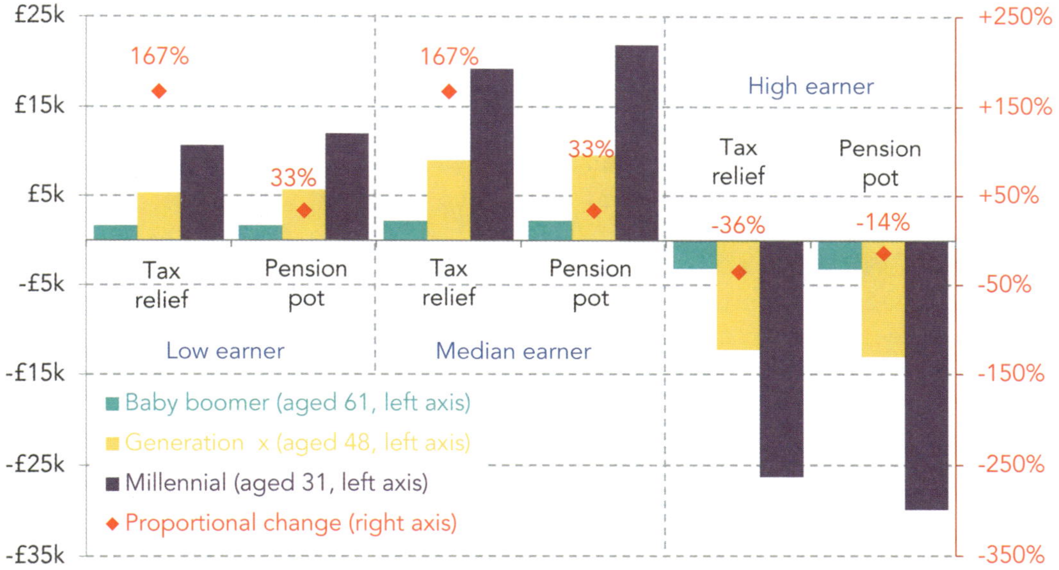

Notes: For full details on the assumptions underpinning these projections, see: *As good as it gets?* (Intergenerational Commission report 12)

Source: RF analysis of OBR, *Fiscal sustainability report – January 2017*, January 2017; RF modelling

Improving the structure of the defined contribution market to reduce longer-term risks

A fundamental challenge to adequate pension provision for younger generations is the level of individual risk they are now being asked to bear – including risks from shifts in investment returns, longevity, and prices. Here, far from making progress, we have gone backwards, not least with the move from defined benefit to defined contribution pensions. Reducing these risks, both in the years when a pension pot is built up, and in how funds are used in retirement, is key to ensuring that the private pension system provides for future generations of pensioners. It should be an explicit public policy objective.

There are two key forms of risk that have been passed to individuals with the widespread shift from DB to DC schemes: the risk around investment returns, and huge uncertainty about how long exactly each of us will live. These are risks that employers and the state usually bore for older generations, but which younger generations are exposed to directly. That is why there is a lot of interest in a middle ground between DB and DC schemes, particularly 'collective defined contribution' (CDC) schemes. This means different things in different countries,[19] but CDCs basically provide a pension savings vehicle that, while not totally insulating individuals from risks around longevity and returns, shares those risks across and within generations. Whereas firms bear most of the risk with DB pensions and individuals bear all the risk in a DC world, risks in a CDC model are borne by scheme members collectively. They pool their contributions in return for a target, but not guaranteed, annual income in retirement.

A collective fund, spanning both the build-up and running down of pension pots, reduces individual risk in two important ways. First, the schemes can pay a target annual income to retirees for however long they live, thereby removing an individual's longevity risk. They can do this by risk-pooling, with those with lower-than-expected lifespans helping to subsidise costs for those with higher-than-expected lifespans. Secondly, a CDC spanning cohorts can smooth short-term variation in investment returns for those reaching retirement at an 'unlucky' point in time. A further advantage of a large fund with a wide age distribution of contributors is that funds can be invested in riskier assets for higher returns than can be achieved for a fund that provides for an individual as they approach retirement.

Ultimately, a CDC comes with a 'pressure valve' that allows target income in retirement, or the level of ongoing contributions, to be adjusted if there are significant shifts in longevity or economic returns. This flexibility was not introduced for DB schemes – which was to the benefit of existing members but made them unattractive for employers in the future. How the burden of any adjustments is distributed is a matter for agreement when creating any new CDC. Employers can still be expected to play an important role in making contributions to the scheme, but are not left carrying the entire risk burden of providing a previously promised pension income in the face of large shocks.

Even if the required legislative framework were already in place, it would likely take a number of years before such schemes could practically be up and running in the UK. And it would take far longer before they reached a steady state, with cohorts spending an entire working life in the scheme. That's why the government should take action now to remove remaining legislative obstacles that stand in the way of their development, and that are, for example, holding back the Royal Mail's attempt to create a CDC scheme.

19 Pensions Policy Institute, *Risk Sharing Pension Plans: The Canadian Experience*, October 2014 and Pensions Policy Institute, *Risk Sharing Pension Plans: The Dutch Experience*, October 2014

However, while it is certainly worth pursuing the establishment of CDC schemes in the medium term, we can more immediately replicate some of the advantages they bring in the accumulation phase in the existing DC market. For example, larger DC schemes provide sufficient economies of scale to allow a sharing of risk across scheme members such that riskier investment strategies can be pursued. In a similar fashion, larger schemes can charge lower running costs. There are also some forms of asset class that are simply inaccessible to all but very large funds – such as the long-term infrastructure projects in the UK which Canadian pension funds invest in.

Policy recommendation

Promote larger pensions schemes better able to share risk among savers, while laying the path for long-term development of 'collective defined contribution' schemes.

- The government should further advance legislation for the development of 'collective defined contribution' pension schemes.
- More immediately, the government should incentivise the defined contribution market to consolidate, in order to share investment risk across individuals and lower operating costs.

A strategy of moving towards consolidation of the DC market can help to bring about higher returns for individuals. Recent improved regulation of master trusts (pension funds covering multiple employers) is a potential first step of a strategy to build up fewer, bigger, pension funds. So far, regulations seek to ensure such schemes are well run and viable, but additional measures could promote wider consolidation of schemes. One such approach is a move towards capping fund management charges, making it more likely that larger, more efficient schemes remain in the long run. Rather than a simple test of viability, the efficiency of scheme management could also be assessed against market leaders, with under-performers encouraged to transfer scheme members into a superior fund.

Similar steps could be taken to allow smaller schemes, or members of smaller schemes, outside of the master trust system to transfer into larger funds. Finally, relating scheme membership to the individual rather than the employer could prevent the proliferation of smaller pots – one for each employment – and encourage a smaller number of large schemes that straddle many firms. The Pensions Dashboards now in development will provide an extremely useful tool for individuals to track their various pension pots and their value.[20] But we believe individuals will be better served if it were also easier to consolidate those pots.

20 See: *pensionsdashboardproject.uk*

Mitigating the risks associated with pension freedoms

The final part of a pension scheme is its primary purpose – providing an income in retirement. But there has been radical change in how people access their pension pots at retirement. The pension freedoms introduced by George Osborne in 2014 have given people far more choice in how they use their pension savings. Before the freedoms were introduced, new retirees were forced to purchase annuities with their DC pension by a fixed age, providing a guaranteed annual income for life that protected them against longevity risk, and (for the small minority who purchased inflation-linked products) the risk of price rises. The government imposed this obligation in order to avoid pensioners purposefully spending down their pension pots in order to become entitled to means-tested benefits. As means-testing was reduced so was the rationale for this intrusion in a personal decision. Now – with pension freedoms in place – people can generally access their pension pots earlier and dispose of their fund as they wish.

There are good arguments for giving pensioners more choice than the previous system provided, but the new approach also brings with it significant risks. For example, research by the Financial Conduct Authority suggests that recent retirees are twice as likely to opt for drawdown products as they are to take an annuity. This matters because they are then bearing the risk of how long they may live.[21]

Worryingly, one-in-three (37 per cent) of those accessing drawdown products does so without seeking financial advice. Overall, the share of products purchased without taking advice has increased from 3 per cent before the freedoms were introduced, to 30 per cent now. Inertia on the part of individuals appears to be a big factor, with 94 per cent of non-advised drawdown sales being to firms' existing customers as people unsurprisingly take the path of least resistance in a very complicated area.[22] For many this will include sensible options like accessing their tax-free lump sum. But a lack of good-quality information, and the sheer complexity of judging between the range of options available to pensioners, is also likely to have played a part.

Providing a more structured path for pensioners to engage with pension freedoms, alongside an easier route for individuals to protect themselves against uncertainty around how long they will live, should therefore be a priority. It would also provide an opportunity to introduce and develop products that do a better job of pooling longevity risk within cohorts before CDC schemes are put into place.

Instead of pension pot providers offering default options to their clients, people could be prompted to choose a product via an independent platform. This would be similar to the price comparison sites that exist for other financial products,

21 Financial Conduct Authority, *Retirement outcomes review: interim report*, July 2017

22 Financial Conduct Authority, *Retirement outcomes review: interim report*, July 2017

and could be delivered via the DWP Pension Wise platform (and ultimately by the new 'Single Financial Guidance Body' being set up by the Financial Guidance and Claims Bill).

More fundamentally, given the move away from annuities, individuals are now being asked to manage their savings in a manner that balances consumption with maintaining an adequate income stream until a very uncertainly timed death. Simply returning to the previous system of inflexible, early and compulsory annuitisation is unattractive. But there is a lot of ground between compulsion and a wholesale move away from guaranteed incomes for life. Instead, we believe a new approach should allow pensioners to benefit from a flexible system, but with a clear default pathway offering at least some guaranteed income for life – reducing a risk that it is rarely sensible for all but the richest individuals to bear. Such a default retirement income product would follow the strategy of auto-enrolment in harnessing inertia while helping to improve retirement outcomes.

This new default pathway should involve people reserving a portion of their pot into a new guaranteed 'Later Life Income' stream, in effect providing an annuity, but one that is purchased at a much later stage of retirement. Such a delay would remove a large part of the longevity-based uncertainty faced by annuity providers previously offering annuities at much earlier ages.

Consider, for example, that 85 per cent of the cohort born in 1953 (currently aged 64-65) still survive, but this will drop to 65 per cent by 2033 (when they will reach age 80).[23] A Later Life Income product purchased at this stage would achieve higher annual payments, thanks to the lower longevity risk premiums in place at age 80. This approach would also avoid the situation where pensioners resent giving almost all of their pension pot away in exchange for an annuity on retirement, when they know there is a risk that an early death makes this a very expensive purchase indeed. And it preserves an element of choice in how to use pension savings over much of retirement. New products should also seek to provide an inflation-indexed Later Life Income that is a competitive alternative to those paid in cash terms.

To further fuel competition and set a default standard, the government should work with large pension fund providers like NEST and The People's Pension to develop quality, low-cost Later Life Income products. This would allow competitive options of this form to be made available as a default option for new retirees, while still providing a range of product choice. That development should start now, in order to enable a product to be introduced by 2020. This new default approach would provide many more individuals with protection against longevity risk, while allowing individuals to retain their current freedoms by simply ignoring such defaults and doing what they choose with their pension savings.

23 RF analysis of ONS, *National Life Tables*

Policy recommendation

Reform pension freedoms by introducing a default product providing a guaranteed income in later life, and stimulate the market in retirement income products.

- The government should, by 2020, introduce a default product for those retiring which includes a 'Later Life Income', ring-fencing a share of pension pots to allow the purchase of a guaranteed income after the age of 80.
- The government should stimulate the market in retirement income products by preventing fund providers directly offering default retirement products when pots mature.

Retirement living standards for future pensioners will depend not only on their private saving and their access to and level of State Pension, but also on their interactions with the welfare state more generally. In particular, experiences will be shaped by the health and social care available to them. These and other challenges to the state's delivery of the intergenerational contract are the topic of the next chapter.

CHAPTER 11

The state – delivering for all generations

We recommend

An extra £2.3 billion of public funding for social care alongside modest user charges on assets, with protections so that no more than a quarter of assets can be depleted.

Supporting the rising health costs of the older population via a new 'NHS levy' that raises £2.3 billion initially, by charging National Insurance on the earnings of those above State Pension age and limited National Insurance on occupational pension income.

A 'citizen's inheritance' of £10,000 for all young adults to support skills, entrepreneurship, housing and pension saving. The citizen's inheritance would be funded by replacing inheritance tax with a lifetime receipts tax that has lower rates, fewer exemptions and is paid by recipients rather than estates.

Our approach to the role of the state

The welfare state is strongly supported by the public, in part reflecting its role in delivering the intergenerational contract. Just as families must rise to new challenges in this regard, if we want to maintain the ties that link the generations (see Box 11.1), so too must the state. Two crucial tasks stand out. The first is to deliver the health and care that older generations need. The second is to support younger generations hit hardest by the aftermath of the financial crisis and facing a harder time building up assets than at any point since World War II.

Delivering health and social care for older generations is no small undertaking. As we saw in Chapter 5, our ageing population – driven by the large baby boomer cohort moving into retirement – is set to push up public spending by £24 billion by 2030 and £63 billion by 2040. Paying for this via borrowing or the usual taxes on income and consumption would put disproportionate costs onto younger and future generations. Both approaches are unsustainable in the long run – neither the national debt nor income tax rates can rise indefinitely – and are clearly generationally unfair.

Cutting back provision would be deeply unfair too – hitting older generations at a stage of life when it is difficult to adapt, and exacerbating our failure to fulfil the generational contract when it comes to provision of a decent system of social care. There is widespread concern that this is the kind of outcome we are heading towards. When adults are asked to list the three topics that are the most worrying for the country, healthcare comes out top. Yet, while it is mentioned in 42 per cent of responses in Britain, it features in just 24 per cent of responses – and is only the fifth most pressing issue – when measured internationally.[1] Addressing this top concern in a way that is generationally fair is therefore a crucial challenge facing the welfare state.

Ensuring Britain has something to offer its young people in the 21st century is equally central to refreshing the intergenerational contract. This means properly discharging the classic roles for future generations of providing education, infrastructure, support in expensive life stages and healthy public finances. But there is more. Younger generations are bearing more risks and holding fewer assets than their predecessors. We need to redress that imbalance if we are to maintain the promise of an asset-owning democracy.

1 B Duffy, *What worries the world? January 2018*, Ipsos MORI, February 2018

Box 11.1 Generational support in our families and communities

Families are providing more intergenerational support than ever, in part as a response to the economic and demographic challenges we've described:

- There are 14 million parents in the UK bringing up children.[1]
- The provision of childcare by grandparents and other relatives has become increasingly important in recent decades, as maternal employment rates have risen.[2]
- 6.5 million people in the UK cared for an ill, older or disabled family member, friend or partner in 2011, an 11 per cent increase on a decade earlier.[3]
- At least a third, and potentially more than half, of first-time buyers have had help from family or friends to purchase a house in recent years.[4] The bank of mum and dad is estimated to have put up £6.5 billion for deposits in 2017, a 30 per cent increase on the previous year.[5]
- Inheritances have been increasing and are set to double over the next two decades. These trends are driven by a number of factors, not least growth in the value of primary residences. But bequest motives also appear to play a key part.[6]

However, as *The Pinch* argued, at the same time as we're spending more time (and money) supporting our own families, we're spending less time supporting different generations in our communities.[7] We need to complement what we do within families with a similar role for public policy. Otherwise there will be new barriers to social mobility and everyone will lose out through a deterioration in the kind of society they live in.

Tackling these kinds of problems is not just for national politicians. More opportunities to mix with and support those in other generations in our communities can have important societal benefits. For example, the work of United for All Ages has demonstrated the value of 'shared sites' such as the co-location of elderly care and childcare facilities.[8] And Homeshare UK promotes the practical, financial and social benefits of schemes that match usually older adults with spare rooms with unrelated adults in need of accommodation, in exchange for moderate support and companionship.[9] Efforts by local government to support endeavours such as these would appear an important complement to the policy choices we focus on in this chapter.

1 Data refers to 2017, and is based on the number of single parents with dependent children plus the number of adults living in cohabiting couples with dependent children. Source: RF analysis of ONS, *Families and households*

2 A Gray, 'The changing availability of grandparents as carers and its implications for childcare policy in the UK', *Journal of Social Policy*, 34(4), October 2005

3 Carers UK, *Facts about carers*, October 2015

4 The 2016-17 *English Housing Survey* suggests that 35 per cent of first-time buyers had help from family or friends. Estimates from the Council of Mortgage Lenders suggest that the proportion of first-time buyers purchasing with assistance was above 50 per cent in 2014, up from around 30 per cent in 2005. Source: MHCLG, *English Housing Survey*; B Clarke, 'New CML data shows nearly half of first-time buyers didn't use the 'bank of mum and dad'', *Council of Mortgage Lenders news*, 5 March 2015

5 Legal & General, *The Bank of Mum and Dad*, August 2017

6 *The million dollar be-question* (Intergenerational Commission report 13)

7 D Willetts, *The Pinch: How the Baby Boomers Took Their Children's Future – And Why They Should Give It Back*, Atlantic Books, September 2010

8 United for All Ages, *Mixing matters: How shared sites can bring older and younger people together and unite Brexit Britain*, January 2018

9 Homeshare UK, *Homeshare UK Sector Report 2017*, September 2017

While families are doing more and adjusting to the 21st century's challenges, the state has not fully adapted. This means that those without family support are at greater risk of missing out. A situation in which the intergenerational contract is increasingly left to families alone could undo the progress made on poverty and quality of life in old age; impose greater risks on young people; and potentially turn today's intergenerational inequalities into tomorrow's intra-generational ones. This chapter is therefore about how government can better play its part in maintaining the contract between the generations.

Underpinning a better-functioning social care system that addresses rising unmet need

Social care – particularly in England, which is the focus of our recommendations in this area[2] – provides the starkest evidence that the services that older people need are increasingly under pressure. Cuts to local authority budgets reduced real-terms spending per adult in England by 13.5 per cent between 2009-10 and 2016-17, with the full impact of these reductions much greater given growing demand for care services associated with the ageing population.[3]

These shifts have a human cost. The number of adults aged 65 and over in England who say that they do not get the care they need stood at 1.2 million in 2016, a figure that has doubled since 2010.[4] These growing levels of unmet need reflect the fact that many local authorities have dealt with tighter budgets by raising eligibility criteria for publicly funded care services, with the vast majority now supporting those with 'substantial' or 'critical' needs only.[5] The fact that families are increasingly dealing with gaps in provision (as demonstrated in Box 11.1) is evidence of the strength of the intergenerational contract, but it comes at an additional human cost when family carers miss days of work or leave employment altogether.[6]

Falling resource and rising unmet need add up to a funding shortfall for social care likely to total at least £2 billion in England.[7] This shortfall persists because there is no consensus about how the cost is best shared between those receiving care and the wider population.

The 2017 Conservative manifesto tried to break this deadlock by bringing additional resources into social care via higher private charges for those receiving it. The proposed mechanism was to include property assets in the means test for domiciliary care, but with a raised threshold (the asset floor). This had the merit of drawing on

2 While our recommendations focus on the English system of social care provision, our directions on changes to public funding would feed through across the nations of Britain.

3 P Simpson, *Public spending on adult social care in England*, Institute for Fiscal Studies, May 2017

4 '1.2m older people don't get the social care they need', *Age UK news*, November 2016

5 National Audit Office, *Adult social care in England: Overview*, March 2014

6 For a discussion of these challenges, see: *A silver lining for the UK economy?* (Intergenerational Commission report 16)

7 L Gardiner, 'Sticking plasters are welcome but, for the sake of all generations, a long-term solution for social care is required', *Resolution Foundation blog*, 10 March 2017

a stock of wealth in Britain that is growing, but is increasingly concentrated within older generations and very unequally distributed *within* them.

A focus on wealth is therefore an effective means for older generations to contribute to the funding of services from which they benefit, while protecting those with the fewest resources. In addition, wealth is also increasingly lightly taxed: Figure 11.1 shows that personal wealth has grown 2.5 times faster than the economy and hence incomes since 1980, but that wealth-related tax revenues have remained flat.

Figure 11.1: Wealth has risen in relation to GDP while wealth taxes have remained flat

Aggregate wealth and wealth-related taxes as proportions of GDP: GB/UK

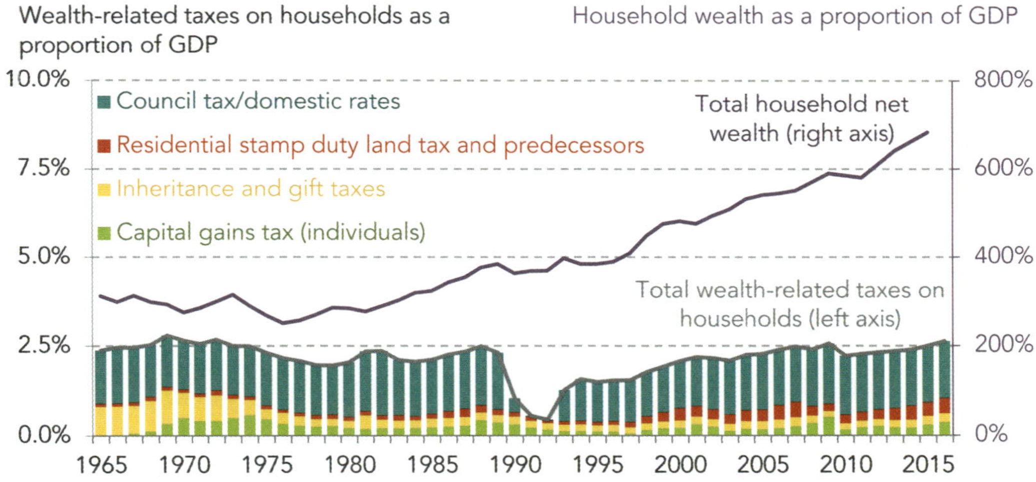

Notes: Total household net wealth covers Great Britain; tax and GDP data cover the UK. See notes to Figure 1 in: *Home affairs* (Intergenerational Commission report 18)

Source: RF analysis of ONS, *Wealth in Great Britain*; ISER, *British Household Panel Survey*; ONS, *UK National Accounts*; D Blake & J Orszag, 'Annual estimates of personal wealth holdings in the United Kingdom since 1948', *Applied Financial Economics*, 9, 1999; OECD.Stat

Nevertheless, the approach to social care funding in the 2017 Conservative manifesto had major drawbacks. At least as initially proposed, without the lifetime costs cap recommended by the Dilnot commission,[8] it would have left individuals with both significant assets and high social care needs exposed to the risk of extremely high costs indeed – potentially losing all but £100,000 of their assets. Even with a cap on lifetime costs (reinstated as a policy during the course of the 2017 General Election campaign), an individual's exposure to the bad luck of needing social care remained substantial.

In theory, because social care need is a risk that private insurance markets are generally not able to protect us against as individuals, a social insurance system largely free at the point of use and funded from wider taxation would have much to recommend

8 Department of Health, *Fairer Care Funding: The Report of the Commission on Funding of Care and Support*, July 2011

it.[9] But this is unlikely to be remotely feasible in the short-to-medium term, given that we face a major fiscal challenge just to pay for the current welfare state. A move to social insurance now would increase these funding pressures and create a strong incentive for lots of need currently met through family and friends to be brought into the state system.

The Intergenerational Commission has not reviewed in detail the design and delivery of social care across the UK. However, we recognise that social care funding has important implications for different generations. More public funding needs to be provided, but in a way that is fair between the generations. And as older generations also have substantial assets, it is right to ask individuals to make a limited contribution towards their own care costs where they are able to do so, but with proper protections.

Policy recommendation

Use £2.3 billion raised from a new progressive property tax to address gaps in public social care funding. Alongside this, introduce user charges on assets so wealthier individuals contribute towards their social care costs in England. However, set the asset floors and cost caps such that no more than a quarter of assets can be depleted.

– £2.3 billion of additional public funding for care should be delivered across Great Britain from 2020 (with funding rising thereafter), drawing on revenues from all administrations adopting the reformed property taxation set out in Chapter 9.[1] This amount of funding – delivered on top of additional revenues currently raised from the social care precept – would go a long way towards addressing shortfalls in England, alongside additional funding in devolved administrations.

– Housing assets should be brought into the scope of the means test across domiciliary and residential care settings in England.

– The government should set the level of the costs cap and asset floor so that no more than a quarter of assets can be depleted – via a £150,000-per-adult asset floor and a £50,000 cost cap.

– So that those paying towards their own domiciliary care are not required to sell their houses, local authorities should have reasonable deferred payment schemes – potentially aligned with deferred payment mechanisms for the new property tax.

1 After the cost of cuts to stamp duty is accounted for.

9 K Barker, *A new settlement for health and social care: Final report*, King's Fund, September 2014

Given that public spending on care is in practice controlled by eligibility criteria and the fees that councils negotiate for services, the result of higher public funding plus more individual charges would be a combination of more people getting the care they need and better-funded (and therefore likely better-quality) care.

Crucially, limited increases in individual contributions towards care costs along the lines we set out would likely not apply to the majority of people requiring care. As Figure 11.2 sets out, over half of adults aged 80 and over have total assets below the proposed threshold of £150,000.[10]

Figure 11.2: Over half of older adults would face no care costs on the basis of their assets under our proposed system

Distribution of family total net property and financial wealth per adult for adults aged 80 and over: GB, 2014-16

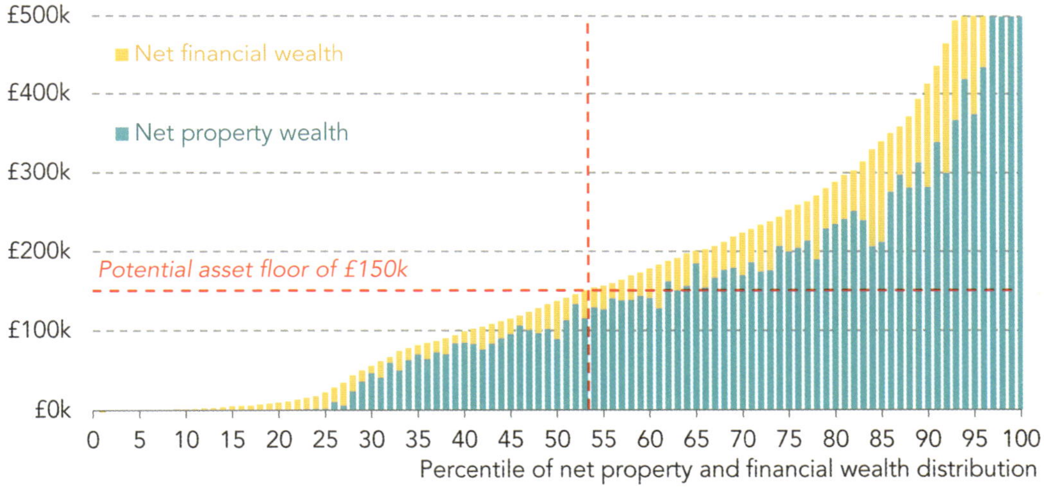

Notes: Data refers to older adults in Great Britain, however social care is a devolved policy area and our policy suggestions are directed at England.

Source: RF analysis of ONS, Wealth and Assets Survey

There would also be a greater degree of individual risk protection than the current system offers for those facing the highest care costs. As an illustration of the potential for risk reduction at the individual level, Figure 11.3 sets out a hypothetical profile of spending on care and proportional asset depletion under different financing systems in a high care costs scenario. While some individuals receiving domiciliary care would pay more, this approach equalises the treatment of different care settings,[11] and means no one would lose more than one-quarter of their assets or pay more than £50,000 in lifetime care costs. By underwriting the long tail of particularly high care costs, this costs cap might also stimulate the development of a private insurance

10 We suggest that the current system for means-testing on the basis of incomes is retained.

11 Currently the asset means test threshold is set at £23,250. For residential care this includes financial assets and property assets (unless someone else still lives in the property); for domiciliary care it includes financial assets only.

market for care, as envisaged when such an approach was originally proposed by the Dilnot commission.[12]

Figure 11.3: A system of care financing with a higher asset floor and a lower costs cap would provide more protection to those with high wealth or care needs

Illustrative example of spend on care and proportion of assets depleted for an individual with lifetime care costs of £150k (split £60k domiciliary, £90k residential), by asset level on going into care and care financing system: England

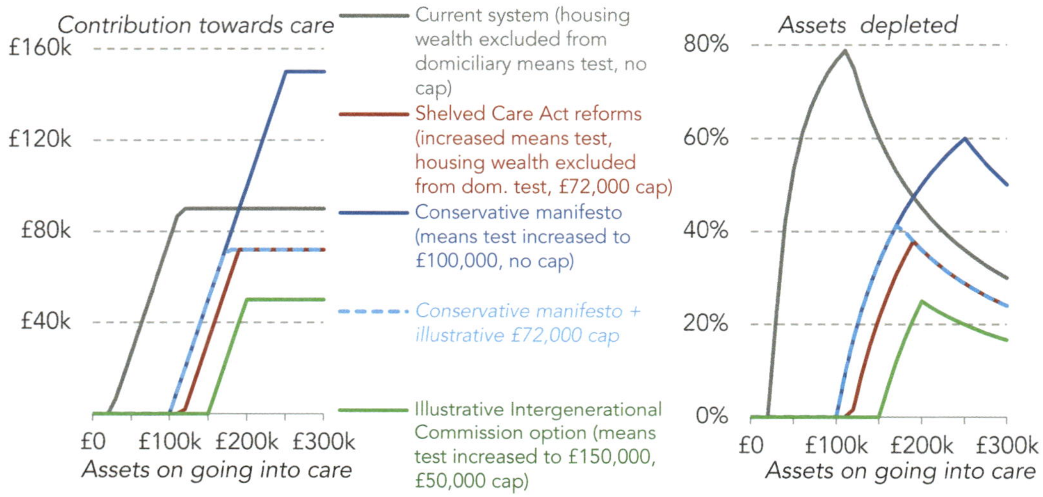

Notes: For simplicity, we assume that assets are all held in property. We assume individual income is just sufficient to cover a contribution to general living costs, but not high enough to affect income means tests. We assume constant prices with no changes to housing value. Currently the asset means test threshold is set at £23,250 across domiciliary and residential care settings, but with property assets excluded in the case of domiciliary care. The 'shelved' Care Act reforms included a means test of £118,000 for residential care and £27,000 for domiciliary care.

Source: RF modelling

There is no perfect approach. But with more collective sharing of costs via public funding and by asking those who have assets to contribute a bit more towards their own care, we can move towards a system that reduces risks for everyone and addresses the startling growth in unmet care needs facing an increasing number of families. And we can do this without imposing unfair burdens on younger generations who face quite enough pressures of their own.

Upholding the NHS for older generations

The NHS faces large funding requirements as well, and there will inevitably be tough decisions ahead around how we manage demand. We welcome the debate that is now opening up about possible new forms of tax to finance the NHS, but these ideas should not inadvertently place unfair burdens on younger generations. We set out new options for revenue-raising in the near term that have the potential to expand in the longer term as needs grow.

12 Department of Health, *Fairer Care Funding: The Report of the Commission on Funding of Care and Support*, July 2011

There is no easy solution, and raising new taxes should never be done lightly. Our search for new revenue sources is underpinned by three insights:

- that the age profile of additional taxation must shift upwards if we are to reduce potential generational inequities in welfare state funding, as set out in Chapter 5;
- that approaches to reform should recognise the growing importance of wealth in British society, its increasing concentration among those older generations that are the heaviest users of the NHS, and how lightly it is taxed at present; and
- that we should pursue a consistent and efficient tax system that is equitable.

With these insights in mind, there is a strong basis for tackling existing age-related inequalities in the tax system that favour older workers. Workers at or over the State Pension age currently pay no employee (or self-employed) National Insurance contributions (NICs). This exemption is now harder to justify given the significant weakening of National Insurance's role in driving a contributory system,[13] and leads to inconsistency in the treatment of otherwise-similar workers. While it is desirable to provide incentives and support for longer working lives – as discussed in Box 8.1 in Chapter 8 – our view is that this anachronism in the tax system can no longer be justified given the fiscal challenge we have set out.

Policy recommendation

As one element of a new 'NHS levy', charge employee and self-employed National Insurance contributions on the earnings of workers over the State Pension age, raising £0.9 billion in 2020.[1]

1 The policy captures Class 1 employee NICs and Class 4 NICs. Revenue estimates include the impact of population growth and rising labour market participation at different ages to 2020-21. For further details, see: *A budget for intergenerational fairness?* (Intergenerational Commission report 11)

Figure 11.4 shows the impact of this policy across both the age distribution and the income distribution of pensioners. Effects are concentrated on younger pensioners, and within the pensioner population they are highly progressive: four-fifths (82 per cent) of the additional revenue raised is drawn from the most affluent fifth of pensioners. Of course, these average effects hide big income reductions for some – an older employee earning £15,000 would be worse off by around £720 per year, for example. But that is only what younger workers are paying already. And it remains the case that both among pensioners and across the population as a whole, this is a measure that overwhelmingly affects better-off households.

13 S Adam & G Loutzenhiser, *Integrating Income Tax and National Insurance: An interim report*, Institute for Fiscal Studies, December 2011

Figure 11.4: NICs on pensioners' employment income is strongly progressive within the pensioner population

Impact of levying employee and self-employed NICs on pensioners' employment income, by age and pensioner income decile: UK, 2020-21

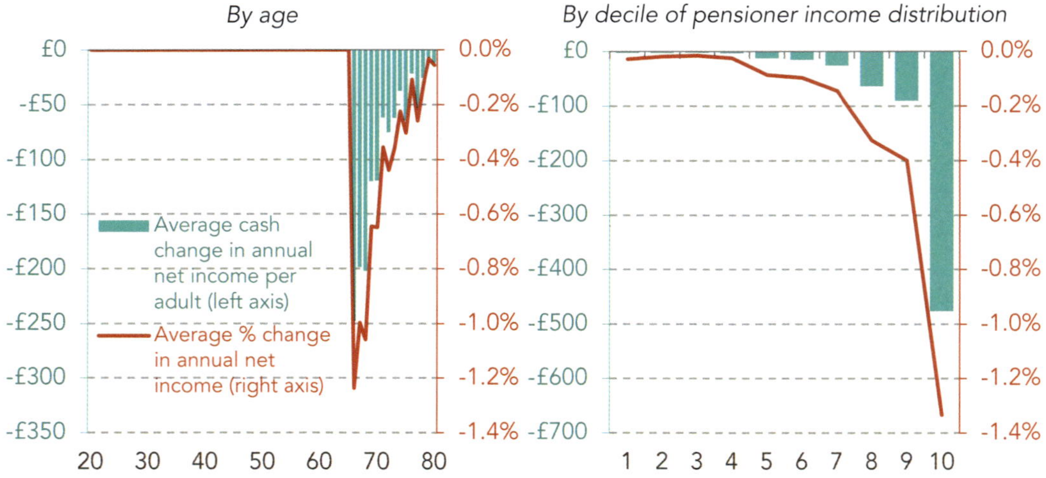

Notes: Pensioner income distribution based on equivalised net household incomes before housing costs of all adults aged 66 and over. See notes to Figure 8 in: *A budget for intergenerational fairness?* (Intergenerational Commission report 11)

Source: RF analysis using the IPPR tax-benefit model; ONS, *National Population Projections (2016-based)*; OBR, *Fiscal sustainability report – January 2017*, January 2017

Given the important but significant challenge of adequately funding the health care needs of older generations, the focus on National Insurance should not stop at pensioners' employment income. Drawing on all three of the points above – the age profile of taxation, the taxation of wealth and the efficiency and equity of the tax system – we see merit in considering the tax treatment of private pension income too.

A large part of the growing wealth concentrated in older generations is in private pension pots, but it is hard to tax as wealth. Instead, the tax treatment of pensions relates to when people are making contributions to them or drawing income from them. Yet there are real deficiencies in the current approach to NICs.[14]

As opposed to income tax, which is generally relieved in the contribution phase and levied in the drawdown phase, NICs are not applied to private pensions when they are drawn down. They are charged on employee contributions, but not on employer contributions. This distinction has a big effect on how much National Insurance is paid, with employer contributions accounting for around three-quarters of the total paid into both defined benefit and defined contribution schemes (having comprised an even larger share in the past when employee contributions to defined benefit schemes were less common).[15]

14 For details, see: S Adam, J Browne & P Johnson, *Pensioners and the tax and benefit system*, Institute for Fiscal Studies, 2012

15 Source: ONS, *Occupational Pension Schemes Survey*

The different treatment of employer and employee contributions does not appear to be justified. This is one reason for our recommendation in the previous chapter that employee NICs on employee contributions be removed as part of rebalancing pensions tax reliefs. But such a move would still leave pensions generously treated in terms of NICs unless we complete the move to a system more similar to that for income tax and switch the incidence of employee NICs to the pensions drawdown phase.

Such an approach has a number of merits. For example, it offers the – generationally fair – opportunity to raise revenue to fund health costs from the cohorts that will disproportionately use these services. An alternative approach – extending NICs to employer contributions in the savings phase for example – would amount to 'grand-fathering' the benefits from a system of relatively light taxation that older cohorts have enjoyed, at the expense of younger ones.

Reforming the system along the lines we suggest would also leave pensions relatively tax-favoured. For example, we do not propose levying *employer* NICs on pension income, and many people will pay a lower rate of tax in retirement than they received tax relief for in working age. In addition, the option of taking a capped tax-free lump sum will remain.

The key challenge to any reform in this area is the issue of 'double taxation' regarding the minority of contributions made by employees that incurred employee NICs in the savings phase. This challenge would dissipate over time as the abolition of employee NICs beds in. And in the short- to medium-term it can be effectively met via a phase-in period at low rates, along with specific measures of redress.

Policy recommendation

As the second element of a new 'NHS levy', place a charge that mirrors employee National Insurance contributions on private occupational pension income, but initially at half the main rate and with a higher starting threshold.

- The levy should be introduced with a lower primary rate (6 per cent) and higher primary threshold (the personal tax allowance, estimated to be £12,360 in 2020) to minimise 'double taxation' of the minority of pension contributions made by employees. This approach would raise £1.4 billion in 2020.[1]

- Beyond this, a redress mechanism should be available for exceptional circumstances so that anyone whose pension pot was disproportionately drawn from employee contributions can be protected from double taxation.

1 Our approach essentially treats all income from occupational pensions combined as a single 'job' for NICs purposes. We exclude personal pensions arranged by individuals to which contributions are made out of income, as these have incurred – and will continue to incur – NICs in the contribution phase.

– Over time – as health needs rise and as the abolition of employee National Insurance on employee pension contributions beds in – the primary rate and threshold should gradually move closer to the rates of employee NICs. This transition would eventually bring annual revenues to above £4 billion.

Like our proposed reforms to NICs on pensioners' employment income, this measure is strongly progressive within the pensioner population.[16] Figure 11.5 shows that four-fifths (78 per cent) of the incidence within the pensioner population falls on the richest fifth of pensioners. Only 14 per cent of pensioners would be affected by this proposal, and only 1 per cent of pensioners in the bottom half of the pensioner income distribution.

Figure 11.5: A NICs-based 'NHS levy' on occupational pension income is progressive within the pensioner population

Impact of levying employee NICs (but with a reduced main rate of 6 per cent, and only on earnings above the personal tax allowance) on occupational pension income, by pensioner income decile: UK, 2020-21

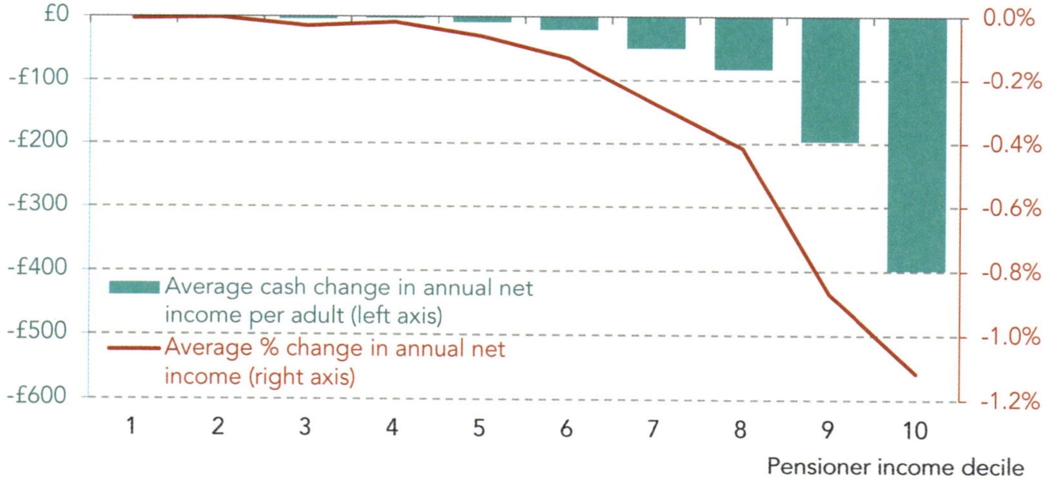

Notes: Distribution based on equivalised net household incomes before housing costs of all adults aged 66 and over. Estimates include the impact of population change at different ages to 2020-21.

Source: RF analysis using the IPPR tax-benefit model; ONS, *National Population Projections (2016-based)*

Changes to taxes are never easy. But properly funding the NHS right across the UK and our social care system in the coming decades is essential if we want to make good on our promise to older generations, quell the public's healthcare anxieties and reshape the intergenerational contract for the challenges of the 21st century. Our approach entails similar levels of additional public funding for healthcare and for social care. These are drawn from the taxation of property, of pension income and of earnings, all of which are concentrated among better-off older adults. Alongside these increased tax revenues we propose a modest expansion of social care charges based on individuals' assets.

16 71 per cent of revenues are drawn from the pensioner population, the remainder coming from those receiving private pensions before State Pension age.

While the revenues we outline do not negate the need for any other tough decisions to be made, they would represent an important step. They also have the potential to deliver more in future. They face up to a key challenge that the welfare state is confronted with in a way that is fair both between and within generations.

Maintaining state support for younger generations that predecessors benefitted from

Delivering the health and care that older generations deserve, need and expect will not be enough to set the intergenerational contract on the right path, even if done in a way that avoids putting extra pressure on the resources of younger generations, as we suggest. Just as important is ensuring that we support members of younger generations as they face today's challenges rather than yesterday's.

The significant new task here is the growing importance of assets in shaping lives and opportunities: we turn to this issue below. But there is also the question of ensuring that we are not reneging on the functions that the welfare state delivered to previous generations.

One of these is providing a safety net to those who experience periods of low income, especially at those life-stages when costs are high and incomes possibly lower – such as when children are young. We showed in Chapter 5 that there are clear short-run differences in the age groups that have borne the brunt of recent tax and welfare changes due to big reductions in working-age benefits. There are many pressures on spending in the coming decades, but our view is that cuts to working-age benefits are being delivered in a way that bears down too heavily on the least well-off members of younger generations. In the case of some of these cuts, a rethink is now required.

The abolition of the cash freeze on most working-age benefits in April next year would mean that they rise by a projected 2.4 per cent. Figure 11.6 shows that more than half the benefits would flow to millennials, who will be aged 21-40 in 2020.

Policy recommendation

Lift the benefits freeze a year early, uprating working-age benefits in line with inflation in April 2019, at a cost of £1.7 billion.[1]

– This change should be funded on the basis that over its lifespan this freeze will have saved the Exchequer around £1.2 billion more than intended when it was introduced in 2015, due to higher-than-expected inflation.[2]

1 For consistency with other costings in this chapter, this figure refers to the cost of the policy in 2020.

2 D Finch, 'Let it go Chancellor. Why Philip Hammond should revisit the benefit freeze in next month's Budget', *Resolution Foundation blog*, 15 October 2017

And the measure is strongly progressive within the millennial generation, boosting incomes by around 1 per cent on average for the poorest fifth.

The current budget is back in surplus and the Chancellor has signalled that he is prepared to increase public spending in this year's Autumn Budget if the public finance outlook remains healthy. As such, now is the time to reduce the pressures that welfare cuts are putting on working-age families.[17]

Figure 11.6: Reversing certain welfare cuts is merited from an intergenerational perspective

Impact of un-freezing working-age benefits in April 2019, by age: UK, 2020-21

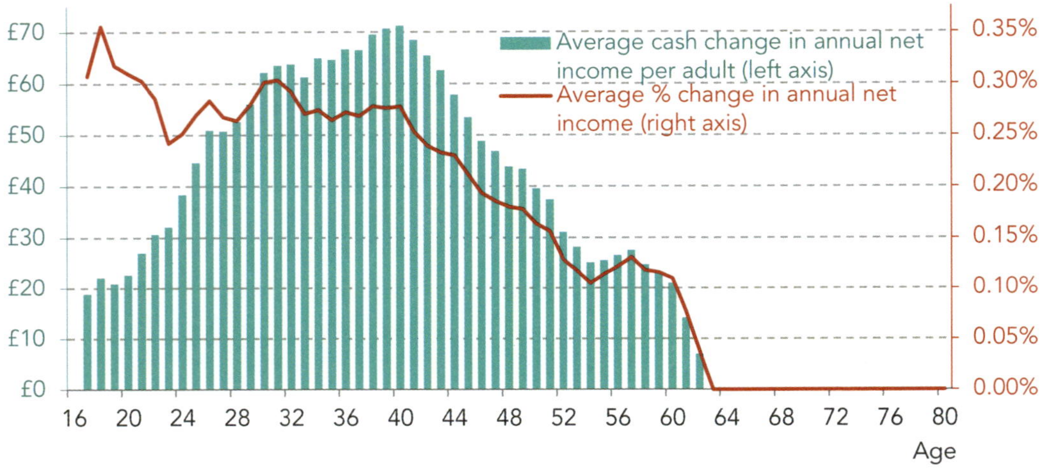

Notes: Estimates include the impact of population change at different ages to 2020-21.

Source: RF analysis using the IPPR tax-benefit model; ONS, *National Population Projections (2016-based)*

But this fiscal turning point should not lead to complacency. As we set out in Chapter 5, national debt is not materially falling and sits at double pre-crisis levels. And UK public investment has been on a downward path for some time. Arresting these trends is a key part of delivering to younger and future generations the healthy public finances and resources that their predecessors were bequeathed. This is essential for the state to maintain the intergenerational contract – a contract that binds many generations and not just those that come into contact with each other during lifetimes.

17 Resolution Foundation, *Sugar Rush: Spring Statement response*, March 2018

Policy recommendation

Maintain the commitment to increase public investment in infrastructure while sustainably reducing debt over the medium term.

Supporting asset accumulation within younger generations

The state's role in funding our healthcare system or providing income support for those in need rests on a deeper responsibility – helping us as individuals to bear risks that are difficult to manage alone. The nation state is the most effective mechanism we have to pool risk. It can also invest in young people when many of them cannot access the resources to do so themselves, ensuring that as a country we have something to offer each young person whatever their background.

We have shown that younger cohorts are losing out on asset accumulation, with lower rates of home ownership and far less access to defined benefit pensions. The vision of the asset-owning democracy is receding. Yet we do not live our lives as individuals, but as families that go to great lengths to mutually support each other, as shown in Box 11.1. One aspect of that support which has grown significantly in recent years and will grow fast in future is intergenerational wealth transfers – be that parental gifts or inheritances. Not only will these become more common, but they will grow in size much faster than our incomes.[18]

The result is that a major and growing factor in our lifetime living standards will be what we inherit, rather than what we earn. This poses challenges: many will not inherit, and those who will are likely to receive this support shortly before retirement rather than in the expensive family-raising years. But there is also an opportunity here to address the lack of assets being built up in younger generations by harnessing some of the greater flow of private intergenerational wealth transfers to deliver a modest asset inheritance for *all* young adults.

There are major weaknesses in the existing approach to taxing gifts and inheritances, contributing to inheritance tax raising only around £5 billion each year. It is charged at 40 per cent on the value of estates at death, but the first £325,000 is excluded. And, since 2007, this £325,000 allowance can be passed to spouses if unused. That gives an effective threshold of £650,000 for many couples (transfers between spouses are tax-exempt too). By 2020, each person will also be allowed to give an additional £175,000 tax-free to direct descendants if in the form of a main residence, taking the combined tax threshold to £1 million for many. This means that while inheritances are rising fast, inheritance tax revenues are projected not to keep up.[19] Lifetime gifts

18 For details, see: *The million dollar be-question* (Intergenerational Commission report 13)

19 *Passing on* (Intergenerational Commission report 21)

are only brought into the scope of the tax if given within seven years of the donor passing away.

Despite raising so little, inheritance tax is unpopular. One reason is its high marginal rate, which leaves some fearing they will lose almost half of their estate. Another is that it is seen as a tax on the thrift and generosity of the giver, rather than on the luck of the recipient. Major exemptions further undermine public support by leaving the system open to accusations that the truly wealthy are able to avoid paying their fair share.

For example, the exemption intended to prevent families being forced to sell family businesses on death has ended up allowing people to easily invest uncapped amounts in companies with which they have no previous link – purely to avoid an inheritance tax bill. Similarly, carve-outs for agricultural assets designed to stop farms being broken up have instead led to some very wealthy individuals buying up huge tracts of land for tax planning purposes. While much attention has focused on the use of trusts to reduce inheritance tax bills, that opportunity has been significantly reduced following reforms in 2006.[20] And crucially, those who are able to can easily plan to minimise or avoid inheritance tax simply by giving earlier in life.

If the state is to respond to the growing importance of income from gifts and inheritances to individuals' lifetime living standards, then the current approach to taxing these transfers cannot be sustained. Significant reform is needed.

Policy recommendation

Abolish inheritance tax and replace it with a lifetime receipts tax with lower rates and fewer exemptions. This should be levied on recipients, with a tax-free allowance to encourage broadly shared inheritances.

- Each recipient should have a lifetime receipts tax allowance of £125,000 (rising with inflation). Beyond this threshold, any new gifts or inheritances received would be taxed – at significantly lower rates than the current system. Lifetime receipts above the allowance and up to £500,000 should be taxed at a basic rate of 20 per cent; with receipts above £500,000 being taxed at 30 per cent. Despite lower rates, this structure would raise an additional £5 billion initially, with revenues rising over time as inheritances grow and the lifetime allowances bed in.
- Transfers between spouses and small gifts (up to £3,000) should remain exempt.
- Within this reform, exemptions should be restricted by: capping the amount of business or agricultural property that an individual can receive tax relief on; limiting those reliefs to

20 For further details, see: *Passing on* (Intergenerational Commission report 21)

'real' farmers and business owners through new tests and extended minimum ownership periods; abolishing the tax-free treatment of pension pots inherited on deaths before the age of 75; and limiting the forgiveness of capital gains tax at death.[1]

1 For further details on these provisions, see: *Passing on* (Intergenerational Commission report 21)

This reform in itself – by switching the incidence of tax to recipients – would encourage the spreading of intergenerational wealth transfers. But on its own it does not go far enough, not least because the timing of receipts for those who get them may very often be quite late in life. That is why, in addition, the extra revenues from the replacement of inheritance tax with a lifetime receipts tax should underpin a modest amount of asset accumulation for all young adults.

Some form of asset ownership, or the ability to rely on parents, plays an important part in young adults' ability to bear risk and take chances on their careers. Evidence from the US shows, for example, that those with well-off parents are much more likely to be innovators (measured in terms of patent-holding).[21] European studies have shown that after controlling for other factors, tolerance for risk increases as wealth increases, with the effects larger at lower levels of wealth. But other background risks reduce these effects – pointing to the importance of policies directly addressing the insecurities young people are facing.[22]

While we have put forward reforms in previous chapters that would support the accumulation of housing wealth, pensions and human capital within younger generations, an essential part of asset ownership or access to parental resources is the scope they provide for individuals to choose which of these ends to pursue. Assets give people options. More widespread asset ownership among the young has a role to play both in reducing the risks they face and encouraging more positive risk-taking – such as retraining, moving jobs or starting companies – that could have economic as well as individual benefits.

Supporting asset accumulation when young has been a policy focus in recent decades – from Labour's Child Trust Fund to the Conservative Party's Help to Buy and Lifetime ISAs. We take inspiration from these approaches, but our view is that some of their significant reliance on 'matching' savings rather than upfront endowments can depress uptake and concentrate it among better-off young adults.[23]

If the state is to play a role in endowing young adults with assets, key questions include the age at which they should be accessed and the degree of restrictions on their use. Our view is that 25 or older is an appropriate age – after formal education, when careers are taking shape, when young adults are old enough to make choices about the careers they

21 A Bell et al., *Who Becomes an Inventor in America? The Importance of Exposure to Innovation*, National Bureau of Economic Research, November 2017

22 L Guiso & M Paiella, 'Risk Aversion, Wealth, and Background Risk', *Journal of the European Economic Association*, 6(6), December 2008

23 For further details, see: *The new wealth of our nation* (Intergenerational Commission report 22)

will pursue and where they will put down roots. To ensure that funds are viewed as assets rather than serving as income, we favour restrictions on use – but ones that are diverse enough to maintain choice on the part of individuals.

As well as a reformed system for taxing intergenerational wealth transfers, this proposal for assets distributed widely across younger generations enables us to maintain the intergenerational contract in the 21st century. Britain will clearly have something to offer all young people, whoever their parents might be.

Policy recommendation

Introduce a 'citizen's inheritance' – an asset endowment to all young adults who entered the labour market during the financial crisis and since – to support skills, entrepreneurship, housing and pension saving.

- From 2030, citizen's inheritances (CIs) of £10,000 should be available from the age of 25 to all British nationals or people born in Britain as restricted-use cash grants, at a cost of £7 billion per year.
- To reflect the experiences of those who entered the labour market during and since the financial crisis, and to minimise cliff edges between recipients and non-recipients, the introduction of CIs should be phased in, starting with 34- and 35-year-olds receiving £1,000 in 2020. Each subsequent year, CI amounts should then rise and be paid to younger groups until the policy reaches a steady-state in 2030, with CIs paid to 25-year-olds only from then on.
- The CI should have four permitted uses: funding education and training (including paying off tuition fee debt); deposits for rental or home purchase; investment in pensions; and start-up costs for new businesses that are also being supported through recognised entrepreneurship schemes.
- CI should count against individuals' £125,000 lifetime receipts tax allowance, ensuring the system is progressive while still bringing forward the timing of 'inheritances' for those set to get one.
- The CI should be funded principally via the new lifetime receipts tax, with additional revenues from terminating existing matched savings schemes – the Help to Buy and Lifetime ISAs – that benefit better-off young adults. The abolition of these schemes is estimated to raise over £1 billion in the medium term.[1]

1 For further details on this policy, see: *The new wealth of our nation* (Intergenerational Commission report 22)

An illustrative roll-out schedule for a citizen's inheritance on this scale is provided in Table 11.1.

Table 11.1: Illustrative roll-out schedule and costs of a citizen's inheritance

Year	Number of recipients	Minimum age of recipients	Birth cohort of recipients	Citizen's inheritance amount	Cost
2020	1,454k	34-35	1985-86	£1,000	£1.5bn
2021	1,447k	33-34	1987-88	£2,000	£2.9bn
2022	1,450k	32-33	1989-90	£3,000	£4.4bn
2023	1,478k	31-32	1991-92	£4,000	£5.9bn
2024	1,430k	30-31	1993-94	£5,000	£7.2bn
2025	1,391k	29-30	1995-96	£6,000	£8.3bn
2026	1,386k	28-29	1997-98	£7,000	£9.7bn
2027	1,351k	27-28	1999-00	£8,000	£10.8bn
2028	1,308k	26-27	2001-02	£9,000	£11.8bn
2029	1,353k	25-26	2003-04	£10,000	£13.5bn
2030	705k	25	2005	£10,000	£7.0bn

Notes: The transition period is shaded yellow, the beginning of the steady-state period is shaded green. For further details, see: *The new wealth of our nation* (Intergenerational Commission report 22)

Source: RF analysis of ONS, *Labour Force Survey*; RF modelling

This approach would have a significant impact on the asset-holdings and opportunities of young adults in Britain. First and foremost, it would markedly increase the assets of the vast majority: as Figure 11.7 shows, the wealth of nearly two-thirds (62 per cent) of 25-29-year-olds in Britain would be at least doubled if a £10,000 CI were handed down today.[24] It would also reduce the Gini coefficient (a measure of inequality on which a higher value represents higher inequality) on net wealth within this age group, from well above to in line with the national average for all ages (0.87 to 0.66).

Figure 11.7: A £10,000 citizen's inheritance would more than double the wealth of nearly two-thirds of adults in their late 20s if they received it today

Distribution of family total net wealth per adult for 25-29-year-olds with and without a £10,000 citizen's inheritance: GB, 2014-16

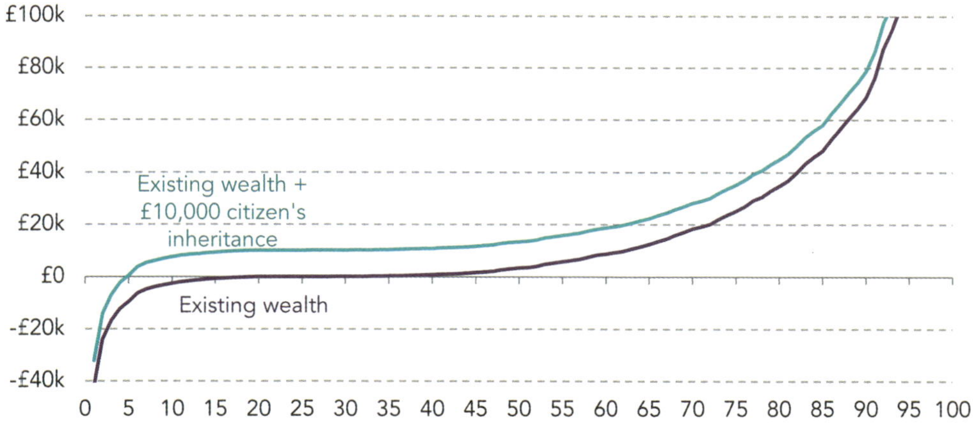

Notes: Excludes physical wealth.

Source: RF analysis of ONS, *Wealth and Assets Survey*

24 It should be noted that we might expect the value of wealth to have grown by the time the citizen's inheritance reaches its £10,000 steady state value in 2030, meaning its impact across the wealth distribution would be lower.

Additionally, a citizen's inheritance would open up significant opportunities in its areas of use. For example, it would provide two-fifths of the average home deposit for a first-time buyer in the UK. In half the regions and nations of the UK, it would cover more than half the average first-time buyer deposit. It would also be more than sufficient to cover multiple rental deposits (typically six weeks' rent). This would help young adults moving between private rented accommodation for reasons such as a new job, and overcome the challenge of putting down a new deposit before the old one has been returned.

A CI would support significant additional education and training, being comparable in generosity to the current loan available for master's degree tuition fees (£10,609 for the 2018-19 academic year). Additionally, it would be sufficient to pay off just under a third of average outstanding student loan debt for the typical graduate who started university in 2012 or later, under the £9,000-per-year tuition fee loan regime. However, this might not be a prudent use of the CI, given that loan repayments are income-contingent rather than resembling conventional debt.

Crucially – and in contrast to most other proposed policy changes for reducing tuition fee debt – a citizen's inheritance would provide support to graduates (whether used to pay off student debt or for other purposes) who have faced increased tuition fees[25] in a way that avoids additional public spending benefiting mainly (higher-earning) graduates at the expense of lower-earning graduates or non-graduates.[26]

As well as helping with costs associated with moving or retraining for work, a CI would support choices about *how* to work by providing a significant amount of the estimated start-up requirements of a new business.[27] Alternatively, saved into a defined contribution pension at age 25, the CI would add an estimated £45,000 to pension pots at the age of 68.[28]

This report has set out the challenges facing young adults, many of whom are building up fewer assets and experiencing little or no living standards progress on their predecessors while also bearing more risks. Assets provide security in and of themselves and act as a potential route to accumulate further assets. They are also a basis for positive risk-taking, for example to get careers moving by retraining or moving for work. For these reasons, a citizen's inheritance at the age at which it is most needed and for all young British adults would represent a bold demonstration that the state's role in delivering the intergenerational contract can evolve for the 21st century.

25 Importantly, it should be noted that these higher costs have come in exchange for the opportunity for more within each cohort to go to university given the lifting of the cap on student numbers. But for those who would have gone to university no matter the fee regime and will earn enough to pay off student debt in full under any fee regime, it should be noted that the proposed roll-out of a CI through cohorts experiencing higher fees than predecessors (the increase to £3,000-per-year tuition fees captured roughly the 1988-93 cohorts, with £9,000-per-year tuition fees thereafter) would provide something in the way of compensation for the higher personal expense they now bear.

26 Proposals such as reducing the interest rate on student loan debt, for example, are regressive within each cohort of graduates because they do not benefit lower earners unlikely to pay off their capital. Wiping out all tuition fee debt would require large amounts of public spending which non-graduates would not benefit from. For a fuller discussion, see: P Johnson, 'A birthday present that could solve the university tuition fees dilemma', *The Times*, 11 July 2017

27 For further details on all of these costings and uses, see: *The new wealth of our nation* (Intergenerational Commission report 22)

28 In line with our analysis in Chapter 4, we assume an average real annual return of 3.6 per cent over working life.

Upholding the intergenerational contract in democratic decision-making

The bold steps outlined in this report might seem a tough ask of politicians. In particular, the sheer size of the baby boomer cohort – some members of which would be asked to contribute more to deliver the changes we call for – and the greater propensity for older adults to vote might appear a stumbling block.

We do not underestimate the challenge of significant change, but in our view these objections can be overdone. First, people do not vote in generational blocs, and are often as concerned for the prospects of their families and neighbours as they are for their own. For example, support for local house building doubled between 2010 and 2016, with the rate of increase in the baby boomer generation the same as at younger ages.[29]

Second, while still large, the age-related turnout gap narrowed in the 2017 General Election, as Figure 11.8 shows. In particular, it was not the 'youth' vote as normally defined but a higher likelihood of voting among those in their 30s that was most significant to turnout increases – exactly the group that our analysis has shown is carrying the hangover of the financial crisis into the family-raising years.[30] So democratic age divides are not as large as they have been.

Figure 11.8: The age-related turnout gap narrowed slightly in the 2017 election

Estimated turnout at General Elections, by age group: UK

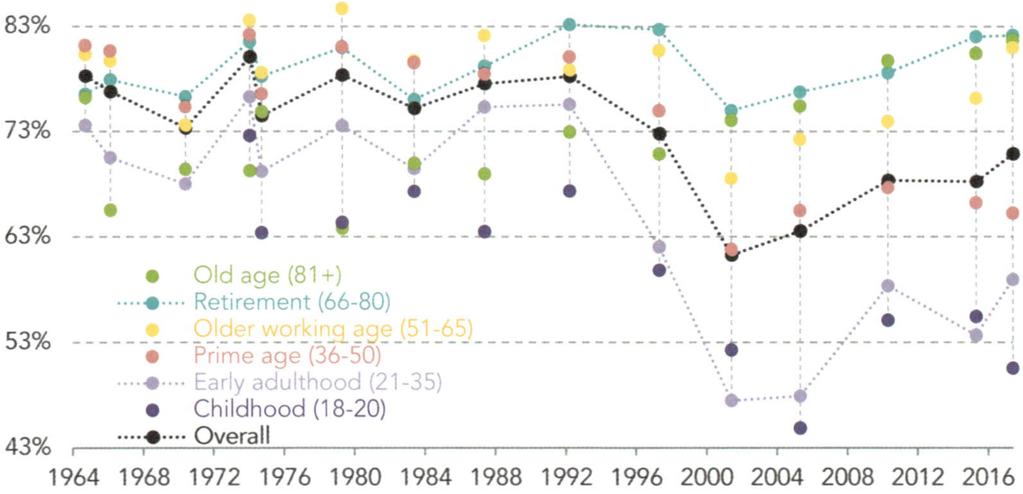

Notes: The measure of turnout used is the number of voters as a share of the eligible population, which excludes non-nationals. For further details, see: *Votey McVoteface* (Intergenerational Commission report 2)

Source: RF analysis of *British Election Study; UK Political Info*; ONS, *Mid-Year Population Estimates*; ONS, *Labour Force Survey*

29 The proportion of adults saying they would support more homes being built in their local area increased from 30 per cent to 58 per cent between 2010 and 2016. Among baby boomers, the proportion rose from 28 per cent to 57 per cent. Source: RF analysis of NatCen, *British Social Attitudes Survey*

30 C Prosser et al., *The myth of the 2017 youthquake election*, British Election Study, January 2018

Nonetheless, given the increasing 'lock-in' effects of voting when first eligible and the decline in first-time-eligible turnout in recent decades,[31] there are steps we could take as part of the electoral process to give the intergenerational contract the best chance to adapt.

Policy recommendation

Engender engagement in the democratic process for each successive cohort by lowering the voting age and automatically registering young adults attending school, college and university to vote.

- The government should set a path for extending the franchise to 16- and 17-year-olds.
- Young adults attending school, college and university should be automatically registered to vote by these institutions. Coupled with a lower voting age, this would mean that the majority of young adults would be in education for their first eligible election, and educational institutions should encourage voting and citizenship education.[1]

1 For further details on these recommendations, see: *Votey McVoteface* (Intergenerational Commission report 2)

We have shown that families are adapting to the challenges facing the intergenerational contract. While fulfilling this contract is something the state has always done, doing it properly today means bold steps to address these new challenges. The policy agenda set out in this chapter is a means for doing so in a way that both older and younger generations can benefit from.

31 *Votey McVoteface* (Intergenerational Commission report 2)

SECTION 5

CONCLUSION

CHAPTER 12

A better, more united Britain

Families do not think in terms of baby boomers, generation X and millennials; their focus is on mums, dads, sons and daughters. That is why the intergenerational contract sits so firmly at the heart of our society. For reasons of both love and self-interest, we go to huge lengths to support each other at different life-stages. We deliver this support naturally through our families, and as a society we have carefully constructed our welfare state to play the same role.

Yet the contract is under threat. Not because of any change in public sentiment – the country continues to wholeheartedly buy into the concept – but rather because of a number of emerging challenges to our ability to deliver on the intergenerational promise. An ageing society brings the advantages of longer lives, but also significant financial pressures that put at serious risk the health and care services that older generations deserve, need and expect. Meanwhile the combination of the fall-out from the financial crisis and deeper, structural shifts in our labour, housing and pensions markets means that 21st century Britain is not living up to its promises for younger generations. Facing tough times, we cannot simply assume young adults will enjoy the living standards progress that seemed to be an inevitable feature of the 20th century.

Over the course of the Intergenerational Commission's two-year investigation, we have gathered much evidence on the challenges facing members of our different generations. And we have uncovered much to celebrate too, about the ways in which families continue to pull together. Increasing numbers care for elderly relatives and the 'bank of mum and dad' now rivals the UK's biggest mortgage lenders in terms of scale. But protecting and strengthening the intergenerational contract requires society, not just our families, to act.

Doing so is no easy task. We cannot wish away the effects of the financial crisis nor our demographic challenges. New thinking and tough choices on a significant scale are required. Some will see these challenges, set them against Britain's unstable political and economic backdrop, and conclude nothing can be done. But as a country we have proved ourselves capable of taking bold action to sustain the intergenerational contract numerous times in the past – introducing the State Pension at the beginning of the 20th century, building homes for the children of the post-war baby boom, and increasing access to university education in the 1990s.

The proposals we have set out in this report are inevitably, at times, difficult. But they are practical and implementable – ours is a policy agenda that Britain can deliver. We do not expect political parties to embrace them immediately, but hope that as the important issues we identify are increasingly recognised, our proposals can be a useful guide to action.

If we once again step up to the challenge of keeping the intergenerational contract strong, we will not only have a better Britain but a more united one.

Our policy recommendations

Jobs and pay – progress in work

Introduce a £1 billion 'Better Jobs Deal' – an active labour market programme offering practical support and funding for younger workers most affected by the financial crisis to take up opportunities to move jobs, change region for work, or train to progress.

Boost pay progression via new sector deals in lower-paying sectors as part of the industrial strategy, and provide new guidance on pay review processes within businesses to improve transparency.

Improve security for self-employed, atypical and the lowest-paid workers via extended statutory rights and greater certainty around working hours.

Enhance the rights of unions to speak to employees in their workplace and encourage innovation in models of worker organising, including reduced union membership rates for the young and better use of technology.

Ensure that apprenticeships are underpinned by rigorous regulation of quality; engage with employers flexibly on T Levels to ensure that the targeted volume of work placements can be delivered; and maintain high-quality specialist technical provision that does not fit neatly within these routes.

Ensure lifelong learning options are available to lower-qualified young people who will not benefit from post-16 technical reforms but who are struggling in today's labour market.

Boost the funding of technical education provision and underpin the 'Better Jobs Deal' by cancelling 1p of the corporation tax cut planned for 2020.

Houses – renovating the market

Introduce indeterminate tenancies as the sole form of private rental contract available in England and Wales, following Scotland's lead.

Introduce light-touch rent stabilisation that limits rent rises to CPI inflation for set three-year periods.

Establish a housing tribunal system which has powers to adjudicate on possession applications and challenges to rent rises.

Bring England into line with the rest of the UK by requiring landlords to register with their local authority.

Revisit housing benefit rules to improve support for younger families on low-to-middle incomes.

Limit future Help to Buy equity loans to those with an annual household income of less than £60,000 a year.

Replace council tax with a progressive property tax – including a tax-free allowance and multiple tax bands – that is related to up-to-date values.

Halve stamp duty so it supports property purchases by first-time buyers and movers and retain a higher tax rate on the purchase of additional properties.

Give city and city-region mayors the authority to limit residential property purchases in housing hot-spots to those resident in the UK.

Introduce a time-limited cut to capital gains tax for owners of additional properties selling to first-time buyers.

Create a unit of highly skilled planners in central government to support local authorities in areas of high housing need, and with a full five-year land supply, to deliver high-quality developments.

Homes England should support five local authorities that are prepared to pilot community land auctions by 2020.

Support the development of the build-to-rent sector by exempting from the stamp duty surcharge on additional properties any institutional investors that either construct build-to-rent properties or buy them within five years of construction.

Reform the viability process to ensure that builders deliver on their up front affordable homes commitments except in exceptional circumstances.

Allow local authorities to raise additional money to build new homes via a property tax building precept and new borrowing flexibilities.

Pensions – saving for tomorrow

Maintain the value of the new State Pension relative to earnings at a slightly higher level than the current position, funded by freezing 'protected payments'.

To maintain fairness between generations, continue to link the State Pension age to longevity, aiming to provide a broadly consistent share of adult life in retirement on average to each cohort.

Develop a system that places requirements on firms and individuals contracting self-employed people to make contributions to their pensions, and provide default routes via which the self-employed can save into pensions.

Lower the auto-enrolment threshold to the equivalent of working 15 hours per week on the National Living Wage – currently just over £6,000 a year.

Narrow the gap between minimum employee and employer auto-enrolment pension contribution over time.

Support further progress on occupational pension saving among low- and middle-earners during a period of rising minimum pension contributions by providing a flat rate of income tax relief; and exempting employee pension contributions from employee National Insurance, funded by capping tax-relieved lump sums drawn at retirement to £40,000.

Promote larger pensions schemes better able to share risk among savers, while laying the path for long-term development of 'collective defined contribution' schemes.

Reform pension freedoms by introducing a default product providing a guaranteed income in later life, and stimulate the market in retirement income products.

The state – delivering for all generations

Use £2.3 billion raised from a new progressive property tax to address gaps in public social care funding. Alongside this, introduce user charges on assets so wealthier individuals contribute towards their social care costs in England. However, set the asset floors and cost caps such that no more than a quarter of assets can be depleted.

As one element of a new 'NHS levy', charge employee and self-employed National Insurance contributions on the earnings of workers over the State Pension age, raising £0.9 billion in 2020.

As the second element of a new 'NHS levy', place a charge that mirrors employee National Insurance contributions on private occupational pension income, but initially at half the main rate and with a higher starting threshold.

Lift the benefits freeze a year early, uprating working-age benefits in line with inflation in April 2019, at a cost of £1.7 billion.

Maintain the commitment to increase public investment in infrastructure while sustainably reducing debt over the medium term.

Abolish inheritance tax and replace it with a lifetime receipts tax with lower rates and fewer exemptions. This should be levied on recipients, with a tax-free allowance to encourage broadly shared inheritances.

Introduce a 'citizen's inheritance' – an asset endowment to all young adults who entered the labour market during the financial crisis and since – to support skills, entrepreneurship, housing and pension saving.

Engender engagement in the democratic process for each successive cohort by lowering the voting age and automatically registering young adults attending school, college and university to vote.

COMMISSIONER BIOGRAPHIES

David Willetts

Executive Chair of the Resolution Foundation (Commission Chair)

The Rt Hon. Lord David Willetts is Executive Chair of the Resolution Foundation. He has served as the Member of Parliament for Havant (1992-2015), as Minister for Universities and Science (2010-14) and previously worked at HM Treasury and the No. 10 Policy Unit.

David is a visiting Professor at King's College London, a board member of UK Research and Innovation, Chair of the British Science Association, a governor of the Ditchley Foundation and a member of the Council of the Institute for Fiscal Studies. He is a board member of the Crick Institute and a trustee of the Science Museum. He is an Honorary Fellow of Nuffield College, Oxford University. David has written widely on economic and social policy. His book *The Pinch* – about fairness between the generations – was published in 2010.

Vidhya Alakeson

Chief Executive of Power to Change

Vidhya Alakeson is the founding Chief Executive of Power to Change, an independent charitable trust that supports the growth of community business across England.

Prior to setting up Power to Change, she was Deputy Chief Executive of the Resolution Foundation, as well as acting as an independent expert supporting the development of personalisation in the NHS. Vidhya worked at the US Department of Health and Human Services in Washington DC during 2006-10 and previously worked at HM Treasury and the Prime Minister's Strategy Unit. She is a trustee of the Young Foundation and member of the Advisory Board of Big Society Capital and Participatory City.

Kate Barker

Chairman of Trustees, British Coal Staff Superannuation Scheme

Dame Kate Barker is Chairman of Trustees for the British Coal Staff Superannuation Scheme, and also a non-executive director of Taylor Wimpey Plc and Man Group Plc. She is an economist and was a member of the Bank of England's Monetary Policy Committee during 2001-10. Prior to this, she was Chief Economic Adviser at the CBI.

Kate has written widely on economics and social policy. Her book, *Housing: Where's the Plan?*, was published in 2014, and in the same year she chaired the Commission on the Future of Health and Social Care in England for the King's Fund. She was awarded a DBE in 2014 for services to the economy.

Torsten Bell

Director of the Resolution Foundation

Torsten is the Director of the Resolution Foundation, a think tank that combines analytical rigour with policy prescriptions to improve the living standards of those in Britain on low to middle incomes.

With a background in economic policy, his focuses include inequality, the labour market, tax and benefits, housing and wealth. Prior to leading the Resolution Foundation, Torsten was Director of Policy for the Labour Party. He has also worked in HM Treasury, as a member of the Council of Economic Advisers during the financial crisis and as a civil servant.

Carolyn Fairbairn

Director General of the CBI

Carolyn Fairbairn has been Director General of the CBI since November 2015. Prior to this, she held a range of senior leadership roles in business, government and the media.

She spent her early career at McKinsey, where she was a leader of the firm's media practice. As BBC Director of Strategy she led the BBC's digital strategy and ran its transmission arm. Carolyn has extensive FTSE board experience as a non-executive director of Lloyds Banking Group, the Vitec Group and Capita Plc. She has also been a director of the Competition and Markets Authority, the UK Statistics Authority, and the Financial Services Authority. During 1995-97 Carolyn was a member of the No. 10 Policy Unit.

Geoffrey Filkin

Chairman of the Centre for Ageing Better

Lord Geoffrey Filkin worked in housing for many years, was a local government Chief Executive and then Chief Executive of the Association of District Councils. He has also founded a number of think tanks and charities, including the New Local Government Network and the 2020 Public Services Trust, and was a government minister in the Lords for four years.

In 2013 he proposed and then chaired a Lords Select Committee on our ageing society. Its influential report, *Ready for Ageing*, was published in March that year. Since then he has worked to found the Centre for Ageing Better and to establish the organisation as an influential independent body to promote the changes needed so that more people benefit from their longer lives.

John Hills

Professor of Social Policy at the London School of Economics

John Hills is Richard Titmuss Professor of Social Policy, Co-Director of the International Inequalities Institute and Chair of the Centre for Analysis of Social Exclusion at the London School of Economics.

His research interests include the distribution of income and wealth, the welfare state, social security, pensions, housing and taxation. Recent books include *Wealth in the UK* (co-author, 2013), *Good Times, Bad Times: The welfare myth of them and us* (2014), and *Social Policy in a Cold Climate* (co-editor, 2016). He was Chair of the National Equality Panel (2008-10), carried out a review of the aims of social housing for the Secretary of State for Communities during 2006-07, and was one of the three members of the UK Pensions Commission from 2003 to 2006.

Paul Johnson

Director of the Institute for Fiscal Studies

Paul Johnson is Director of the Institute for Fiscal Studies and a visiting professor in the Department of Economics at University College London.

He has worked and published extensively on economics and policy, with a focus on the income distribution, the public finances, tax, social security and education. Paul has also worked at HM Treasury, the Department for Education and the Financial Services Authority. During 2004-07 he was deputy head of the Government Economic Service. Paul is currently also a member of the Committee on Climate Change and of the Banking Standards Board. He was an editor of the Mirrlees review of the UK tax system.

Sarah O'Connor

Investigations Correspondent and columnist at the Financial Times

Sarah O'Connor writes about the changing world of work for the Financial Times, where she is an investigations correspondent and columnist. Sarah joined the Financial Times in 2007 as a graduate trainee, and in the decade since she has covered the US economy from Washington DC, the UK economy from London and the financial crisis from Reykjavik.

Her investigation into algorithmic management won Financial/Economic Story of the Year at the 2017 Foreign Press Association Awards, while her regular op-ed column won Economics Commentator of the Year at the 2017 Comment Awards.

Frances O'Grady

General Secretary of the TUC

Frances O'Grady is the first female General Secretary of the Trades Union Congress.

She joined as campaigns officer in 1994, and launched the TUC's Organising Academy in 1997. Frances headed up the TUC's organisation department in 1999, reorganising local skills projects into unionlearn which now helps 250,000 workers into learning every year. As Deputy General Secretary from 2003, Frances led on the environment, industrial policy, the NHS and winning an agreement covering the 2012 Olympics.

She has served as a member of the Low Pay Commission, the High Pay Centre and the Resolution Foundation's Commission on Living Standards.

Ben Page

Chief Executive of Ipsos MORI

Ben Page is Chief Executive of Ipsos MORI. Since joining in 1987, Ben has worked in MORI's private sector business on corporate reputation and consumer research, for companies like Shell, BAE Systems, and Sky TV. He has also worked closely with both Conservative and Labour ministers and senior policy makers across government. He has led on work for No. 10 Downing Street, the Home Office and the Department of Health, as well as a wide range of local authorities and NHS Trusts.

Ben is a fellow of the Academy of Social Sciences and serves on advisory groups at the King's Fund, the Institute for Public Policy Research and the Social Market Foundation, and is a trustee at the Centre for London.

Nigel Wilson

Group Chief Executive of Legal & General

Nigel Wilson was appointed Group Chief Executive of Legal & General in 2012, having joined as Group Chief Financial Officer in 2009.

Nigel won the Most Admired Leader award at Britain's Most Admired Companies Awards 2017, for Management Today. During 2015-16 he was a member of the Prime Minister's Business Advisory Group. He was also City AM Business Personality of the Year in 2014. Nigel was Senior Independent Director (SID) of Capita Plc during 2009-12, and was SID and Chairman of Halfords Group Plc during 2006-11. Other previous appointments include Group Commercial Director of Dixons Group Plc; Managing Director of Stanhope Properties Plc; and Managing Director of Viridian Capital.